MANAGING ORGANIZATIONAL CHANGE

MANAGING ORGANIZATIONAL CHANGE

Third Edition

Patrick E. Connor, Linda K. Lake,
and Richard W. Stackman

Westport, Connecticut
London

Library of Congress Cataloging-in-Publication Data

Connor, Patrick E.
Managing organizational change / Patrick E. Connor, Linda K. Lake, and Richard W. Stackman.—3rd ed.
p. cm.
Includes bibliographical references and index.
ISBN 1-56720-509-7 (alk. paper)—ISBN 1-56720-510-0 (pbk. : alk. paper)
1. Organizational change. I. Lake, Linda K. II. Stackman, Richard W. III. Title.

HD58.8 .C653 2003
658.4'06—dc21 2002029869

British Library Cataloguing in Publication Data is available.

Library of Congress Catalog Card Number: 2002029869
ISBN: 1-56720-509-7
1-56720-510-0 (pbk.)

First published in 2003

Praeger Publishers, 88 Post Road West, Westport, CT 06881
An imprint of Greenwood Publishing Group, Inc.
www.praeger.com

Printed in the United States of America

The paper used in this book complies with the Permanent Paper Standard issued by the National Information Standards Organization (Z39.48-1984).

10 9 8 7 6 5 4 3 2 1

The authors and publisher gratefully acknowledge permission to use the following:

Excerpts from "John Henry." Collected, adapted and arranged by John A. Lomax and Alan Lomax. TRO—© Copyright 1934 (Renewed) Ludlow Music, Inc., New York, NY. Used by permission.

Every reasonable effort has been made to trace the owners of copyright materials in this book, but in some instances this has proven impossible. The author and publisher will be glad to receive information leading to more complete acknowledgments in subsequent printings of the book, and in the meantime extend their apologies for any omissions.

To our families

We must be the change we wish to see in the world.

—Mohandas Gandhi

There is a certain relief in change, even though it be from bad to worse, as I have found in traveling in a stage-coach, that it is often a comfort to shift one's position and be bruised in a new place.

—Washington Irving

If we do not change our direction, we are likely to end up where we are headed.

—Ancient Chinese proverb

Toto, something tells me we're not in Kansas anymore.

—Dorothy in *The Wizard of Oz* by L. Frank Baum

No one wants to be the one to initiate change, but once it is started, everyone wants a say.

—Unknown

A great wind is blowing and that gives you either imagination or a headache.

—Catherine the Great

Contents

Tables, Figures, and Questionnaires

TABLES

FIGURES

QUESTIONNAIRES

Preface

Among the three of us, we have owned and operated our own company and worked in aerospace firms, mental-health agencies, computer-manufacturing plants, universities, credit bureaus, newspapers, travel-service organizations, and one state penitentiary. Whatever their many differences (and their similarities are far greater than their differences), these organizations all share a modern characteristic: all of them are continually changing. And by our very presence at these organizations, we have been students of organizational change.

Working in these places over the years has given us a respect for the difficulties that people encounter in facing the changes they experience. We therefore wrote the two previous editions with four objectives in mind, and these objectives remain unchanged here.

Our first objective is to help people understand organizational change. We try to meet that objective by describing a number of critical elements that are involved in any change process. These elements are reflected in the bulk of the chapter titles. In this edition particularly we have emphasized the dynamic character of change through examples. Change is a process, not an event, and we have endeavored to capture that flavor here. In revising this book, we too grappled with change as a process. The initial outline to the latest version of this book included extensive discussion of the "new" economy; however, before principal revisions could start, the dot-com bubble burst, and even more dramatically the United States and the world began dealing with increased threats of terrorism and the aftermath of September 11th.

Our second objective is to help people constructively deal with changes in and about organizations. The biggest barriers to any change effort include (1) lack of management visibility and support, (2) employee resistance to change, and (3) inadequate change-management skills. To that end we have described a number of managerial actions that can and perhaps should be taken. We have also devoted a chapter to the larger issue of formulating change policies, as well as a chapter describing some broad-scale aspects in the conduct of a change program.

The third objective reflects our experience and interest in what is usually called macro analysis of organizations. Most volumes on change management emphasize an organization-development (OD) approach. For us, OD is an important set of assumptions, methods, and procedures for managing organizational change. But it is not the complete set. Dealing successfully with change requires a variety of perspectives; our intent is to offer a managerial one.

A fourth objective—still relevant today—emerged since the original publication of this book. In just the past half-dozen years organizations have found themselves caught up primarily in a whirlwind of at least four kinds of forces: forces of quality, globalization, technology, and diversity. We have attempted to recognize the importance of those forces throughout our examination of change throughout the book, including the examples.

All of these objectives stem from a basic point of view that we hold, a view that any reader of this book should understand. The point of view has two parts. First: Put simply, we see organizations as human instruments—instruments that are designed and employed to do a job (build a car, cure the sick, educate the young, construct a dam). As with any human situation, these instruments are subject to change. Second: We view management as an art and science of exercising options. This is true whether the subject is managing change, formulating strategies, or resolving conflict. Our view is that in carrying out these responsibilities, managers are continually confronted with an array of choices, as well as many possible ways to select from among those choices.

We owe a debt of gratitude to a number of individuals for assisting with this project. Dating back to the publication of the first edition, we thank Craig Lundberg for his advice, suggestions, and encouragement. Anthony Buono also gave generously of his time to offer suggestions and criticisms. We are also grateful for the ideas and recommendations suggested by Carole Napolitano, Joseph Garcia, Jean DeLuca, and Kenneth Keleman.

We also appreciate the assistance of Carri L. McBride, Marcia Finch, and Jim Kephart and the continuing contributions made by the students in Connor's "Managing Organizational Change" seminars. We have learned a lot about the subject from those discussions. We are especially grateful to the tireless and engaged efforts of Mary Stout. Thank you, Mary.

Lake is grateful to numerous colleagues who tolerated, even encouraged, her efforts to bend and manipulate change theory into practical, daily use. She also thanks her coauthor, Patrick Connor, for getting her intrigued by the formal study of organizations and the changes they undergo. Her gratitude runs deep and covers the opportunity to work on this project.

The substantive revisions that resulted in this third edition fell to Richard Stackman, who joins Connor and Lake as a coauthor. University of Washington, Tacoma, students Johanna Noedel, Robert Reichard, Douglas Willis, and especially Paul Majack provided research assistance. The friendship, support, and confidence continuously displayed by Connor, and that of Craig Pinder, continue to be instrumental in the development of Stackman's voice as a scholar.

Finally, we cherish our families, to whom we dedicate this book.

MANAGING ORGANIZATIONAL CHANGE

1
Managing Organizational Change

Consider the following premise: change is the norm in organizational life. If this premise is valid, then the job of organizational leaders is not so much managing the day-to-day operations of an organization, but rather guiding it through constant change. In essence, their primary job is to create stability in the midst of change.

It is an understatement to acknowledge that the new millennium has brought about rapid, unforeseen changes for organizations. At the start of 2000, the U.S. economy was enjoying its longest economic boom on record. Managers in organizations were focused on keeping up with new technologies and competing in a global marketplace while ensuring that their organizations did not fall behind the competition. At the start of 2002, companies had been coping with the rapid erosion of profits and the collapse of stock prices, a sudden spike in energy costs in the previous year, and horrific terrorist attacks on U.S. soil.

What are the common elements of these best-of-times and worst-of-times scenarios? One possible answer: uncertainty and survival. All change is about ensuring organizational survival, and, whether the economy is strengthening or weakening, uncertainty exists because the consequences of changing are usually less well known than the consequences of *not* changing. Change is precipitated by (1) dissatisfaction with the status quo, (2) a strong desire (or need) to move to a more desirable condition, or (3) the appeal of a well-thought-out strategy for realizing a vision.[1] The underlying forces producing the need to change are many. We avoid the temptation of listing dozens and note instead the following seven.

Diversity. The monopoly in business of white, middle-class, middle-aged males has been eroded. Increasingly, women, people of color, the physically disabled, and other so-called minorities are finding that their organizational influence is growing. This is happening in both the workplace and the marketplace. Statistics bear out these claims. For instance, about 65 percent of the *Fortune* 1,000 companies have at least one member of an ethnic minority on their board of directors, up from 55 percent in 1998.[2] It is now considered the norm that maintaining a diverse workplace is not only the right thing to do but also creates a competitive advantage.

Globalization. Multinational alliances—the European Community, Canada/U.S./Mexico, and the Pacific Rim are the most potent examples—seem to be here to stay. Add China, the single-largest global market, to the mix and we find that there is virtually no industry that is not feeling increased competition from either members of those alliances or from other countries. Deciding on the best markets to enter and then establishing oneself in new cultures can be formidable tasks.

Consumers. At the personal level, consumers are changing what they want. For one thing, they are demanding higher quality and greater value for their money. This translates into a demand for more choice and more personalized product diversity. Second, they are demanding more services to go along with the products. Third, in much of the developed world, demand is shifting away from durable goods toward services, and therefore toward less use of materials. This last point corresponds with the demand by many consumers for environmentally friendly products from environmentally conscious organizations.

Employment practices.[3] Lifetime employment, once a goal of both companies and individuals, is giving way to flexible employment systems that consist of temporary and contingent employees, contractors, and consultants. Companies are also utilizing seniors past the age of sixty-five due to society's increasing willingness to value age and wisdom along with youth and energy. Such companies place higher value on experience, corporate memory, and know-how, all traits older individuals are likely to possess.

Economic health. At the societal level, so-called economic revitalization is an important item on many states' agendas. The way this agenda item is pursued is changing dramatically, however.[4] Many communities are shifting their emphasis away from trying to entice old, established manufacturing plants to move in, and toward trying to create an economic, cultural, and educational climate that attracts new, entrepreneurial companies. For example, Tacoma, Washington, is enjoying a rebirth thanks to economic, cultural, and educational changes. The 1990 introduction of a University of Washington campus in the downtown core has sparked major redevelopment, including construction of two new museums. With Tacoma dubbed the nation's "most-wired city" thanks to infrastructure investments by two high-speed Internet companies, community leaders have focused on luring technology-based companies to augment its corporate base in the sectors of transportation (Port of Tacoma), health care (MultiCare and Regence BlueShield), and finance (Frank Russell).

Technology. To comprehend the effect of technology advances, consider the computer you were using just ten years ago. What were you using it for? How fast was your computer? When did you start surfing the Internet? What products or services do you now purchase armed with a computer and a credit card?

Moore's law—attributed to Gordon E. Moore, one of the cofounders of Intel—states that processors will double in performance every eighteen months, getting cheaper along the way.[5] The development and continually increasing performance of processors at lower costs have, as we all know, changed the game for most people in most industries. In general, the widespread use of computers in business has allowed two things to happen. First, organizations have been able to decentralize their operations down to a much lower level than ever thought possible:

> Microelectronics allows us to decentralize our systems to a level at which they can provide support capability to individual workers. This change may appear in the form of a modular management or office work station that offers a menu of services on command. Or it may appear in the form of an "intelligent toolbox" in which people carry the resources of their profession wherever they go, just as plumbers or carpenters carry their tools with them today.[6]

Second, the microchip has changed people's thinking not only about *how* to do a job, but also about *what* jobs to do. In the banking industry, for example, the introduction of computers was seen as the death knell for a large number of jobs, yet the opposite occurred. "From 1973 to 1980, employment in banking in California rose about 10% a year, despite computers and automated tellers. Why? *Because the banks used the new technologies to offer new services previously undreamed of.*"[7] From a production and inventory-management standpoint, Dell Computers downloads new orders hourly and automatically reschedules the assembly line every two hours.[8] By using technology, Dell reduces inventory and labor costs while maximizing efficiency and reducing overhead costs. Finally, online spending in the United States in 2001 was estimated at over $30 billion, compared to a meager $1–$2 billion in 1998.[9]

The past. In many ways organizations are captives to their pasts. Many of the problems organizations currently face can be traced to changes made in the past.[10] For example, many organizations that downsized in the 1980s and 1990s lost critical institutional knowledge, primarily through early retirements. The people who understood the company's culture and customers were no longer around, and many companies quickly rehired their own retirees as consultants.

SO WHAT?

These examples, and this book, are about change. In fact, as the title suggests, this book is about a particular kind of change, the kind that occurs in organizations.

The point of all the preceding discussion of changes in our society is that much of what happens in this society is the result of organizations' actions. As Amitai Etzioni has said,

> We are born in organizations, educated by organizations, and most of us spend much of our lives working for organizations. We spend much of our leisure time paying, playing, and praying in organizations. Most of us will die in an organization and when

the time comes for burial, the largest organization of all—the state—must grant official permission.[11]

Thus, most of the ways that we will respond to the types of changes described previously will be with and within organizations. Additionally, we are not interested here in merely describing how organizational changes take place. Rather, we are concerned with how managers can conduct changes in ways that are beneficial to their organizations and the people who populate them. Unfortunately, we must acknowledge here and now that change is often mismanaged and beset by unexpected developments. Changing organizations is difficult, and one could argue that it is even a miracle that effective change occurs at all. And it isn't going to get any easier in the future:

> The Industrial Age company—already challenged by disruptions of technology, ever more power consumers, relentless margin pressure, and a horde of unorthodox newcomers—will, in the next few years, give way to the post-industrial company. What will the post-Industrial Age company look like? A few things are certain: It will have to balance optimization *and* innovation, focus *and* experimentation, discipline *and* passion, evolution *and* revolution. . . . Accommodating these paradoxes will require ambidextrous leaders.[12]

The phrase "accommodating these paradoxes" is particularly potent. There is a paradox that all managers face when leading change efforts. That paradox involves creating effective change while providing stability. Considering the paradox—change *and* stability—one should quickly understand (and not underestimate) the challenges managers face.

The purpose of this chapter is to introduce the major ideas involved in change management. We do so first by describing a "natural" change process, so called because it represents what would happen if there were no managerial intervention. We then present a model of managed change. This model guides the flow of the book and offers one way for a manager to create order in what can be a chaotic process. Finally, we offer a brief preview of the direction that the rest of the book takes.

It is risky to provide extended examples in a book, as they can quickly become dated. But we have decided to focus on four companies—specifically, Napster, Ford, Microsoft, and General Electric. The changing stories of these companies should not only help to highlight key points, but they should also spark discussion especially if recent business press is also considered as you work your way through this latest edition.

"NATURAL" ORGANIZATIONAL CHANGE

Figure 1.1 illustrates what may be called a natural, unmanaged change process. The process is natural in this sense: However it starts, it would progress on its own to some organizational conclusion, regardless of whether it is ever

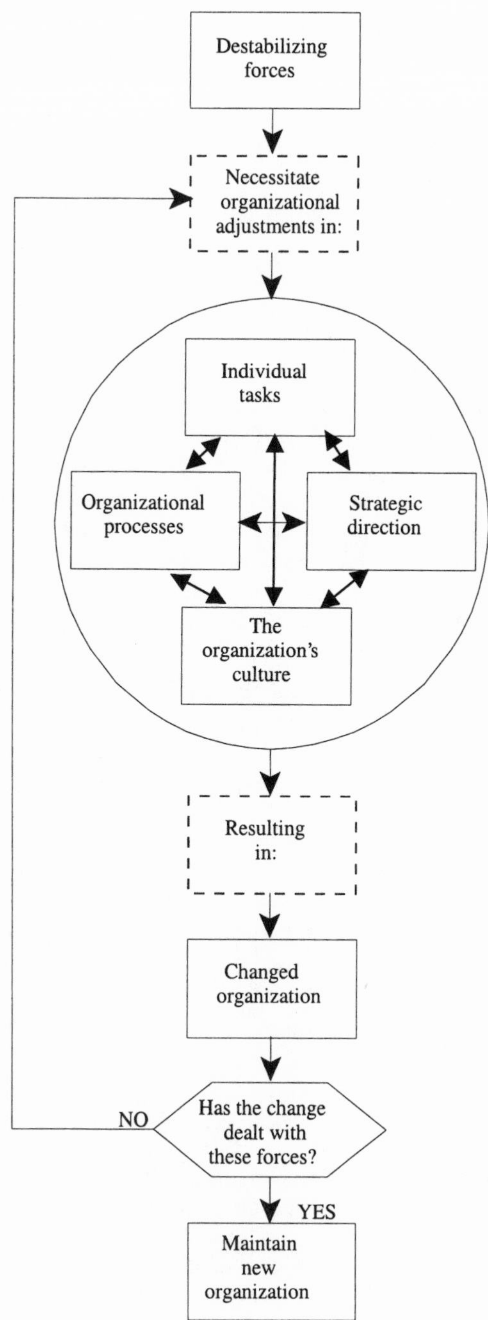

Figure 1.1 Unmanaged Change Process

interfered with. Consider the following sequence of events. Starting at the top of the figure, the idea is that somehow, for some reason, disrupting or disequilibrating forces begin acting to destabilize the organization.

Destabilizing forces may originate outside the firm, such as when a competitor introduces a new product or a regulatory agency exerts pressure regarding consumer safety. The forces may also come from within, such as when a new CEO is hired, a new goal is established, or a lead engineer returns from a conference with new knowledge to be applied to a current project. Their origins—from within or without—are not material right now, because the issue is the same: They are forces disrupting the organization's status quo.

In turn, these forces necessitate some sort of organizational adjustment so that the disruption or disequilibrium can be dealt with. The forms that such adjustments may take are many and varied, of course. As we discuss in chapter 3, we find adjustments occurring in one or more of four organizational elements: (1) in tasks performed by individuals; (2) in various organizational processes, such as communication, decision making, control, and so forth; (3) in the overall strategic direction taken by the organization over the long run; and (4) in the organization's dominant values, norms, and customs—otherwise known as its culture. With no guidance or direction from management, the form of those adjustments will develop according to custom, convenience (paths of least resistance, for example), power differences among groups affected, or whim.

Whatever form(s) the adjustments do take, the result is a changed organization. If the adjustments have adequately dealt with the destabilizing forces, then the new—changed—organization will be maintained. If not, then the cycle begins again, and further organizational adjustments will occur.

MANAGING CHANGE

For our purposes, figure 1.1 is not sufficient. As noted earlier, our intent is to examine the purposeful aspects of organizational change. There is an important distinction between change as a phenomenon and changing, as a set of actions.[13] This view is consistent with Karl Weick's concern that processes can best be understood in their active tense:

> The idea of process implies impermanence. The image of organizations that we prefer is one which argues that organizations keep falling apart and that they require chronic rebuilding. . . . The fact that this [rebuilding] is problematic, must be engineered, and can be bungled needs to be kept uppermost in organizational theorizing.[14]

Figure 1.2 is figure 1.1 with a management overlay imposed. This figure is in the active tense, the *changing-managing* model. The figure shows that selecting strategies for managing change is one of the key intervention points in the change-management process.

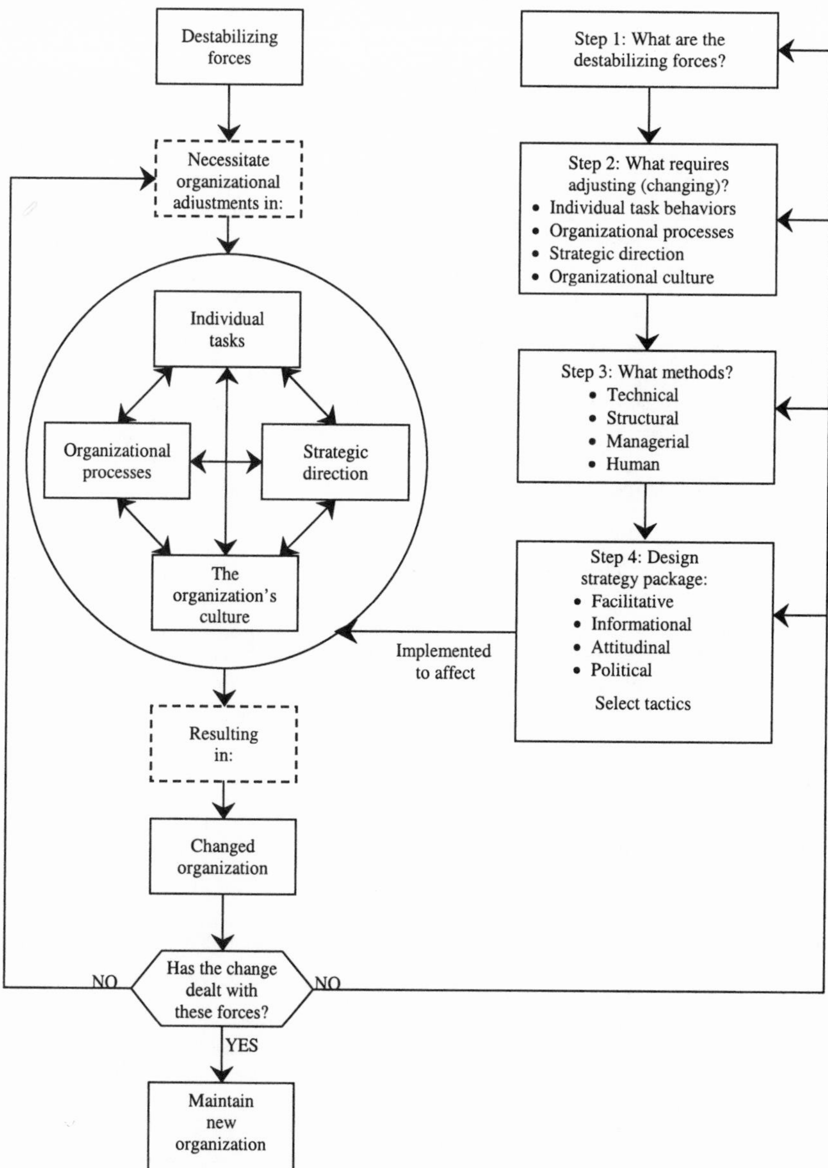

Figure 1.2 Managed Change

Destabilizing Forces

However, figure 1.2 also indicates that choosing change strategies cannot logically begin until three other important decisions are made. First, the identity, nature, and source of the destabilizing sources have to be diagnosed. Do they originate from outside the organization—such as from the marketplace, the regulatory community, or the labor market? Or do they provoke from within—for example, from a need to increase efficiency, or because it becomes apparent that first-line supervisors need to increase their managerial knowledge and skills if the organization is to have a competent middle management in the next three to five years?

Diagnosing and understanding these forces is essential if the next questions are to be answered intelligently. One cannot hope to decide which aspects of the organization need to be changed, or what method of change or package of strategies is appropriate, if the originating forces are not clearly identified and understood. This is the purpose behind the discussion in chapter 2.

Objects of Change

The second key question to ask is *what* is to be changed? As we noted earlier, and as we develop further in chapter 3, four major organizational properties are typical objects of change:

- Frequently, the way a person performs a particular job needs to be modified. Different raw materials, new equipment, better procedures—these all can serve to alter *individual task behaviors*.
- At the organizational level, methods of control, information transmittal, and decision making may need revising in the face of new circumstances. Such *organizational processes* as these are therefore a second object of change.
- More broadly, management may need to modify the organization's *strategic direction*—which services it will provide to which clients; which markets it will compete in with which products.
- Finally, management may decide that certain critical organizational assumptions, norms, ideals, and customs need revising. The enterprise's *organizational culture* thus becomes an object of change.

Methods of Change

A third major question also must be answered: *How* is the change to be made? As we discuss in chapters 4 and 5, four distinct methods are available:

- The way in which materials, intellectual resources, and production operations are treated may be altered. This is a *technological* method.
- In addition, relationships may be modified—for example, functional, role, or reporting relationships. This is a *structural* method.

- Administrative actions also can be taken. For example, the organization's reward system can be used to stimulate a change, or labor-management cooperation can provide a means for change to occur in a positive and constructive manner. These are examples of a *managerial* method.
- Finally, human beings can be changed: They can be selected, retrained, transferred, replaced, fired. We call this a *human* method of change.

Change Strategies

As figure 1.2 shows, these questions—what are the destabilizing forces, what is to be changed, and by what method(s) is the change to occur—constitute only the first broad steps in managing a change process. A fourth step requires choosing the strategies that will be most appropriate and useful for accomplishing that change.

The term *strategy* means a general design or plan of action. We identify four major strategies that managers can use in conducting organizational change; they are discussed in some detail in chapter 6.

The people on whom the change is having a direct impact are called *change recipients. Facilitative* strategies make it easier for change recipients to accomplish a given change or series of changes. For example, change recipients may be offered resources that will aid them in making the change. Basically, facilitative strategies are used in situations in which the recipients have some sense of what they want to do but lack the means to do it.

When using *informational* strategies, change managers offer knowledge, facts, and opinions so that change recipients can make rational decisions and take the resulting action. Change managers assume here that recipients will act rationally in the face of facts, and given adequate information will recognize the problem and develop solutions in agreement with one another because the facts are so compelling.

An attitude is "an orientation towards certain objects (including persons—others and oneself) or situations. . . . [A]n attitude results from the application of a general value to concrete objects or situations."[15] *Attitudinal* strategies are based on the belief that people's attitudes determine their actions in any situation. To change an action one must change an attitude. These strategies focus on changing attitudes of both individuals and groups.

Finally, political activities in organizations concern acquiring, developing, and using resources to accomplish one's purpose. *Political* strategies rely on this notion. They involve giving, withholding, competing for, or bargaining for scarce resources so as to accomplish the change program's objectives.

Maxims for Change

As we develop further in chapter 6, the selection of strategies is critical to successful change management. However, since change strategies are almost never used singly and there are no guarantees as to their success, we must think not so much of selecting a single strategy as selecting a strategy *package*. A strategy package consists of the first strategy to be used, the second, the third, and so on, until eventually the final strategy is reached. This package also includes the tactics to be employed to carry out each strategy as the change agent learns from his mistakes along the way.

To guide our thinking about change strategies, therefore, we offer the following maxims:

1. *Designing a strategy package is a necessary part of change management.* It is not enough to know the object and method of change. If a diagnosis of the destabilizing forces leads to a decision to change specific task behaviors, for example, by a technological method, then "selecting a strategy" means designing the set of means for implementing that change. Without a deliberate design for a strategy package, the process is haphazard, even random.

2. *No one strategy package fits all situations.* Some managers seem to believe that their favorite strategy (and often the only one they ever use) is always appropriate and always best. However, many variables can affect the success of a particular approach in a particular situation. Employees eventually tire of the flavor of the month.

The major variables, or criteria, for selecting strategies are identified and discussed in chapter 6. For now, suffice it to say that the choice of a specific strategy package will depend on a number of things. For example: How quickly does the change have to be implemented? What degree of planning is necessary? How many people need to be involved? What sort of resistance is likely to be encountered? How clear is the gap between current performance and desired performance? Who has what knowledge relevant to the proposed change? What are people's expectations regarding the change? Who will be in charge of implementing the change, and how much knowledge, skill, power, authority, and so forth will that person have?[16]

It is highly unlikely that these several criteria will lead a change manager to the same conclusion time after time about which strategy package to select. In other words, the same change strategy is not indicated in all situations.

3. *The choice of a strategy package is guided by an understanding and consideration of key aspects of the change situation.* In many ways, this is an extension of maxim 2. The aspects to be considered become guidelines for choosing the type of strategies and tactics that will be most appropriate. As shown in chapter 6, we find that the key criteria to consider are the time available to effect the change, the extensiveness of the proposed change, the characteristics of the change recipient, and the resources available to those wanting to implement the change.

4. *Choosing a strategy package really means designing a series of strategies, their order of conduct, and the tactics employed to carry out each one.* When the change recipient consists of two or more subgroups, several strategies might be applied simultaneously, each aimed at a different subgroup. This might also

be true when there is only one group, but several somewhat different objectives to be met. For example, one strategy could be used to ensure that the change takes place quickly, while a second could be applied over a longer time period, and a third employed to ensure that the recipient group members completely understand the rationale for the change. In managing change, one cannot forget that the organization is a system of multiple, interrelated parts. The impact of changes to one part migrating to other parts of the organization—whether intended or unintended—must be considered. Additionally, managers must exercise caution that one strategy does not cancel out or interfere with a previously used change strategy, a concurrent one, or one intended for later use.

Summary

Let's summarize the preceding discussion: Figure 1.2 shows that managing change concerns a number of issues, which include identifying the destabilizing forces, choosing what to change, selecting the appropriate methods to use, designing the most effective change strategies, and implementing those strategies with the correct tactics. Moreover, the figure emphasizes a serial logic. Step 4's accomplishment requires that steps 1, 2, and 3 have all been executed. Step 3 requires the same of steps 1 and 2, and so on.

The result of these steps is a changed organization, depicted on the left-hand side of figure 1.2. Of course, this is the best-case scenario that ignores that change can be messy, or it can be completely derailed. We cannot insure that, before concluding a planned change process, one may not have to start again at the beginning. At the conclusion of the planned change, if the question "Has the change dealt adequately with the forces?" is answered in the negative, the response is to go back to one of the preceding four steps. In some cases, management may need to cycle all the way back to the original question: "What are the destabilizing forces?"

THE PLAN OF THE BOOK

As noted earlier, the model of managing change sketched in figure 1.2 serves as a broad guide to the structure and content of this book. Chapter 2 discusses the overall idea of a diagnostic approach to change, sources of destabilizing forces, and organizations' orientation or predisposition to change.

Chapter 3 concerns itself with the major objects of change: task behavior, organizational processes, strategic direction, and culture. Chapters 4 and 5 develop four key methods for conducting change: technological, structural, managerial, and human.

Chapter 6 has to do with designing strategy packages. The principal strategies for implementing a change program are discussed, together with the criteria for selecting different strategies and tactics in different situations.

Chapter 7 describes the three major players in change processes: change managers, or those with overall responsibilities for designing the change and seeing that it occurs successfully; change agents, or those who are directly involved in conducting a change; and change recipients, or those people in the organization on whom the change is being visited. We also introduce the concept of *change allies,* who in seemingly invisible ways aid the change process.

Chapters 8 and 9 are integrating chapters, designed to pull the previous segments of the discussion together. Chapter 8 is concerned with policy questions in change management. Issues are raised concerning the relative desirability of change versus stability, the availability and allocation of scarce resources, and the problems involved in managing while a change program is in progress.

Chapter 9 expands the basic change model presented here. It relates the various elements and processes involved in change to one another and also provides sample diagnostics to assist in managing a change process while considering the question "What is success in the management of change?"

We bring our treatment to a close by considering some ethical issues in managing change. Chapter 10 discusses ethical problems that may arise in four major areas: strategy selection, recipient selection, management responsibility, and manipulation. We conclude by suggesting a number of values and ethical guidelines that anyone responsible for designing and implementing change could fruitfully follow.

Finally, this book provides readers some extended examples that focus on specific organizations, or current concepts or theories associated with change. These examples appear in the "Focus On" boxes in each chapter.

The selected "Focus On" example for this chapter is Napster.

Focus On: Napster

Shawn Fanning is credited with pioneering peer-to-peer computing and launching the Napster craze while a freshman at Northeastern University. Peer-to-peer computing allows two people to share information by simply hooking up the contents of their computers into a global information index that anyone else can also access. The simplicity of the idea is that every computer becomes a receiver and a sender of information, which is stored and accessed from individual computers, not a central server.

In the beginning, the primary users of the Napster software were students who traded music online. If you wanted a copy of the new Jennifer Lopez song, you loaded the Napster software and began a search of computers that had the song stored on their hard drives. The search provided you numerous options and versions, and you selected the version you desired with a simple press-and-click of your mouse. The person from whom you were securing the song was never part of the process, and once the song was on your computer, others could obtain a copy from you.

But peer-to-peer computing isn't just about trading music; it's about trading information—all types of information, including books, films, and magazines. Whatever can be stored on a computer can be traded.

Today, Napster represents more than a company that fought for its survival and lost following legal battles with the recording industry. Napster symbolizes the power of an idea that has brought about and will continue to drive change. From a simple idea about a different architecture for exchanging information between computers, Napster has brought about changes at the individual, organizational, and industry levels.

Consider the following:

In June 1999, Fanning provided the software to a mere 30 friends. In just a few days the Napster software had been downloaded by 3,000 to 4,000 people. Before a 2001 court order forced Napster to suspend the ability for individuals to share files, it was estimated that more than 80 million people had downloaded the Napster software onto their computers.

Additionally, Napster was credited with driving consumer demand for more powerful computers and greater bandwidth. CD burners became standard equipment on 70% of all new computers, and by March 2001, installation of DSL and cable Internet services had grown by 150 percent. Remember, speed in downloading information from the Web is critical. Take Napster (or its growing number of clones) out of the mix, and the Internet service industry feared that the growth of DSL and cable modems would slow.

By January 2001, with Napster accounting for upward of 60 percent of universities' bandwidth on a daily basis, more than 120 U.S. universities had started regulating Internet use or banning Napster altogether.

Napster ran afoul of the major record label companies because of concern over depressed sales and copyright infringement as royalties for music composers, publishers, and artists were not being collected. Why would anyone buy a new CD when they could download the music for free? The paradox is this: At the very time that record companies were losing royalty revenues because people were downloading music for free and thus not buying new CDs, Napster had provided those companies with a new distribution channel for their products. (And remember, not just the record companies could take advantage of this new technology; magazine and book publishers and TV and movie firms could also.)

The challenge today for Napster, the Napster clones that may face their own legal challenges, and the recording industry is producing a copyright-secure process that makes it easy to transfer music online while generating royalties. Of course, the question remains as to whether individuals are willing to pay for such a service.

For Napster specifically, new clones have outpaced it with respect to reliability and searching features—something Napster will have to copy. To be legit, Napster will have to secure licenses from major record labels. Questions remain as to whether Napster can ever generate revenues. One idea is to charge a monthly subscription fee, with a portion of that fee going to the record industry. Simple math illustrates that if 20 million users pay a minimum of $100 a year in subscriptions to download music, $2 billion would be generated.

For the recording industry, the record labels have banded together into two consortia and have created their own Napster-like sites—MusicNet and pressplay. These two mutually exclusive sites provide access to 85 percent of the recording industry's music collection, meaning an individual would have to subscribe to both to have access to the majority of the recording industry's music collection. Moreover, neither service currently allows music to be burned to CDs or loaded onto portable players, which is seen as a fatal flaw.

Ultimately, it may be the advent of new technology that reconciles industry concerns with consumer wants. One such advancement is digital rights management (DRM). DRM makes sure you have paid a "toll" before you can access music and ensures that anyone else you pass it on to pays a toll as well. For example, let's say you pay 50 cents for a download, and you share the download with another user. That person pays another 50 cents, but—get this—you get 10 percent of that fee for sharing the download legitimately.

Sources: S. E. Ante (2001), Now, Napster can get down to business, *Business Week*, Feb. 26, p. 35; S. E. Ante (2001), The day the music died, *Business Week*, Jan. 22, p. 14; S. E. Ante (2000), Inside Napster, *Business Week*, Aug. 14, pp. 112–121; W. Cohen (2001), Digital music fans face a battle of the bands, *Fortune*, Oct. 29, pp. 34–35; J. Ewing (2001), Bertelsmann says play it again, Napster, *Business Week*, Nov. 12, p. 12; J. Ewing (2000), A new net powerhouse?: Bertelsmann's deal with Napster could kick-start a bold plan for the media and entertainment giant, *Business Week*, Nov. 13, pp. 46–52; R. Grover & T. Lowry (2001), Can't get no . . .: The recording industry tries, and it tries, but will post-Napster models work?, *Business Week*, Sept. 3, pp. 78–79; R. Harris (2001), Napster's relaunch on hold until next year, *Washington Post*, Oct. 29, www.washtech.com/news/media/13427-1.html; A. Kover (2000), Napster: The hot idea of the year, *Fortune*, June 26, pp. 128–136; A. Kover (2000), Who's afraid of this kid?, *Fortune*, March 20, pp. 129–130.

NOTES

1. K. N. Dervitsiotis (1998), The challenge of management organizational change: Exploring the relationship of re-engineering, developing learning organizations and total quality management, *Total Quality Management*, pp. 109-122.

2. S. N. Mehta (2001), What minority employees really want, *Fortune*, July 20, pp. 181-186.

3. This discussion relies on J. A. Challenger (2001), The transformed workplace: How you can survive, *The Futurist*, November-December, pp. 24–28.

4. W. F. Miller (1985), Emerging technologies and their implications for Oregon, Legislative Conference on the Economy, Oregon Council on Economic Education, Menlo Park, CA: SRI International, January 9, 7-10.

5. C. Edwards & I. Sager (2001), Intel: Can CEO Craig Barrett reverse the slide? *Business Week*, October 15, pp. 80-90.

6. Miller, p. 19.

7. Miller, p. 33 (emphasis added).

8. L. Walker (2001), Plugged in for maximum efficiency, *Washington Post*, June 20, p. G1.

9. J. Brown (2001), Shoppers are beating a path to the web, *Business Week*, December 24, p. 41.

10. D. Ancona, T. Kochan, M. Scully, J. Van Maanen, & D. E. Westney (1999), Module 8 overview: Organizational change and transformation, in *Managing for the future: Organizational behavior and processes* (2d ed.), Cincinnati: South-Western, p. 2.

11. A. Etzioni (1964), *Modern organizations*, Englewood Cliffs, NJ: Prentice-Hall, p. 1.

12. G. Hamel (2001), What CEOs can learn from America, *Fortune*, November 12, 2001, p. 140.

13. R. Chin (1961), The utility of system models and developmental models for practitioners, in W. G. Bennis, K. D. Benne, & R. Chin (Eds.), *The planning of change*, New York: Holt, Rinehart and Winston, pp. 201–214.

14. K. E. Weick (1979), *The social psychology of organizing* (2d. ed.), Reading, MA: Addison–Wesley, p. 44.

15. G. A.Theodorson & A. G. Theodorson (1969), *A modern dictionary of sociology*, New York: Thomas Y. Crowell, p. 19.

16. J. P. Kotter & L. A. Schlesinger (1979), Choosing strategies for change, *Harvard Business Review*, March-April, pp. 106–114; J. R. Gordon (1993), *Organizational behavior*, Boston: Allyn and Bacon, pp. 678–690.

2

Getting Started

Although organizational change may sometimes seem to sprout from nowhere, to tumble along with no apparent purpose, and to lack any semblance of a plan, that is not strictly true. Even the most haphazard change effort can be seen to have some structure to it. The current change may seem to be tangled up with the one that came before it or the one that follows it, but some order can be made of it, if only to identify a beginning, a middle, and an end.

Order or stability in the midst of change should not be underestimated. People—even if they are open to change—seek a better understanding of what is going to happen or what might happen.

The purpose of this chapter is to provide some order within change. As a starting point, we first present a diagnostic approach to organizational change, emphasizing its usefulness as a managerial tool—not only at the beginning of change but at a number of points during it as well. Next we look at some of the causes or sources of change in organizations. Completing our discussion of getting change started, we look at organizations' typical orientation to change—either as initiators of change or as adaptors to those changes that occur. The example of Napster (see "Focus On: Napster" in chapter 1) exemplifies both initiation of change (i.e., what Napster itself started) and adaptation to change (i.e., the recording companies' response).

DIAGNOSTIC APPROACH TO CHANGE

In an effort to make organizations operate more effectively, organization members propose and implement changes constantly. How do they decide when to make changes, what to change, and how to change it? Whether or not they are aware of it, they engage in some form of organizational diagnosis. In other words, they study what currently exists, compare that to whatever state they wish existed, and from that information determine what actions to take to make their wishes a reality. Finally, when everything is all in place, they evaluate whether it was a good change and whether it was done well.

This diagnosing is often done informally, and incompletely. Invariably, those charged with the diagnosis face a sense of urgency to do something now, and consequently, they circumvent the process in the interest of getting the changes implemented as soon as possible. When the diagnosis is omitted or improperly conducted, symptoms are mistaken for problems, causes are masked or ignored, and the choice of a future course is only a guess. By rushing the diagnosis—if it is completed at all—the conclusions drawn and the actions taken are frequently not as good or as effective as they might be, and the actions taken may be the seeds of future problems.

In contrast, conducting conscious, systematic diagnostic efforts at a variety of points in the change process can positively affect the success of that process.[1] This diagnosis should consider the past history of change efforts (both successful and unsuccessful ones) in the organization as well as the timing of any change(s) with respect to the organization's capacity to change.[2] When diagnosis is properly conducted, essential problems are recognized and understood, their causes are illuminated, and a future course for change is indicated. Most important, a full understanding of the problem—and thus the reasons for any proposed change—is easier to communicate. Clear and consistent communication can mean the difference between the need for change being accepted and supported by organizational stakeholders, and the emergence of resistance to block needed change.

Diagnostic Efforts

Diagnosis is essentially a matter of gathering and analyzing information to understand how an organization is functioning at a particular time.[3] Figure 2.1 illustrates a generalized diagnostic model that we use in discussing the beginning of a change and call upon repeatedly throughout our treatment of organizational change.

Diagnosis consists of four basic parts: formulating the problem statement, gathering information about the problem, analyzing the information, and deriving suggestions for future actions. Each phase of the diagnosis builds upon the preceding phases. Failure to thoroughly conduct any of the early phases will have negative effects on the success of the subsequent phases.

Formulating a problem statement can begin as simply as making comments such as "Orders are getting filled late," "Morale is certainly low in here," "Our inventory costs are certainly high," or "With all these people and all this equipment, we should be doing better." Correctly framing a problem statement frequently requires several iterations of questioning and feeding back answers to various organizational members. Finding the right problem to diagnose is a crucial part of the entire change program.

Gathering information may include looking at paperwork, observing people's routines, or conducting interviews. Organization-development practitioners have numerous methods and techniques for gathering information. Among

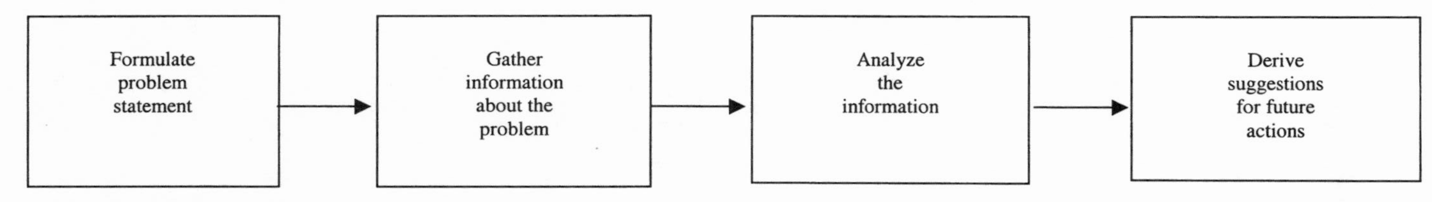

Figure 2.1 Diagnostic Model

them are questionnaires, interviews, observations, engaging participants in discussion of issues, and unobtrusive measures such as examining company records.[4] Critical to gathering information, of course, is a focus on reliable and valid measurement.

Analysis of the information must include first an examination of whether it is the right information and whether there is enough of it. If not, more data gathering is required. Once the validity of the information is confirmed, then analysis moves to comparing the way things are currently being handled with some sort of idealized standards or operating procedures.

Finally, this comparison, which has been based on gathered information, leads to suggestions for further actions. Those actions are the steps required to move the organization from the current state to the idealized future state.

Organizational diagnosis may be orchestrated or led by a single individual but requires the involvement of all interested stakeholders—both internal and external. Diagnostics will be most successful when everyone cooperates sufficiently to provide the best information possible. Since later application of resources is based on the diagnostic findings, organizations are well advised to spend sufficient time and energy and to gain cooperation at this stage of a change effort. Organization-development practitioners believe that gathering organizational data and feeding it back to organization members improves the quality of the data and creates a common way of thinking and talking about the facts.[5]

Diagnostic efforts can, and should, be applied both when a change strategist (defined here as the person charged with identifying the need for change, creating a vision for a desired outcome, and deciding what change is feasible[6]) believes the organization is in need of remediation or healing and when the organization would benefit from development into new areas or new ways of doing things for a more generalized improvement. Remedial diagnosis concentrates efforts on finding problems and their causes. Diagnosis for developmental purposes focuses on assessing the organization in preparation for proactively changing organizational elements to increase effectiveness.[7] Whether the outcome is remedial or developmental, diagnostic activities provide a focus for examining, understanding, and treating the organizational situation at hand.

Diagnosis and Organizational Models

This generalized diagnostic model can be applied in different situations, so the actual form the diagnostic effort takes depends on key aspects of those situations. Two of those key aspects relate to models. The model of organizations and the model of organizational change held by the person conducting the diagnosis have the greatest influences on the form of the diagnostic effort.[8]

Each of us holds a model of organizations. We have some notion of what the important parts or elements of an organization are. Further, we have beliefs about how those parts are related, and how they function relative to one another.

We demonstrate the existence of our organizational model in our dealings with an organization. A person moving into a new house or apartment has to call the local power, telephone, and cable companies and ask to speak to someone in new accounts at each organization. If there are later problems with billing or service, the call is made to billing or customer-service departments. A model of organizations may also include a belief about the efficiency of organizations. Some believe that small companies work rapidly to comply with requests, whereas large ones are slow and inefficient. Imagine the same apartment dweller interested in arranging local phone service, long-distance phone service, cable television, and a high-speed Internet connection. In some locales, one company provides all four services; unfortunately, the organizational structure as established by the company requires the individual to call four separate phone numbers to arrange for these services. When there are service-related problems, complaints must be made directly to the offending department.

Most organizational models rely on an open systems view. Such a perspective locates the organization within a larger environment, with highly permeable boundaries between them. Environmental resources first pass into the organization, are transformed, and then are returned to the environment as products or output. The organization is considered only one subsystem of a larger system, related to and influencing many other subsystems. An organizational model based on such a systems perspective shapes the diagnostic effort to include aspects of the environment and all parts of the organization, not just the troubled part.[9] A manager making a change in one component of an organization necessarily will anticipate the effects of that change on other organizational components—including suppliers, customers, and community representatives—and apply diagnostic and other resources to it. Such changes may also affect suppliers, customers, or both, for example.[10] *Connections*—those strategic relationships nurtured by collaboration—are considered to be one of the "three Cs" for world-class companies competing in the twenty-first century.[11] Just as connections are vital to effective change, so too are the remaining two Cs—*concepts* (i.e., the ideas and technologies driven by innovations) and *competence* (i.e., skills and abilities utilized to effectively and efficiently bring about change).

Organizational Change Models and Diagnosis

As noted previously, a model of organizational change has two components. We have already introduced the first component—the organizational model and its definitions of organizational elements and their interrelationships. The second component is a set of beliefs about how change begins, progresses, and ends. When beliefs about change are superimposed on the organizational model, the result is the organizational change model. Our model of organizational change—presented in chapter 1—includes aspects of our organizational model. Both the objects and methods of change relate to specific components and relationships from our organizational model. Tasks, organizational processes, managerial objectives, and culture are all important elements of organizations. An organization can be changed by changing any of those components. The importance of this to our discussion of diagnosis is that diagnostic efforts will be applied only to those elements that are recognized parts of our organizational model.

There are other models of change that guide people's actions. Some managers may see a change they are making in production processes as an isolated change designed to increase production. If they believe that production processes do not affect people, they will not apply diagnostics to that aspect (i.e., the people) because they believe there is no "people" problem that requires a solution.

Another component of our change model is that a need exists to maintain the new system—to institutionalize the change. We therefore would apply diagnostics to determine how to accomplish the institutionalization before evaluating whether it had been accomplished. However, some other change models simply assume that after a change has been implemented, it will remain in place, intact, until the next change is formally made. In that case, the diagnostics applied would be governed by that assumption, and no effort to examine and support it would be made.

It seems clear that the form and the use of diagnostic efforts depend on the user's models of organizations and of organizational change. A final illustration of that is offered. The corporate offices of one medium-sized company were being moved to a building in a different suburb of a city. Those working on the move believed that people would be affected by the change in location, which was an outward sign that their organizational model contained people and setting as two of its components. They assumed that people would be concerned about transportation to the new office, since many lived relatively near the old site. Because of this assumption they conducted a diagnosis in the form of asking the workforce to complete questionnaires as to whether transportation was a problem, and how they'd like to solve that problem.

Management also believed that people would be concerned about housing, since many of the workers were apartment dwellers and relatively free to move closer to the new office. They went through a quick diagnostic procedure, producing the solution of having a chamber of commerce representative use company time to offer information about the new suburb and its services, particularly the type and cost of available housing.

The diagnostic effort was important because the results of that effort influenced where additional company resources were applied. In essence, *this really is the whole point* of using diagnostics. It is simply a way of determining where to apply company resources to effect and sustain change, and what those resources should be. If diagnosis is done properly, those allocations will result in high-quality, appropriate solutions to change problems.

In the following chapters, some sample diagnostics will be offered. Our approach is to offer a sampling of the types of diagnostic efforts that could be useful at each stage of organizational change. In chapter 9, when the full process of managing a change is described, some sample diagnostics will be suggested.

SOURCES OF CHANGE

In this section, we look at another aspect of the beginnings of a change in an organization—the sources of change.

External sources of change are the business's or industry's social, political/legal, economic, and technological environments. The degree to which these environments can stimulate change in a particular organization depends on both the organization and the extent of its interaction with the world outside its doors.

There are three important *internal* sources of change. The first is the professionals who work for the organization but retain outside affiliations. From those affiliations, they gain knowledge they then apply to existing internal situations. A second internal source is the establishment of new organizational goals. Existing means must be changed in order for the organization to achieve the new goals. Finally, having excess organizational resources fosters additional organizational changes. The antithesis is also true. A reduction in resources can result in changes as operating budgets are reduced or departments are reorganized.

Although we have divided external sources from internal ones, that division is admittedly somewhat artificial. The internal sources we discuss here obviously had some part of their origin in the world external to the organization. We wish to emphasize that the primary impetus for change is either external or internal. Either the environment is the primary source of a change, or factors inside the organization are the greatest stimulus for change.

External Sources of Change

Change in an organization can be stimulated by sources essentially external to that organization. Among those sources are social changes, the political/legal environment, economic conditions, and technological developments.[12] Table 2.1 lists those sources and offers examples of some resulting organizational changes.

Social changes in the organization's environment are changes in the beliefs, values, attitudes, opinions, and lifestyles of society as a whole. At a superficial level, changes in social attitudes can bring about new requirements for products. Indeed, some companies are geared to making yearly, seasonal, or even monthly changes in products or packaging to meet what they interpret as society's desires for different cars, different clothes, or the latest colors in home appliances. Although these changes in products require changes in production

Table 2.1
External Sources of Organizational Change

Social	
Value of a clean environment	Government policing agencies proliferate.
	New pollution-reduction technologies are developed.
	Companies assume the full costs of conducting their business.
Value of gender equality and inclusion of diversity	Greater numbers of women and minorities enter the workforce, with an increase in power and technical level of competence.
	Companies develop new product lines for working women and mothers.
	Product-marketing strategies are changed to appeal to women and people of diverse racial backgrounds and sexual orientations.
Political/Legal	
Conservatives in power	Businesses have capital with which to expand.
Liberals in power	Businesses are highly regulated and are required to provide or return benefits to workers.
Deregulation of industry	Banks and transportation firms operate more competitively.
Economic	
Expanding economy	Businesses expand; conglomerates flourish.
Recession	Layoffs, cutbacks, divestitures, and business failures are common.
Technological Developments	
Improved communications	Organizations can reach their customers and clients in a greater variety of ways.
Improved transportation	Businesses reduce raw materials and finished-goods inventories, shipping just in time to make schedules.

schedules, machinery configurations, materials ordering, and advertising campaigns, companies deal with them by applying procedures established for implementing these routine changes as they are created. In these companies, such changes are anticipated and dealt with in a programmed fashion.[13]

Changes in beliefs and values held by society can be sources of more profound and unprogrammed changes. The push in the 1970s and 1980s for a cleaner environment was an important impetus for change in a number of large and small corporations as well as in agencies of city, state, and federal governments worldwide. What began as an external change in values relative to the world's physical environment resulted in numerous organizational changes. Governmental agencies grew; new technologies were developed to reduce pollution; and millions of corporate dollars were spent as legal, engineering, and even clerical departments responded to the regulations that came into being. Some companies went out of business because of the increasingly popular beliefs in saving certain aspects of the dwindling natural environment even at the cost of profits and jobs. Ford Motor Company provides an example. Upon his appointment as chairman of the board, Bill Ford Jr. outlined his goal of making the company more environmentally friendly and socially responsible.[14]

Another profound source of social environmental change has been the movement for more equitable representation of people of diversity in the workplace. Because of this movement, companies have changed employee search and promotion practices to bring women and people from diverse racial and ethnic groups into a greater variety of organizational positions. In many places, they have also had to retire old prejudices in hiring and promoting people with nontraditional sexual orientations.

Each year, *Fortune* magazine publishes an issue highlighting the "Fifty Best Companies for Minorities." Each company that appears on this list demonstrates diversity at every level—from its new hires to its suppliers to the charities it supports.[15] *Fortune* also pays attention to the diversity within the upper ranks as well as the existence of role models. A recent issue noted that much progress has been made, but much work remains to be done. One survey reported that a staggering 45 percent of minority executives say they have been the targets of racial or cultural jokes at work.[16] Coca-Cola faced a class-action lawsuit that got its start when a small group of African American employees began meeting in each other's living rooms to share frustrations at what they saw as lack of opportunity.[17]

The increase in the acceptance of diversity has led to second-tier opportunities. Advertising has catered increasingly to diverse racial and ethnic groups by picturing members of those groups in marketing materials and in targeting products specifically to those groups. Some companies are responding to the greater numbers of women in the workforce by changing product lines and marketing strategies. More and more products are being introduced to take full advantage of women's changing social and economic status. Hotel and travel businesses, prepared-food companies, and clothing manufacturers have changed their product lines in order to develop, produce, and advertise products aimed at working women and their families. Finally, as people with nontraditional sexual orientations express their diversity and show their economic power, travel agencies, cruise lines, hotels, and other leisure-time establishments target programs specifically to them.

The political/legal environment is a second important external source of change. Social change has been aided by political and legal forces. The political/ legal environment, swinging from conservative to moderate to liberal and back again, can on its own serve as a potent source for change. For instance, the probusiness policies of the Reagan administration (also favored by the two Bush administrations) created a favorable corporate tax structure that resulted in corporations with additional capital to use for expansion. The expansion projects were the internal changes generated by an outside source of change for those companies. In other times, the political climate results in governmental agencies' gaining stringent control or implementing new oversight policies over certain industries. Following the bankruptcy of Enron in 2001, the Securities and Exchange Commission began to look more closely at how best to regulate accounting firms responsible for auditing the books of publicly traded firms. Widespread public concern over the accounting firms' ability to be self-policing became evident given the accounting firms' "incestuous professional relationships" by serving as consultants to, and generating substantial revenues from, their audit clients.[18]

On the other hand, the relaxation of laws regulating airlines, banks, and telecommunications services have been tremendous sources of change in companies that provide those services. Some companies have responded creatively and have thrived. Others have failed without the protection of regulation.

The entire banking industry has undergone major changes—though with mixed results—to take full advantage of deregulation. Banks changed their cultures to become marketing organizations as competition across state borders rather than protectionism within states became the norm. Banks recruited into their operations people in professions that were new to the industry. These marketers, salespersons, financial planners, and strategic planners became the new leaders in banking, emphasizing the increasing importance of their orientations to how business should be conducted. Loan representatives who used to wait for customers to ask for loans are now pounding the pavement, selling their services in a suddenly competitive marketplace. Furthermore, the larger banks—Citigroup and Chase, for example—sought to be full-service financial institutions through the ownership of investment houses.

Economic conditions can also be external sources of change for corporations. For many years, people in the United States believed the economy would continue to get better and better. The economy was so strong an influence that it affected managerial outlook and actions. Executives in both private industry and governmental agencies believed their enterprises would continue to grow and generate greater shareholder wealth. More recently, organizations have had to learn to live with the contraction rather than expansion of their operations.

Focus On: Ford

As the new millennium approached, Ford Motor Company was considered the strongest and best-managed U.S. automaker. Thanks to aggressive management and lofty goals, Ford was set to become the number-one U.S. automaker in 2001—a title it hadn't held since the 1920s.

In the driver's seat (pun intended) was president and CEO Jacques Nasser, whose vision was to transform the venerable carmaker into a consumer-focused corporation intent on developing long-lasting relationships with car buyers. Nasser viewed Ford's perennial number-two position as a result of Ford's inability to please customers. To accomplish his task, Nasser hired in outsiders with customer service experience.

Armed with cash reserves that stood at a whopping $23 billion in January 1999, Nasser went on a $13 billion buying spree—acquiring controlling interests in such companies as Volvo and Jaguar. He also initiated gut-wrenching cultural changes—including a performance-appraisal system copied from General Electric—that he hoped would result in a growth-oriented consumer powerhouse focused on anticipating the wants and needs of car buyers. Ford was to become nimble and Internet-savvy. Another Nasser initiative was providing Ford employees with their own laptops.

Nasser's ultimate goal was to turn Ford into the leading consumer company for automotive products and services. Nasser wanted Ford to have a hand in the nearly $68,000 in revenues that a $20,000 car generates from the sales price, maintenance, spare parts, gas, and insurance.

Bill Ford Jr. had assumed the title of chairman of the board with his own goals. His intent was to make the company more environmentally friendly and socially responsible. Touting "sustainable manufacturing," Ford Motor Company was to become the model for production techniques that minimized long-term environmental damage. Gone were the days of moving on and building new sites. Ford would no longer abandon sites, though it was easier and cheaper to start over at a new location. Instead, current sites would receive makeovers, resulting in factories that were more productive and more pleasant to work in, with increased flexible equipment, fewer workstations, and new processes. Web-based PCs would allow factory workers to share factory-floor concerns with suppliers and engineers, creating the need for more computer-literate employees. Part inventories would be cut in half to a mere 12 hours.

How quickly a company's fortunes can change.

By October 2001, Ford's cash reserves stood at $4.1 billion. The company known for its tagline "Quality Is Job One" was producing vehicles with more defects on average than its six largest competitors. Its U.S. market share (23.1%) was down 1.7 percentage points in the first half of 2001 alone. Plants operated at less than 80 percent of capacity, and so many new car and light truck models had been delayed that future sales were jeopardized.

And let's not forget the Firestone tire debacle—with a cost estimate of $3.5 billion for two separate tire recalls and the never-ending bad press.

By November 2001, Nasser was out and Bill Ford was in as CEO. Ford's deep problems—quality snafus, the Firestone debacle, a lack of exciting vehicles, and a brain drain—had been transferred to the great-grandson of founder Henry Ford. Seemingly overnight, the grand plans that were to transform Ford into a true powerhouse were no longer front and center.

Sources: W. Brown (2001), Ford just doesn't get it, *Washington Post,* Nov. 2, www.washingtonpost.com/wp-dyn/articles/A30175–2001Nov2.html; J. Green (2000), Ford's PC plan: Slow to boot, *Business Week,* Sept. 11, p. 14; K. Kerwin & J. Muller (2001), Bill takes the wheel, *Business Week,* Nov. 12, pp. 50–52; K. Kerwin & K. Naughton (1999), Remaking Ford, *Business Week,* Oct. 11, pp. 132–142; B. Morris (2000), This Ford is different: Idealist on board, *Fortune,* April 3, pp. 122–136; J. Muller (2001), Ford: Why it's worse than you think, *Business Week,* June 25, pp. 80–89; J. Muller (2000), A Ford redesign, *Business Week,* Nov. 13, pp. 78–88; F. Swoboda (2002), Ford to cut 35,000 jobs, *Washington Post,* Jan. 11, www.washingtonpost.com/wp-dyn/articles/A30898–2002Jan11.html; A. Taylor III (2001), What's behind Ford's fall?, *Fortune,* Oct. 29, pp. 104–108; A. Taylor III (2001), First crunch time for Jac, *Fortune,* June 25, pp. 34–36.

Fortunes change quickly for organizations (see "Focus On: Ford"). Ford, the darling of the U.S. automotive industry as the new millennium dawned, announced at the start of 2002 the trimming of 35,000 jobs (out of a companywide 345,000), the closing of five plants, the elimination of four car models, the cutting of its annual dividend to shareholders, and the suspension of bonuses for managers and matching contributions to salaried employees' 401(K) savings.[19] In similar circumstances, some companies dismiss entire divisions or sell subsidiary companies. Smaller companies reduce their workforce, cut salaries and wages, restrict their product lines or services, and reduce hours. Some companies never return to their prerecession structures—either because conditions never improve adequately, or they gained greater efficiency by making the changes that were required.

Finally, technological developments affect organizations on two levels. At the first level is the environment in general. Over the last century, general technological developments have included the internal combustion engine, electric lights, telephones, transistors, computers, and supersonic transport.

These general developments have had an effect on all industries, and on all organizations.

The second type of technological developments are those that occur in a particular company's own industry. Hospitals fifty years ago were essentially big buildings with beds and clean linen. The technology was centered on what the people—the nurses and doctors—could do directly for their patients. Surgery and medicines were a relatively minor aspect of the technology. Today, medical technology is far more complex and is changing rapidly. New diagnostic equipment, new drugs, and refined means of caring for patients appear in rapid succession. Those machines and drugs play an enormous part in today's patient care. Developing medical technology has caused major changes in how the business of a hospital is conducted as well as the need for ongoing training for medical staff.

Internal Sources of Change

Continuing our discussion of the sources of organizational change, we now look at internal sources. Again, we note some arbitrariness in labeling sources as either external or internal. However, the following three sources originate primarily from inside an organization. Table 2.2 lists the three sources and offers examples of some resulting organizational changes.

Table 2.2
Internal Sources of Organizational Change

Sources	Resulting Changes
Professional associations	New methods of performing work in the specialty are applied.
	New organizational processes are designed to accommodate the new methods.
New organizational goals	New tasks for individuals and organizational units are required to meet the new goals.
	New people are hired to accomplish the new tasks.
	The organization revises its organizational structures to accommodate new tasks.
Excess organizational resources	Extra services for employees, such as cafeterias and fitness facilities, are added.
	Organizations provide employee training in areas not essential to organizational success.
	Firms search for new ways to do business or new areas to be in.

Professional associations are vehicles by which people can relate with members of their professions outside their organizations. Through membership in professional organizations, subscriptions to professional journals, and attendance at conventions and lectures, professionals continually learn of new developments in their specialties. Engineers bring back to their companies the latest technical information to either apply directly or develop further for later use. Managers learn new managerial techniques, new ways of designing organizations, and new areas of economic opportunity, which they apply to their own companies.

What is particularly significant about changes brought about through professional associations is that their consequences are usually not limited to the technical specialty of the professional introducing them. For instance, a nurse may return from a convention with a new way of administering medication to patients with a particular disease. The implementation of that one new procedure results in numerous other changes: changes to work schedules as one floor nurse devotes an entire shift to carrying out the new procedures, and other nurses rearrange their routines; a change in supply houses as a source for the new drugs and equipment; and a change in physicians to those who know or are receptive to the new technique. All of this happens because one nurse attends one seminar.

Engineers, managers, and scientists might be expected, because of their positions and roles within companies, to bring in changes resulting from their professional associations. However, people in numerous other positions, such as the nurse in the preceding example, can also be the instrument of change. Secretaries return from meetings with news of office-automation equipment and procedures; salespeople at seminars learn of new telemarketing techniques; and plumbers learn of new materials to use in existing applications.

Another internal source of change in organizations is the adoption of new organizational goals. If an organization previously provided one kind of product, a switch to a sufficiently different product results in considerable internal changes. Many large telephone companies have broadened their scopes to become telecommunications companies. Qwest now provides not only standard landline telephone services, it also has cellular phone and DSL services and is a partner in both satellite and cable TV companies. This shift in goals from providing a single product to providing several diverse (though related) products resulted in numerous changes. Structurally, under its ownership umbrella it has to have different companies, each with its own profit responsibilities and upper management. Different types of employees were brought into the various operating companies. And new markets with their additional, but very different, regulatory requirements necessitated putting structures and people in place to deal with them.

Excess organizational resources, in the form of profits and even perhaps idle time for some managers and workers, are produced when a company is operating smoothly and successfully. These excess resources can often stimulate a search for new ideas to use in the company. The search is supplementary to daily operations and doesn't disrupt existing activities.[20] Again, the reverse is also true: the *lack* of—instead of excess—organizational resources can be a source of change. A lack of resources can lead to downsizing, layoffs, outsourcing, elimination of training opportunities, moving production oversees, and so forth.

Changes brought about because of the excess resources vary, because different companies choose to use those resources in different ways. Some companies provide extra services for their employees. Company-owned cafeterias, fitness centers, jogging tracks, and day care centers are increasingly common. Other companies provide supervisory and management training, assertiveness classes, career and values-clarification seminars, or job-development courses. Such amenities are expected in a general way to enhance employee productivity but are not absolutely essential to the company's functioning.

Companies may also choose to apply their excess resources to finding new ways of doing business, finding new business domains to enter, or developing new technologies to exploit. The changes that these decisions in turn cause are seen in the addition of new divisions, employees, locations, products, and services. They in turn require alterations in structure and the addition of new professional specialties and managerial procedures.

ORIENTATION TO CHANGE

This chapter has dealt with the beginnings of change—the application of diagnosis to organizational change, and the external and internal sources of change. The final aspect of the beginnings of change that we consider is the issue of how an organization typically views change. Some organizations are seemingly ever ready to make changes—frequently initiating and generally embracing change. Others attempt to avoid, delay, or stop it—changing infrequently, reluctantly adapting to the changes around them, but never initiating changes.

Some characteristics prepare an organization to be innovative and receptive to change, and some tend to cause it to resist or avoid change. There are both structural and cultural characteristics of importance to how an organization views change. There may be no better example of an organization that proactively embraced change—both structurally and culturally—than General Electric under the leadership of Jack Welch. Welch's mandate was that GE remain in a line of business only if it could be number one or two in the industry; otherwise the business would be sold. The rule also drove acquisitions at GE, and executives' performance and compensation were tied in part to their ability to deliver on that mandate.

Structural Characteristics

Certain organizational structures are less well suited to change than are other structures.[21] Bureaucratic organizations have long been considered resistant to change and innovation. They have a number of structural attributes that lead to this result.[22]

Bureaucracies develop formalized policies and procedures to govern daily activities. Once committed to paper, these policies and procedures not only establish the behaviors specifically associated with them, but also tend to become models for later policies. To change behavior that relies on formal rules, new rules must be developed and applied. The process of developing the new rules is also formalized, so that changes in the way activities are conducted take a great deal of time and effort.

In addition, bureaucratic structures typically require that members follow proper communication channels, making it difficult for, say, an accountant in the Northwest regional office to submit a suggestion for change to the operations managers in the East Coast division. Even if the change could be accomplished, the news that an opportunity or a need exists cannot be effectively communicated.

Bureaucracies also frequently require that a strict accounting of both short- and long-term plans be submitted long in advance so that these plans may be approved or disapproved at every step up the hierarchy. Because performance is then measured by the accomplishment of those plans, there is no incentive to break out in new directions to take advantage of new developments as they appear.

Structural factors affect a bureaucratic organization's ability to change.[23] In fact, that structure perpetuates a continuation of past practices through its policies and its organization. We cover this topic more completely in chapter 4, where organizational structure is considered as a method of change.

Cultural Characteristics

Some organizations' norms direct them to either encourage or resist change. When faced with identical opportunities or incentives to change, two companies might respond differently, according to the prevailing norms. Employees in one might respond in typical fashion by ignoring the information, working harder and harder to do business as they always have done it, discounting warnings to change, and generally resisting change efforts. Employees in the other company, working under norms for responding quickly and being first in the industry to do things in a new way, provide suggestions and information during the diagnosis and make the changes rapidly, leading all others in the field.

A company where the norm is "Do whatever it takes to get the job done" or "It doesn't matter what it costs; do what you have to do (within reason)" facilitates movement in new directions. Encouragement to try new ideas, even those that might fail, leads to more changes than does the admonition to propose only those changes that are sure to succeed.

Some companies highly value innovation—being the first to use a new process, produce a new product, or enter a new market. Some companies were early adopters, with employees toting every manner of cellular phone, pager, PDA, laptop, and other wireless communication device as they went to meetings, rode the elevator, and ate their lunch. Microsoft Corporation has pushed its value of innovation to become a leader in the computer software industry. The company does not simply wait to see what the others are doing and then copy it. Rather, by being first with their products, they try to set the industry standards. They exhibit this value in their treatment of employees as well. In addition to the somewhat common perk of free juices and soft drinks, most employees receive their own offices, often with windows. Employees also have their pick of company-maintained basketball and volleyball courts and football fields. Microsoft is one of the first companies to extend insurance and other benefits to employees' same-sex partners, just as they do to husbands and wives. The Microsoft goal is clearly to lead while others follow. Microsoft's future strategy is discussed in chapter 3.

Companies that value change and innovation utilize internal resources to ensure that they do change. In an effort to spot environmental elements or occurrences to actively engage, they place people in positions to survey the environment. Companies valuing change actively seek even faint signs of a need or opportunity to change; they do not wait passively to hear what is happening around them. To do so, they hire people who also understand and value change.

Earlier in this chapter we mentioned professional associations as sources of change in organizations. The effects mentioned were by-products of the associations' existence. However, some of these associations have as their goal the instigation of change within the industry they serve. The new culture they espouse is one of active interest in change.

A state association of hospital administrators becomes dissatisfied with the way a particular state agency reimburses for indigents' medical care. Rather than waiting for each member to return to his or her hospital and individually effect changes, the association uses its collective resources to make changes at the legislative level. This organization has chosen to change not only the way it has typically done business—influencing the profession through its members—but also the way an entire industry carries out its work. This exemplifies the new cultural norms operating within this organization. Another example is the Teachers Insurance and Annuity Association/College Retirement Equities Fund (TIAA-CREF). As the world's largest pension fund, with $255 billion in assets, CREF is considered a master at pushing changes in the way corporations govern themselves—specifically with respect to the number of inside versus outside board of director members—through quiet, behind-the-scenes diplomacy.[24]

Sometimes an organization's culture causes it to typically resist change when its business or environment indicates that a different set of norms is more appropriate. We discuss this topic in more detail in chapter 3, where organizational culture is viewed as an object of change.

A FINAL WORD ABOUT GETTING STARTED

At the beginning of this chapter we said that organizational change has a beginning, a middle, and an end. While we believe that it helps anyone participating in a change to understand that, and this understanding is essential to functioning as a change agent, it must be acknowledged that the end of one change is often the beginning of another. The changes may be spaced so closely that they appear to never end. With the external and internal forces that operate today, we believe that everyone in organizations should strive to be prepared for repeated, even continual, change.

Metaphors can often be of use in understanding complex actions and forces. On this topic, we like a boating metaphor. Some organizational changes are like a sailing voyage from one port to another. The captain (change manager) commands the boat, and the crew help. When the weather turns bad, the crew (change recipients) make various adjustments (changes) and the boat eventually gets to port (change is complete).[25] Other changes are more like a whitewater raft trip. It sails not a calm ocean but a river of permanent white water.[26] This contrast of organizational change as either an episodic or ongoing activity still allows the use of diagnostics, of recognizing whether the change is externally generated or sprouts on board, and lets us look at how well prepared the boat and crew are to weather the voyage. It's sometimes just a good idea to know whether you're going to be on the water for a long, long time or land at your intended destination after a three-hour cruise.

NOTES

1. J. R. Gordon (1983), *A diagnostic approach to organizational behavior,* Newton, MA: Allyn and Bacon.

2. A. M. Pettigrew, R. W. Woodman, & K. S. Cameron (2001), Studying organizational change and development: Challenges for future research, *Academy of Management Journal,* 44, pp. 697–713.

3. T. G. Cummings & C. G. Worley (2001), *Organization development and change* (7th ed.), St. Paul, MN: West.

4. D. Nadler (1977), *Feedback and organization development: Using data-based methods,* Reading, MA: Addison-Wesley, p. 119; R. Axelrod (2000), *Terms of engagement,* San Francisco: Berrett-Koehler, p. 16.

5. A. O. Manzini (1988), *Organizational diagnosis: A practical approach to company problem-solving and growth,* New York: AMACOM, p. 11.

6. R. M. Kanter, B. A. Stein, & T. D. Jick (1999), The challenges of execution: Roles and tasks in the change process, in D. Ancona, T. Kochan, M. Scully, J. Van Maanen, & D. E. Westney (Eds.), *Managing for the future: Organizational behavior and process* (2d ed.). Cincinnati, OH: South-Western, p. 16.

7. Ibid., p. 15.

8. D. A. Nadler & M. T. Tushman (1980), A model for diagnosing organizational behavior, *Organizational Dynamics,* 9 (Autumn), pp. 35–51.

9. Discussion relating open systems theory to organizational diagnosis can be found in: M. R. Weisbord (1982), Organizational diagnosis: Six places to look for trouble with or without a theory, in M. S. Plovnick, R. E. Fry, & W. W. Burke (Eds.), *Organizational development: Exercises, cases, and readings,* Boston: Little, Brown, 1982; Cummings & Worley, 2001; and M. Beer (1980), *Organization change and development,* Santa Monica, CA: Goodyear.

10. Axelrod, 2000, p. 45.

11. R. M. Kanter (1999), Change is everyone's job: Managing the extended enterprise in a globally connected world, *Organizational Dynamics,* 28, pp. 7–23.

12. This discussion relies on J. A. Pearce & R. B. Robinson (1982), *Strategic management: Strategy formulation and implementation,* Homewood, IL: Richard D. Irwin.

13. For a more complete description of routine innovation, see K. E. Knight (1967), A descriptive model of the intra-firm innovation process, *Journal of Business,* 40 (October), pp. 478–496.

14. B. Morris (2000), This Ford is different: Idealist on board, *Fortune,* April 3, pp. 122–136.

15. S. A. Mehta (2000), What minority employees really want, *Fortune,* July 10, pp. 180–186.

16. Ibid.

17. A. Harrington (2000), Coke denied . . .: Prevention is the best defense, *Fortune,* July 10, p. 188.

18. L. Lavelle (2000), The Big Five's credibility gap is getting wider, *Business Week,* October 30, pp. 90–92.

19. F. Swoboda (2002), "Ford to cut 35,000 jobs," *Washington Post,* www.washingtonpost.com/wp-dyn/articles/A30898–2002Jan11.html, January 11.

20. R. M. Cyert & J. G. March (1963), *A behavioral theory of the firm,* Englewood Cliffs, NJ: Prentice-Hall.

21. S. Becker & T. Whisler (1967), The innovative organization: A selective view of current theory and research, *Journal of Business,* 40 (October), pp. 462–469.

22. For a discussion of bureaucratic organizations and their characteristic ways of doing business, see: A. Downs (1966), *Inside bureaucracy,* Boston: Little, Brown.

23. R. L. Daft (1982), Bureaucratic versus nonbureaucratic structure and the process of innovation and change, in S. R. Bacharach (Ed.), *Research in the Sociology of Organizations,* Greenwich, CT: JAI Press.

24. J. A. Byrne (1999), The Teddy Roosevelt of corporate governance, *Business Week,* May 31, pp. 75–78.

25. S. P. Robbins (1993), *Organizational behavior: Concepts, controversies, and applications,* Englewood Cliffs, NJ: Prentice-Hall, p. 691.

26. Found in Ibid., p. 692, and based on a perspective in P. B. Vaill (1989), *Managing as a performing art: New ideas for a world of chaotic change,* San Francisco: Jossey-Bass.

3

Objects of Change

Not all organizational changes are startling or earth-shattering. Many are routine and predictable. To manage a change event successfully, regardless of how spontaneous or planned it may be, one must understand the basic elements of change: what is being changed, and how the change occurs. In other words, one must understand both the object (the *what*) and the method (the *how*) of change.

What is being changed? Frequently, the way a person performs a particular job needs to be modified. Different raw materials, new equipment, and more efficient procedures can affect and alter individual task behaviors, or how people actually perform their jobs. At the organizational level, methods of control, information transmittal, and decision making may need revising in the face of new circumstances. Such organizational processes as these are therefore a second object of change. More broadly, management may need to modify the firm's goals, or even its strategic direction or domain. Finally, management may decide that certain critical organizational values, norms, or customs need revising. The enterprise's organizational culture thus becomes an object of change.

The purpose of this chapter is to describe the typical objects of organizational change efforts. The purpose of the next chapter, chapter 4, is to discuss the methods of change. There, four distinct approaches are involved. First, the way in which materials or production processes are treated may be altered; this is a technological method. In addition, relationships may be modified—for example, authority, functional, or role relationships. This is a structural method, the second approach. Third, administrative actions can be revised; personnel practices, reward and evaluation systems, and information/control systems are all examples of managerial methods. Finally, people themselves can be changed; they can be selected, retrained, transferred, replaced, or fired.

These objects and methods, or what is changed and how, form a basic descriptive system for studying organizational change, as illustrated in figure 3.1. As the figure indicates, *objects* of change are distinct from the *methods* used, although they are not completely independent, of course. Organizations are

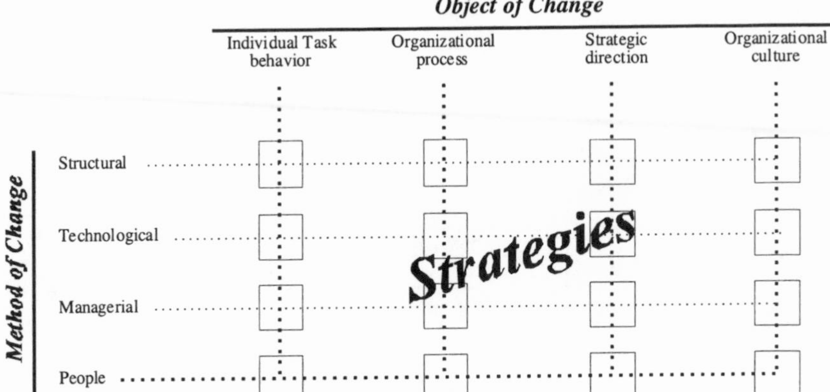

Figure 3.1 Classification System of Organizational Change

complicated, ambiguous, and even deceptive, and therefore, as with everything else, a manager's selection of a particular object of change might be influenced by his or her confidence in a certain method.[1] Still, it is useful to understand that *what* is changed is not the same thing as *how* the change is done. Taken together, changing a desired object by means of a particular method is likely to require a specific set of strategies. The strategies that are available, as well as their strengths and weaknesses, are discussed in chapter 6. As will be evident, our view is that different strategies are more (or less) effective in different cells of figure 3.1.

OBJECTS OF CHANGE

Organizational changes can have several kinds of impacts. For one thing, they can affect individuals and their jobs, such as the CPA who has a new set of accounting procedures to follow, or the social worker whose caseloads have doubled because of a drastic reduction in state or federal funds. Who actually does the work and where it is done are two objects of change. Many organizations now rely on temporary workers or have outsourced certain "back-office" functions (e.g., payroll, accounts receivable) to lower costs and to focus on the functions most relevant to the organization.[2] Changes can also take place in the ways in which decisions are made, performance is measured and appraised, or career paths are charted; these kinds of changes affect fundamental organizational processes. Changes can occur in a company's long-range goals, in the clientele that a state agency serves, or in the products that a manufacturing firm produces. These are changes in the organization's strategic direction. Finally, changes can affect such things as the ways in which people share information with (or withhold it from) each other, encourage (or discourage) experimentation, or support (or oppose) other work groups in the organization. These are examples of changes affecting norms, which is a way of saying that changes can affect an organization's culture.

INDIVIDUAL TASK BEHAVIOR

Changes are made in individual task behavior frequently. Work is of central importance both to individuals and to society at large:

> That importance is basically instrumental: work is engaged in primarily for the sake of its product, the goods and services that it generates. But it is no less true that work is often valued for its own sake, that for many people it meets the need for meaningful activity, as defined by others and as experienced by themselves. For many others, however, the work experience is unpleasant and it's marked with severe disadvantages. These people persist at work only because they see no alternative way to meet basic needs. If this is both obvious and undesirable, it follows that we should be concerned with ways to make work more meaningful and satisfying, and to do so without paying an unacceptable social price in terms of diminished quantity or quality.[3]

Historically, attempts to change task behavior centered on simplifying jobs, frequently to a highly routine, predictable, and programmed extreme, in attempts to increase efficiency. Taylor's scientific management is a good example of this approach.[4] Corporate and governmental organizations have been emphasizing production and service quality, as reflected in the popularity of the total quality management (TQM) and continuous improvement process (CIP) movements.[5] Change attempts associated with this development have emphasized complexity, multiple dimensions of the task, and human factors. Table 3.1 illustrates these ideas.[6]

Basically, the trends suggested in table 3.1 have developed because over the past several years change events have been focused on a number of particular task characteristics. We can use the job characteristics model, shown in figure 3.2, to identify and examine those characteristics.[7] According to the basic model, five core job dimensions create three critical psychological states that in turn lead to a number of beneficial personal and work outcomes. We note that these links among the job dimensions, psychological states, and outcomes are not exactly the same for everyone, of course, because an individual's knowledge and skill, desire to grow and develop, and satisfaction with the work context will affect them.

In any event, the job characteristics that are the most common objects of change attempts are those identified in the figure: skill variety, task identity, task significance, autonomy, and feedback.

Skill Variety

One of the most common objects of change is a job's *skill variety.* Management often wants to have a worker use either more or less skill variety,

Table 3.1
Historical Themes in Work Design

From an early focus on:	To a contemporary focus on:
Job simplification	Increasing job scope
Single jobs	Multiple, related jobs
Job components only	Human and organizational factors, too
Managerially designated job features	Perceived and subjectively experienced features as well
External controls (supervisors, procedure manuals)	Self-controlled individuals; self-regulating groups and units
Low risk taking	Innovation and creativity
Production outcomes	Several types of both work and personal outcomes

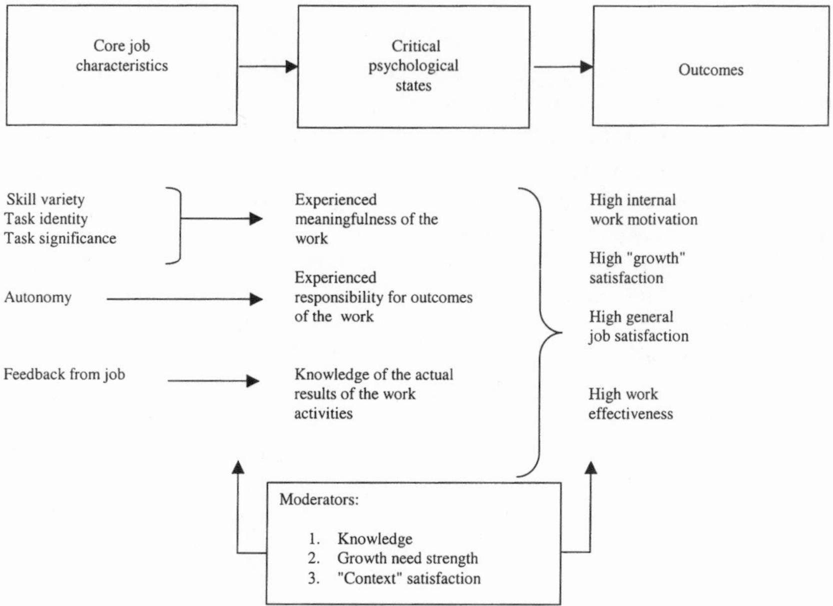

Figure 3.2 The Job Characteristics Model

Source: J. R. Hackman & G. R. Oldham (1980), *Work redesign*, Reading, MA: Addison-Wesley, p. 90. *Work redesign* by Hackman/Oldham. © Reprinted by permission of Pearson Education, Inc., Upper Saddle River, NJ.

depending on whether they want to make the job less difficult, change the number of different activities that the worker has to perform, or increase the meaningfulness of the work for the employee. Skill variety is the degree to which a job requires a variety of activities in carrying out the work. As figure 3.2 illustrates, the more skills a job requires an individual to use, the greater the skill variety and the greater the meaningfulness the worker experiences from doing that job.

We use the word variety deliberately. Skill variety does not mean using the same skill a large number of times; it means using several different skills to perform a given job.

Some jobs involve only one or two activities and therefore require only one or two skills to perform. Several summers ago, for example, one of us observed a railroad section gang in operation. This was a group of people whose task was to repair a broken section of railroad track. Accomplishing this mission involved several jobs: the old track was taken up and removed, the old broken ties were discarded, new gravel was shoveled and raked into the bed, and new ties and rails were laid. The job design for this task was simple: one person, one job. A single individual performed each job. For example, one person picked up a couple of new ties, carried them over to where they were to be placed, laid them down, and then went back for a couple more while someone else set those into place.

The point of this example is that each job had a low level of skill variety. Picking up a railroad tie, carrying it, and setting it down are not highly varied activities, and performing these activities does not demand a large variety of skills.

In contrast, observe a skilled cabinetmaker at work: the wood has to be selected according to criteria that are not always obvious; she then has to perform some sophisticated designing, calculating, and measuring; the wood is cut, planed, and finished; finally, the cabinet has to be hung, often to fit in with cabinets and counters that are already in the room. In short, the job of cabinetmaking involves a great number of activities that require many different skills to perform. It is clear that this is a high-skill-variety job.

Task Identity

A second common object of management's change efforts concerns the "wholeness" of a job. The idea here is that some jobs are performed piecemeal, and others are performed as a whole. Thus an employee may perform one small task, and then the job travels to another, who then adds another part. Conversely, a worker may assemble a complete product, performing all of the tasks required. *Task identity* is the degree to which the task is completed either as an identifiable whole, or in parts. The more a worker perceives a job as a whole task to be done from beginning to end, the greater the task identity and the greater the meaningfulness that he or she experiences.

In our previous example, each member of the railroad section gang probably experienced fairly low task identity. Each person was performing only a part of the overall job. On the other hand, the cabinetmaker's job had fairly high task identity—especially, in the example, since all of the various tasks from measuring the room to hanging the completed cabinet were performed by one individual.

Task Significance

Some tasks have more human significance than others. Either they affect a large number of people, both inside and outside the immediate organization, or their impact is more substantial on people's lives or work. For example, a technician who checks switches on a 777 airliner may be performing essentially the same task as someone who examines connections in a television set. Most people would agree, however, that the first task's human significance is greater: *Task significance* is the degree to which the job has a substantial impact on the lives or work of others.

One of the reasons that management may want to change workers' task significance is to increase the sense that the work is important, not trivial. The idea is that the more important the workers see their work, the more effectively they will perform it. Several years ago an American astronaut visited the aerospace company where his space capsule was being built. At the end of his visit he was chatting in the cafeteria with a roomful of production workers. Someone asked him if he had anything to say to those assembled. Thinking of the ride he would take in a few weeks, he laughed and said, "Yeah. Do good work." His remark became the company's official slogan for the next three years.

Skill variety, task identity, and task significance are frequent objects of change attempts because they relate to the *meaningfulness* that employees get from their jobs. The argument is that when a task requires an individual to stretch, either mentally or skillwise, that person is likely to get more out of performing it. Games, puzzles, and challenging sports are popular precisely because of this quality.

Similarly, if an individual can produce a whole product, not just a small and often nonidentifiable piece of it, that person is likely to get more meaning from the job. And if a person understands that what she or he does will affect other people, and that effect may be critical to those people's well-being, then the individual's sense of job meaning will likely be enhanced.

To summarize, then, management may wish to change the skill variety, task identity, or task significance of a job if they want to increase the meaningfulness of that job for their employees. Of course, employees can also seek for themselves ways to increase the meaningfulness of their jobs. Either way, employees today expect more from their workplace in comparison to previous generations—be it a sense of meaning or a chance to express themselves as individuals.[8]

Autonomy

Sometimes management may want to change the degree of latitude that workers have in carrying out their tasks. For example, it may be difficult to spell out specific rules or regulations that dictate the precise way a job should be performed. Or perhaps several variations have proved to be equally effective. Management may therefore decide to change—in this case, increase—the level of *autonomy* that the workers have.

This job characteristic refers to the amount of discretion that workers have in the performance of their tasks. When and how the job is to be performed is the essence of autonomy. Autonomy, then, is the degree to which the job provides freedom, independence, and discretion to the individual in scheduling the work and in determining the procedures for carrying it out. Referring again to figure 3.2, we said that skill variety, task identity, and task significance are important because they affect the meaningfulness that people get from their work. Autonomy is an important job characteristic because it often affects the sense of responsibility or ownership that individuals have for their work and its outcomes. As J. Richard Hackman puts it, "To the extent that autonomy is high, work outcomes will be viewed by workers as depending . . . on their *own* efforts, initiatives, and decisions, rather than on the adequacy of instructions from the boss or on a manual of job procedures."[9] Management can then expect those outcomes to be high-performance ones.

Feedback

The sense of ownership and responsibility that people can get from increased autonomy can happen only if they are knowledgeable about the outcomes of their work. *Feedback* is the job characteristic that allows them to acquire that knowledge. If management wants workers to have a better understanding of the effects of their work, feedback may be increased. More information then will be supplied, or supplied more frequently, so that understanding can be enhanced. Feedback is the degree to which carrying out the task results in the individual's obtaining direct and clear information about the impact and effectiveness of the work.

Performance evaluations, weekly department meetings, production graphs posted on the wall—these are all examples of performance feedback. We know one manufacturing company, for instance, in which each department receives output data, broken down by department, on a daily basis. As we might expect, there is a reasonably spirited competition among the various departments, a competition recognized, sanctioned, and rewarded by corporate management.

Many a winning departmental worker has enjoyed a night at the theatre or a ballgame at company expense.

ORGANIZATIONAL PROCESSES

Frequently managers want to change basic organizational processes. We obviously cannot examine here every type of process that occurs in most formal enterprises. We can, however, single out some especially important processes—control, reward, appraisal, and decision.

Control Processes

The essence of control is to ensure that planned actions take place as they are supposed to. This assurance takes two forms: preemptive and reactive.

Preemptive control is anticipatory; it involves attempts to influence the organization's environment, to shape its direction. Change attempts therefore may be aimed at such influencing and shaping methods. Advertising, for example, which is used to influence consumers' attitudes toward the company's products, may be an object of change. Similarly, lobbying efforts of a state educational agency may undergo change in the face of shifting economic and political realities.

Reactive control is regulatory; it focuses on operations and their deviation from standards. Typically there are four steps in a reactive control process, as illustrated in figure 3.3.[10] Once (1) standards are established (which should be done consistent with organizational goals and policies), the reactive control system is in operation.

Obviously, any of the control steps in the figure is a likely object of change: (2) the way in which performance is measured, or the measures themselves; (3) the methods by which performance is compared to standards, including the time frames that are used; and (4) the criteria employed in evaluating any deviations, as well as the means by which the performance is corrected or the standards modified.

At a broader level, an organization-wide control system may be changed. For instance, the avowed purpose of TQM programs, of course, is to ensure that the customer's needs are met promptly, accurately, and consistently.[11] Introducing such a program usually means substantial change:

> [E]fforts at continuous organizational, product, and service improvement take a system-wide focus that includes process and product control, as well as attempts to empower workers with the responsibility and authority for attaining the desired outcomes. Getting and using customer feedback, assuring vendor and supplier quality, using [statistical controls], and designing experiments in quality improvement accompany the changing role of employees.[12]

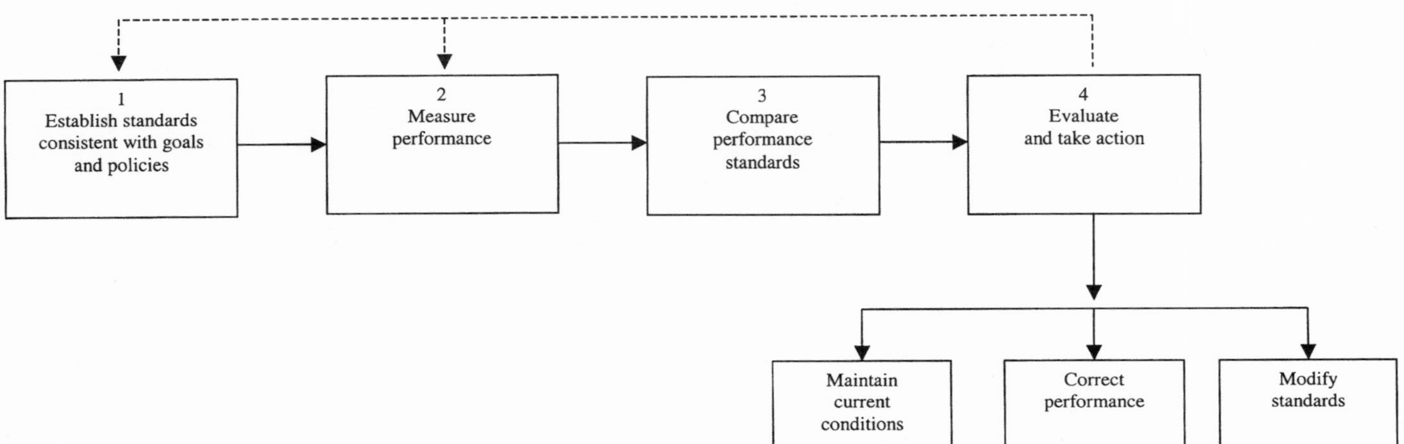

Figure 3.3 Steps in the Reactive Control Process

Consequently, the implementation of an organization-wide control system could likely affect the work (e.g., skill variety, task identity, or task significance) actually done by employees.

Reward Processes

One of the most significant ways in which an organization and its members can be affected is a change to the reward system. Who gets rewarded, the behavior that earns rewards, and how the rewards are given are all crucial matters to most members of most organizations. This is especially true for organizations that use remuneration as a basis of control and whose members obey primarily for utilitarian reasons. As Daniel Katz and Robert L. Kahn note,

> Work is largely an instrumental activity, rewarded in industrialized societies by money and in others by barter or direct share in the product. In societies that have a money economy, money becomes an almost universal reinforcer, and is so recognized. [And so the question is, can] the reward structure be effectively used as the primary target of . . . organizational change?[13]

The answer to this question seems to be yes. In general, profit sharing has been combined with an incentive-pay system to affect both total employee pay *and* satisfaction.[14] The basic conclusion that we can draw with respect to reward systems is that changing how employees are rewarded in turn affects the organization's climate, its supervision, and the interpersonal relations within it. Reward systems are potent objects of change.

Appraisal Processes

If an organization's reward system is to be an effective object of change, the appraisal process must be included in the change effort. In other words, if people are going to be rewarded differently—on the basis of different criteria, or for different behaviors—then the criteria need to be applied properly and the behaviors must be assessed accurately.

Performance appraisal is the process of setting those criteria and applying them. Evaluating people's performance in an organization is seldom straightforward or simple, of course. To do a good job of it, a manager must know, understand, and communicate management's expectations for performing a particular job; monitor the way in which an employee does the job, as well as the results; compare the behavior and results with those expectations; and then measure the match (or gap) between them. In addition, the manager must also provide feedback to the employee. This last part of the process can raise strong feelings, to say the least.

Despite—or perhaps because of—all of this, appraisal processes are crucial to an organization. In fact, the evidence is overwhelming: Installing an organization-wide appraisal system has dramatic implications for employee-management relations, job satisfaction, authority relationships, power distribution, employee commitment, and a host of other organizational characteristics.

Of course, if changing the appraisal process is to be successful, the new objectives, duties, task procedures, and performance criteria must be realistic, understandable, and acceptable to all parties. As mentioned earlier, an appraisal system involves a great deal, ranging from establishing organizational objectives to recruiting new employees to designing training-and-development programs. The point, in other words, is that instituting a new appraisal process may well involve changing more than procedure; it may require changing basic managerial philosophy.

There may be no better example of this than General Electric—the organization discussed in chapter 4—and its "vitality curve." Every year each GE business ranks its executives and managers. The leaders of each business are forced to identify the people in their organizations whom they consider to be in the top 20 percent, the middle 70 percent, and the bottom 10 percent. The appraisal scheme, named after the "vital middle 70 percent," requires managers to weed out their worst performers; employees rated in the bottom 10 percent are given a year to improve their performance.

It is a process that works for GE; however, Jack Welch, the chairman and CEO of GE from 1981 to 2001, freely admits that he wouldn't inject such a plan into an organization without a "performance culture" already in place.[15] Even he had trouble, at times, ranking one out of every ten direct reports in the bottom category; however, according to Welch, the process, as outlined, worked (and continues to work) because GE spent over a decade building a culture with candor and openness at every level. Such a commitment to building this kind of culture was lacking at Ford Motor Company, which could explain why Jacques Nasser, the ousted CEO of Ford, met with such strong resistance when he attempted to implement a similar appraisal process.

Decision Processes

For years, decision making in organizations was considered to be an issue of centralization, or the degree to which decision-making authority is distributed throughout the organization's membership. Within the last several years, however, a slightly different view has been emerging. The issue is not how much, on average, employees participate in organizational decisions. Rather, the issue is who participates how much in what decisions. As Katz and Kahn put it, "On what is one to take part, and in what degree, and how?"[16] For us, then, the process called decision making concerns who contributes, how much they contribute, the way in which they contribute, and which decisions they contribute to.

Another way to say this is that people who make different types of decisions exercise different types of influence. In turn, people who hold different organizational positions are often required to exercise different types of influence.

Because of this, upper-level managers are probably most concerned with decisions about organizational resources; middle-level managers are most concerned with coordination issues; and lower-level supervisors are most concerned with decisions related to task performance.[17] Since decision making is central to organizational functioning, changing it is critical to organizational effectiveness. And "changing" may mean anything from altering basic resource-distribution criteria to revising the way that task assignments are made.

An example of a decision-process change is that reported by Nancy Morse and Edward Reimer.[18] They experimented with an ongoing organization, changing a major variable: "In this experiment the objective was to change the role structure with respect to decision making and its accompanying activities so that the lower hierarchical levels in the structure would have more power and responsibility for carrying on the work of the organization."[19] For the most part, the experiment produced changes in a variety of employee characteristics: self-actualization, satisfaction with supervision, liking for the company, job satisfaction, and liking for the change.

Another way in which decision processes can be the object of a change effort is altering the decision rule used. When several people join in making a decision, they tend to follow some basic governing rules, such as the following:[20]

- *Consensus rule.* Everyone involved in making the decision must agree with the proposed decision.
- *Majority rule.* At least one-half of the people involved must agree with the proposed decision.
- *Plurality rule.* More people must agree with the proposed decision than support any alternative decisions.

Thus, when decision processes are the general object of organizational change, the rule by which decisions are made may be the specific object. Different decision rules affect both the decision's quality and people's acceptance of it; therefore, changing the rule may well change important aspects of the decision process.

STRATEGIC DIRECTION

At the broadest level, change can be implemented in the overall direction that an organization takes. At such a level, change is exceptionally difficult to manage and far-reaching in its effects.

Years ago, James Thompson argued that organizations do more than merely react to environmental demands, opportunities, and pressures. Rather, they actively "engage" the environment, establishing a *domain.* A domain "consists of claims which an organization stakes out for itself."[21] These claims are set forth mainly in terms of the products or services that the organization produces and their actual or potential consumers:

Thus universities are universities, but their domains may range considerably; some offer astronomy courses, others do not; some serve local populations, others are international; some offer student housing and graduate education, others do not. No two firms in the oil industry are identical in terms of domain. Some refine petroleum and market gasoline and other derivatives; others buy and market gasoline and oil. Some operate in a regional territory; others are national or international. Some provide credit cards; others are cash and carry.[22]

The idea of domain is so important because it indicates the basic identity of the enterprise. Who it is, what it is trying to do, and whom it is trying to serve—these issues are central to an organization's *raison d'être.* Attempts to change organizational domains are therefore attempts to change organizational identity. It is this shared identity—given its centrality, distinctiveness, and enduring nature to the organizational stakeholders—that makes collective action a reality,[23] and thus makes changes to the identity difficult, as organizations are prone to ego defenses that work to maintain the continuity of an existing identity.[24] While success is not assured, Microsoft (see "Focus On: Microsoft") provides one recent example of a company intent on reinventing itself.

Focus On: Microsoft

By any measurement standard—be it market capitalization, cash flow, market share dominance, or continuing product development and redevelopment—Microsoft is one of the most successful companies of the past twenty years. Microsoft is an industry—and economic—leader. And there is little doubt that Microsoft intends to remain a leader.

Through an aggressive acquisition strategy (e.g., Microsoft acquired ninety-two companies between 1995 and 1999) and ongoing product development and redevelopment (e.g., the launching of its Windows XP operating system and the Xbox game system), Microsoft weathered the dot-com bust and its ongoing legal wrangling with the federal government over antitrust issues. Today, Microsoft remains the undisputed champion in computing operating systems and office software, and it's the Windows and Office divisions that produce the financial resources for Microsoft's continued growth. In 2001, Microsoft had cash reserves of $30 billion, and those reserves were growing by $1 billion a month.

Yet by the late 1990s, Microsoft was turning into a lumbering dinosaur. Analysts saw Microsoft as a technology follower, not a leader. With its 30,000 employees, 183 different product lines, and five layers of management, Microsoft had become bureaucratic. The company was mired in red tape, best exemplified by the company's requirement that all major decisions ultimately needed the approval of chairman Bill Gates and CEO Steve Ballmer.

It came as no surprise that by 1999, after nine months as CEO and conducting 100 in-depth interviews throughout Microsoft, Ballmer felt it was time to reinvent Microsoft. One immediate change now allows Ballmer's lieutenants the freedom to run their businesses and spend their budgets as they see fit, as long as they meet revenue and profit goals.

Microsoft's rallying cry through the '80s and '90s was to put a PC on every desk and in every home. The new rallying cry is to give people the power to do anything they want, anywhere they want, and on any device. Microsoft's new vision is to make the PC as easy to use as a TV or telephone. To achieve this, Gates and Ballmer concluded that the company's strategic direction had to change. Such a profound strategic change is also resulting in changes to Microsoft's culture and organizational processes, and individuals' tasks and responsibilities.

Today, Microsoft is *attempting* to reinvent itself from a software titan to an Internet titan. Though Microsoft will continue to develop Windows software for PCs and servers, the company intends to position itself on the cutting edge of the Internet. New software is being developed that will link servers, PCs, cell phones, handheld computers, TV set-top boxes, and other devices. Microsoft is moving away from traditional software applications purchased at computer stores to software delivered as services over the Web. Consumers will buy subscriptions over the net, not software on CDs. With a click of the mouse, you (or everyone in your company) will be able to use the latest version of any software. Consider that it took Microsoft fifteen months just to upgrade its own 50,000 PCs to the Windows 2000 operating system.

Make no mistake about it: becoming an Internet titan is a fundamental shift in Microsoft's identity. No longer is software seen as a product; software is now a service. To accomplish this change, Microsoft has taken the following steps, among others:

- Applied XML, a programming language that creates tighter links between products, prices, and other information on the Web.
- Created a separate business division (.Net) that is not tied to Windows and its office-product software. .Net will let unrelated Web sites "talk" to one another and to programs that run on every device, including PCs and TV set-top boxes. Thanks to .Net's tying everything together, a consumer can get full word-processing and spreadsheet capabilities, more than enough storage space on a remote server, and online support. Examples of the potential for .Net include (1) aggregating an individual's financial information from various Web sites onto one screen, and (2) purchasing a plane ticket online and then having the flight schedule automatically show up on your computer's daily calendar and PalmPilot.
- In 2001, altered the responsibilities of its top three executives to increase flexibility. The president, Richard Belluzzo, was to manage sales, customer support, finance, and other operations. The CEO, Steve Ballmer, was to focus on strategy, marketing, and being the company's public face. The chairman, Bill Gates, was to be the chief software architect. Barely a year later, Belluzzo had restruc-

tured himself out of a job as the main business units gained more responsibility and autonomy over their fiscal and operational performance.

- Now emphasizes security and privacy across all its products. Microsoft announced at the start of 2002 that the new philosophy of "trustworthy computing" had become the company's highest priority. Gates wanted to ensure that computer users can safely venture across an increasingly Internet-connected world. Ensuring security and privacy is so critical that Microsoft will not launch any new product or include any new feature if it fails security tests. To underscore the importance of security and privacy, the compensation plans (i.e., raises and bonuses) for Microsoft engineers will be tied to how secure products are.

Microsoft is clearly focused on creating an Internet strategy that will ultimately allow individuals to (1) tell the computer what to do, (2) find stuff quickly and easily, (3) create interactive Web pages, and (4) utilize digital photography and three-dimensional imaging. The question remains as to whether Microsoft will succeed in becoming an Internet titan. Ultimate success depends on Microsoft's ability to generate sales and profits; however, the company freely admits it has no clear answer as to how it will accomplish this. History itself provides no guidance, either. Rarely has one company dominated one epoch and gained the upper hand in the next as it has attempted to manage the "highly delicate balance between milking the past and mining the future" (see Greene, Oct. 30, 2000, p. 152).

Sources: J. Greene (2001), Microsoft: How it became stronger than ever, *Business Week,* June 4, pp. 74–85; J. Greene (2000), Microsoft's big bet, *Business Week,* Oct. 20, pp. 152–163; D. I. Hooper & T. Bridis (2002), Microsoft makes security job No. 1, *Tacoma News Tribune,* Jan. 17, p. A3; A. Lin (2002), Microsoft's president leaving, *Tacoma News Tribune,* April 4, pp. D1–D2; M. Moeller (1999), Remaking Microsoft: Why America's most successful company needed an overhaul, *Business Week,* May 17, pp. 106–116; B. Schlender (2001), Microsoft: The beast is back, *Fortune,* June 11, pp. 74–86; B. Schlender (2000), Damn the torpedoes! Full speed ahead, *Fortune,* July 10, pp. 98–110.

Some organizations, however, have successfully navigated a change in corporate direction. The Phillip Morris Company, by means of product diversification, is one example.[25] After the U.S. Surgeon General linked smoking to lung cancer in the 1960s, almost all of the tobacco companies looked for product lines that would sustain them in a time of declining tobacco sales. Most merely bought other companies and treated them as subsidiaries. This allowed them to spread their risk over a more diversified base. But Phillip Morris did something different.

Over the years Phillip Morris had demonstrated a remarkable ability to create an image for a product—cigarettes—that was basically undifferentiated. This ability allowed it to build a commanding market share. For example, the image created for Marlboro as the preferred smoke for rugged, masculine, outdoor types lifted the brand to the number-one selling position in the United States. So, instead of merely buying other firms and treating them as investments, Phillip Morris sought opportunities where they could apply their expertise in advertising and image creation.

As noted, this expertise is most effective with products that are basically undifferentiated. Thus, the company sought to develop first by purchasing Miller Beer. At the time, Miller was an also-ran in the beer market. Moreover, given the trend of consolidation in the industry as well as the coming emergence of microbreweries, it was widely predicted that the brand would disappear in the not-too-distant future. Phillip Morris not only provided immense amounts of cash for advertising (from tobacco revenues), but it also moved its experts into Miller to run the company and to build market share.

It may have been a stroke of luck, but one of Miller's subsidiaries happened to have a so-called "light" beer. Management had not succeeded, however, in marketing it with the theme of diet and weight control. The new owners changed the theme: Miller Lite was now the beer for young, active, athletic people who wished to remain quick and agile. This complemented the new image of Miller Genuine Draft as the choice of attractive, hardworking, upper-blue-collar types: "Miller Time" raised Miller to the position of second-largest brewer in the United States, behind Anheuser-Busch.[26]

Phillip Morris's success with Miller is a result of change in corporate direction, not merely portfolio building. Not only was the acquired company's direction changed, but the parent company also made basic changes: in management (moving key people to the subsidiaries), in the use of funds (both for advertising and for tremendous expansion), and in taking an active part in managing the new business as an integral part of the overall organization.

Consumers are a second major basis for strategic change. A firm's management may decide to market its products to a different group of customers from their current ones, or an agency may decide to offer its services to a different clientele. In either case, the organization will likely undergo a change in strategic direction.

In one case, a successful manufacturing firm failed because it tried to change customers. La Plante-Choate Inc., located in Cedar Rapids, Iowa, manufactured tractor-drawn scrapers and bulldozers (the blade and operating mechanism, not the tractor itself). All of their production was sold to Caterpillar Tractor Co. or through Caterpillar's dealers.[27]

Shortly after the end of World War II, Caterpillar decided to integrate and manufacture their own accessories. They offered to buy several of their suppliers, including La Plante-Choate. L.C. declined the offer, and because they were well known to earthmoving contractors, they decided to enter the tractor and prime mover business and compete for the customers of Caterpillar and others.

This decision necessitated daunting changes in every facet of the company. Because all of their products had been sold to Caterpillar, they had no separate dealer network, no distribution channels—in fact, no marketing department to speak of. All of these had to be created from scratch.

The technology for making scrapers and dozers was mostly cutting, shaping, and welding heavy steel. On the other hand, making prime movers required machining, assembling, and other fabrication operations. These processes in turn required more labor, of higher skills; new production equipment; larger plants; and different engineering abilities. Purchasing, which was a fairly simple matter before, had to be expanded to deal with suppliers of engines, radiators, tires, gears, and myriad other items.

With the number and magnitude of these changes, it would seem that La Plante was doomed. The functional departments, however, performed almost miraculously. A marketing department was formed, and it secured a respectable dealer network. Engineering took only two years to design a prime mover that outperformed its competitors. Production and purchasing managed to get the necessary equipment and supplies, and labor was acquired and trained to start limited production.

Despite this excellent performance at the functional levels, however, La Plante-Choate did not succeed. Perhaps the change was too great, too all-encompassing, to manage. Perhaps, and this might be even more important, the company simply did not have the resources to successfully challenge the entrenched giants for their customers.

Whatever the reasons for Phillip Morris's success or La Plante-Choate's failure, the impacts are similar. Changing an organization's strategic direction means changing products, services, customers, or any combination of these. And in addition, it often means changing the firm's structure, its management, or even its collective self-identity.

ORGANIZATIONAL CULTURE

In 1982 a pair of management consultants published one of the most influential books of the past several years. Thomas J. Peters and Robert H. Waterman's *In Search of Excellence*[28] made one major point, a point that they drove home with example after example. This was that companies that enjoy excellent management have one thing in common: a shared understanding of their value systems, what their companies stand for. Following the lead of that analysis, academicians and consultants alike have been able to identify several of the beliefs that characterize the particularly "excellent" organization:[29]

- A clear, shared vision connects the corporate vision with day-to-day decisions and work.
- The leadership consistently communicates and reinforces the vision and values.

- Involved employees are a valued asset, not a cost. They assume responsibility for work, control their work environment, and are accountable for the outcomes.
- Employees maintain an external focus (customer, supplier, general public, community, and so forth).
- Management understands what competencies are required to accomplish strategic objectives, and where competence adds value.
- The organization is structured so that employees are able to respond quickly and positively to a changing environment.
- Good measurements reinforce shared values.
- All members—top to bottom, managers and nonmanagers alike—are in alignment with overall goals and strategies.

Whether one buys the argument that Peters and Waterman emphasized is not really the point here. In fact, a number of their exemplars of excellence have encountered some major difficulties in the last decade. What is of interest, however, is what they and their successors identify by this "excellent" belief system: the organization's culture. Thus, the fourth and broadest aspect of an enterprise that may be a candidate for change is its culture. It is worth emphasizing the phrase "broadest aspect" of an enterprise because it foreshadows the difficulties that arise when attempts are made to change an organization's culture. We begin our discussion of culture by first defining the term before describing its features, but we remind you to consider the following—the difficulties experienced by the exemplars first outlined in *In Search of Excellence* may have been the result of changes occurring in the organizations' environments that required possible changes to the companies' cultures.

Organizational Culture Defined

Organizational culture has been defined in a variety of ways. Some have related it to shared values; others say that it is a pattern of beliefs and expectations shared by the organization's members. A more encompassing view holds that

> Culture is the set of values, guiding beliefs, understandings, and ways of thinking that is shared by members of an organization and is taught to new members as correct. It represents the unwritten, feeling part of the organization. Cultures serve two critical functions in organizations: (1) to integrate members so they know how to relate to one another, and (2) to help the organization adapt to the external environment.[30]

We can describe the nature of organizational culture at four levels, ranging from the most basic (and hidden) to the most explicit. Our description follows Hunt's,[31] in which he likened the organization's culture to a peeled onion; this conception is shown in figure 3.4. As we "peel" the cultural onion, we go from the most visible indicators to the core assumptions that are shared by members of the organization.

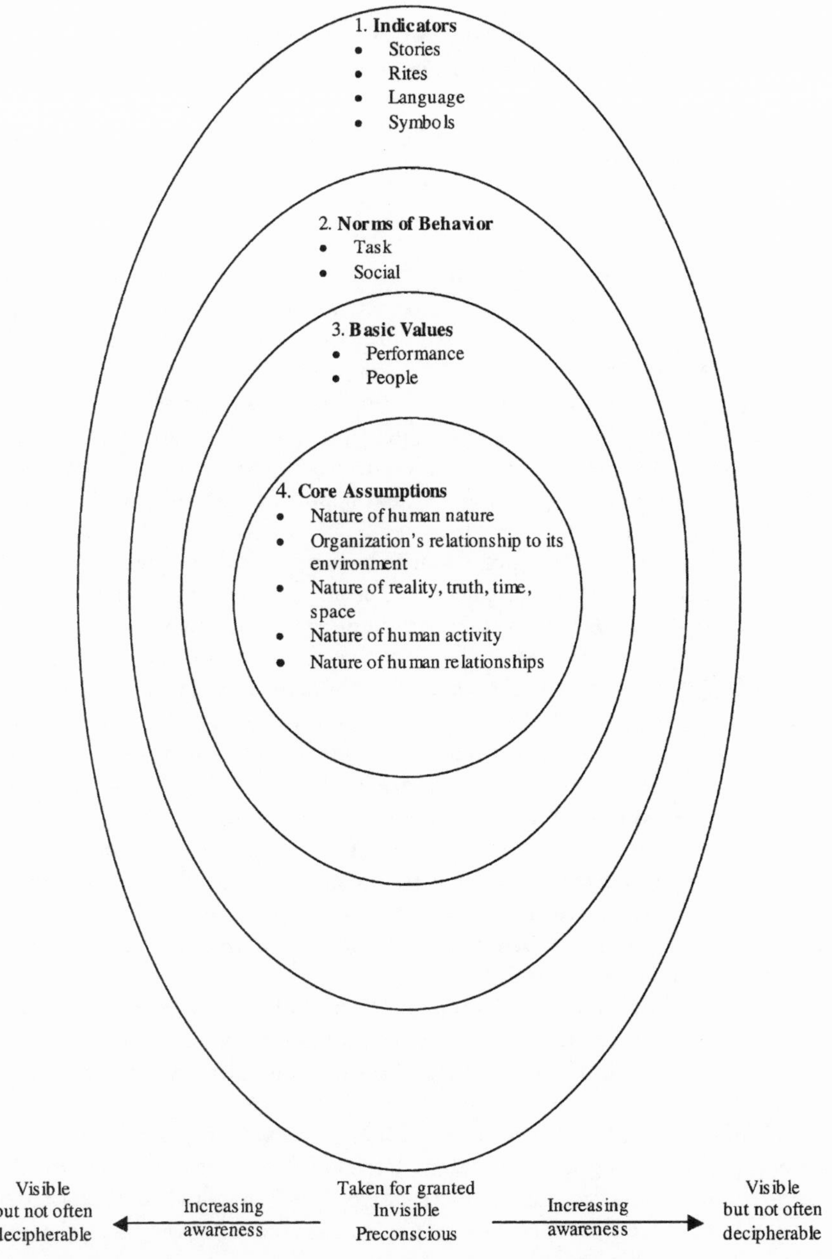

Figure 3.4 A Peeled-Onion Conception of Organizational Culture

Source: Adapted from J. G. Hunt (1991), *Leadership: A new synthesis,* Newbury Park, CA: Sage, p. 227. Copyright © 1991. Reprinted by permission of Sage Publications, Inc.

Indicators

At the surface level are the observable behaviors and visible artifacts: for example, tales that are passed on to new employees, company slogans and logos, office layout, and so forth. In particular, one can use four major indicators to describe (or understand) an organization's culture: stories, rites, language, and symbols.[32]

Stories

A story is "the narration of an event or series of events, either true or fictitious."[33] Organizational stories are usually narrations about how people reacted at a particular time to a particular set of circumstances. Often, the actions they took are then embellished and justified in the stories that evolve.

Stories serve at least three purposes: to inform new employees about the organization, to affirm important values and norms, and to reveal what is unique about the organization's function in society. A story usually focuses on a single event (or sequence of events) that happened sometime in the organization's past.

One encounters several types of stories in various firms and agencies. Joanne Martin and her colleagues have described seven common story types that "occur with great regularity in a wide variety of organizational contexts":[34]

- *Are the rules for everyone?* This is known as the rule-breaking story. Here, a very-high-status employee, such as the president or chairman of the board, encounters a low-status (frequently new) employee whose job it is to enforce a rule—for example, admitting only those personnel to a work area who have a specific identification badge. The story tells whether the bigwig complied with the rule or pulled rank and entered the work area anyway.
- *Is the big boss human?* In this type of story a high-status person is given a chance to do something that equalizes his or her status with that of others: clean up after the company picnic, ride the company bus instead of going separately in a limousine. The story tells whether the big boss did the thing or refused to do it.
- *Can the little person rise to the top?* Stories of this type concern whether a low-status employee receives a deserved promotion because of demonstrated abilities, regardless of his or her original status. In its extreme form, this is the familiar Horatio Alger story.
- *Will I get fired?* This type of story concerns reductions in staff. Low-status employees fear losing their job; high-status employees have to make the decision. A major reorganization in the early 1990s resulted in IBM—an *In Search of Excellence* exemplar—breaking its tradition of never having laid off employees in its history.
- *Will the organization help me when I have to move?* These stories tell whether the company helps employees deal with the difficulties they encounter when they move from one location to another. The theme of the stories usually

concerns personal difficulties (such as paying rent on two places while waiting for the children to get out of school, helping the spouse find a job) rather than work-related problems.

• *How will the boss react to mistakes?* In these stories a mistake has been made, the boss has found out, and a confrontation takes place. One version of the story tells of the boss who says, "*I* gave you the go-ahead on that project, and so we *both* made the mistake." The other version tells of the subordinate who lost a major contract and thereafter disappeared into the dark recesses of the company, never to be seen again.

• *How will the organization deal with obstacles?* These stories deal with problems. The problems can be external, such as a fire, earthquake, or blizzard; technical, such as a breakdown of the telephone system; or organizational, such as management's not allowing the air-conditioning system to operate so as to save on power costs. A company owner in Massachusetts has become a legend for continuing to pay his employees after a devastating fire destroyed his factory.

When the story concerns an organizational hero—either the Big Boss or the Little Person—the hero is portrayed as having strongly developed character traits, especially courage and wisdom. Even more important, however, heroes embody the values and behavior that made the company a success, and thus are the values and behavior that people should be emulating today. In short, stories portray the organization's history while tying it to the present.

Rites

Rites indicate what is really important. The order in which agenda items are placed, the way people greet one another, the hoopla and fanfare of sales meetings, and the solemn reading of highly detailed written reports are all rites in which every organization engages.

Some rites can be seen in many management practices: employee promotion announcements, long-range planning processes, and performance evaluations are three clear examples. Some are social: attendance and behavior at the boss's annual Christmas party, making final contract decisions at the country club, going out for beer on Friday afternoons after work.

These are all rites that one can observe. But what meanings are conveyed? To have a particular item on a meeting agenda may signal in one company that it is significant enough to be considered by the important people who attend. In another firm, where decisions are not really made in these meetings, the appearance of the item means something different.

The meaning of the weekly after-work beer could be that all employees get access to all others, and that people from different levels in the company can exchange ideas and opinions. On the other hand, it could be an opportunity for managers to catch subordinates displaying unseemly behavior.

As we saw in the case of stories, organizational rites tend to take on certain patterns. In fact, six basic patterns have been observed. They range from the familiar rites of passage—as when a freshman pledge is awarded full status in the sorority, or when the graduate student passes the departmental qualifying examinations—to rites of integration, such as the annual meeting in the cafeteria where the president delivers the state-of-the-company address.[35] Table 3.2 summarizes the six most common types of organizational rites.

Language

Most organizations have a language that enables members to communicate efficiently and meaningfully. It can be heard in everyday technical use as well as in informal jargon and slang. It can also be heard in songs, jokes, or accepted proverbs ("We'll play by any rules, as long as they apply to everyone"; "publish or perish"). Governmental bureaucracies have a particularly strong reputation for developing (and nurturing?) their own unique language. This seems especially true of military organizations, as illustrated by new recruits' encounters with the U.S. Navy:

They enlist at the AFEES (Armed Forces Examining and Entrance Station), otherwise known as a home town recruiting station. They then go to a RTC (Recruit Training Command) at the nearest NTC (Naval Training Center). Here the Navy puts them through the transition from civilian to military life with a busy schedule of lectures

Table 3.2
Types of Rites Found in Organizations

Types of Rites	Function Served
Rites of passage	Help people move into new roles and statuses Example: Basic training in the military
Rites of degradation	Dissolve social identities and the power that goes with them Example: Firing and replacing the top executive
Rites of enhancement	Enhance social identities and the power that goes with them Example: Award banquet for star salespeople
Rites of renewal	Revitalize social structures and improve organizational functioning Example: Annual management retreat
Rites of conflict reduction	Reduce conflict and aggression Example: Collective bargaining
Rites of integration	Reinforce feelings of togetherness and bonding Example: Office holiday party

Source: Adapted from H. M. Trice & J. M. Beyer (1984), Studying organizational cultures through rites and ceremonials, *Academy of Management Review,* 9 (October), p. 657; and (1993), *The cultures of work organizations*, Englewood Cliffs, NJ: Prentice-Hall, p. 111. *Cultures of Work Organizations* by Trice/Beyer. © Reprinted by permission of Pearson Education, Inc., Upper Saddle River, NJ.

and drills on the Navy's traditions, customs, and regulations. Here they learn the first key words in their new vocabulary, such as CC (Company Commander), the POD (Plan of the Day), BI (Barracks Inspection), EPO (Educational Petty Officer), MD (Military Drill), TOD (Term of the Day), TAD (Temporary Additional Duty). Newly enlisted recruits are given three tests: the ASVAB (Armed Services Vocational Aptitude Battery), the NFQU (Nuclear Field Qualification Tests), and the FLAT (Foreign Language Aptitude Test). They also receive a four digit NEC (Navy Enlisted Classification), which codifies their incoming skills, qualifications, and aptitudes.[36]

In brief, the vocabulary of an organization's language contains words that convey meanings inside the organization that they would not have outside. We know one company, for example, that is a high-energy sales firm. Its managers routinely refer to people's "hot button," which is its euphemism for an employee's particular motivating factor. There is little doubt that language is a potent means for transmitting organizational culture.

Symbols

Finally, symbols provide the most explicit indicator of an enterprise's culture. Obvious examples are seen in corporate logos, slogans, insignias, office furnishings, emblems, and so forth. "Like a good neighbor, State Farm is there" is an example of an organization's attempt to convey a certain sense or belief about itself. Similarly, Merrill Lynch's bull evokes meanings, emotions, and beliefs about that company. The symbol is both clear in its portrayal of strength, and ambiguous as to what specifically it has to do with the brokerage's abilities and products.

Internal symbols are also important in conveying an organization's culture. Does top management have the top floor in the office building? Does a first-line supervisor have a closed office or one with movable walls approximately half-height? One of us worked for a company that prided itself on its Spartan efficiency. Family pictures—of spouse, children, and so forth—were not allowed in an employee's office cubicle. However, each person was given the choice of either a plant or a painting, but not both. These restrictions, too, are all symbolic.

Norms of Behavior

At the second level of figure 3.4's peeled onion is the set of norms that guide members' behavior. Basically, norms are rules or codes that indicate proper and improper action; they provide guides for playing the organizational game. They describe what is really important in the organization, what behavior will get someone in trouble, and what will get one ahead.

In any organization there can be thousands of norms. They might include how to dress, how hard to work, how to measure success, how to deal with each other, and how much time should be spent in the office on a Saturday. In other words, norms cover a wide spectrum of behavior. However, it is generally helpful to think of them as relating to two distinct aspects of organizational life: They can be distinguished as to whether they guide the technical aspects of work or guide social and interpersonal relationships. This distinction is a common one, often referred to as task versus people orientations.

More specifically, four major categories of norms shape an organization's culture: task-support norms, task-innovation norms, social-relationship norms, and personal-freedom norms. These have been identified and studied by Ralph H. Kilmann and Mary J. Saxton:[37]

Task-Support Norms

Task-support norms guide people's behavior toward each other in a technical dimension. "Share information with other work groups" is a norm that encourages people to cooperate with each other in performing tasks. This kind of norm is especially important in fast-moving high-technology firms. In contrast is the "Stick to your own task" view. This statement tells people to work by themselves. Usually such a norm leaves cross-group cooperation to the supervisory levels.

Management may wish to change task-support norms because of a change in technology. If, for example, a job changes so that two or three workers now have to coordinate their individual tasks, it does not make much sense to encourage them to stick to their own business; the task-support norm has to change.

Task-Innovation Norms

Task-innovation norms are also technical in nature. Such norms guide people with respect to experimentation. A new employee does not have to be told too often, "We've always done it this way," to understand that the firm is committed to maintaining the status quo. Creativity and innovation are not encouraged in that company.

Companies that survive in an industry undergoing abrupt changes may do so because they embrace a norm of innovation among their employees. The norm at 3M has been for employees to spend up to 15 percent of the workweek on anything they want as long as it is product related.[38] In 2000, 3M generated $5.6 billion in sales—a third of its total revenues—from products that didn't exist just four years earlier.[39]

Managers who wish to introduce and reinforce a norm of innovation have to recognize an important truth. They have to do all they can to reduce or even eliminate the stigma usually associated with failure. 3M has been able to do just this. The discovery of an adhesive that didn't stick all that well could have been deemed a failure in a company that brought us Scotch tape. Instead, that adhesive has been used in what many consider one of the single-greatest office product inventions of the last half of the twentieth century—the Post-It note.

Social-Relationship Norms

Social-relationship norms refer to the firm's social dimension. They guide people's interpersonal behavior. Some companies encourage their employees to socialize off the job; some make it plain that such relationships are not desirable. "I see those people all day at work—no way am I going to spend my free time with them, too!" exemplifies the sentiment in the latter firms.

Organizations that require a great deal of collaboration and nonformal communication encourage strong social-relationship norms. If managers wish to stimulate the formation of such norms, they will probably have to introduce some company activities that involve the employees (e.g., softball teams) and/or the families of employees, not just the employees themselves. We know one firm, for instance, that regularly treats its members to a day's outing on the company yacht. This serves both as a reward and as a norm reinforcer.

Personal-Freedom Norms

Personal freedom is the fourth category of norms identified by Kilmann and Saxton. These norms also concern the social aspects of organizational life. They govern the degree of personal autonomy that individuals enjoy in the organization.

We spoke earlier of autonomy as an element of individual task behavior. We said that it concerns the amount of discretion that workers have in performing their tasks. Personal-freedom norms refer to such discretion companywide. Translated into action, they concern the degree to which people are encouraged to express their personal preferences, even if those preferences may be at odds with conventional wisdom. Such norms encourage individuals to believe in either their own values or the organization's.

Changing personal-freedom norms is no small matter. How do we encourage employees to speak out when they used to be punished, even slightly, for doing so? How do we discourage such expression when previously it was reinforced, even rewarded? Of course, speaking out is not the only basis on which personal-freedom norms rest. Dress codes, hair length, and informal versus formal communication channels all relate to the degree of autonomy that individuals have.

In our society, personal freedom is a delicate issue. It is no less so in organizations. Changing organizational culture by changing personal freedom is tricky business. Careers have risen and fallen because of people's ability (or inability) to assess these norms and their impact. We are all familiar with the lesson in movie mogul Sam Goldwyn's classic comment: "I don't want any yes-men around me. I want everybody to tell me the truth, even if it costs them their jobs."

Basic Values

The third level of our cultural onion is considerably below the surface and contains the basic values that underlie the stories, symbols, norms, and so forth that make the organization the kind of place it is. By its nature, the concept of values is not very precise. It comes as no surprise, therefore, to learn that it has been described in many ways. In fact, the comment made by Clyde Kluckholn et al. is still true today, half a century later:

> Reading the voluminous, and often vague and diffuse, literature on the subject in the various fields of learning, one finds values considered as attitudes, motivations, objects, measurable quantities, substantive areas of behavior, affect-laden customs or traditions, and relationships such as those between individuals, groups, objects, events.[40]

Still, a reasonable consensus has developed about a working definition of values. Kluckholn et al. defined values as a conception of the desirable that influences the selections one makes from available means and ends. Building on this foundation, Rokeach defines values as "abstract ideals, positive or negative, not tied to any specific object or situation, representing a person's beliefs about modes of conduct and ideal terminal modes. [They] guide actions and judgments across specific objects and situations."[41] In short, values are ideals, either explicit or implicit, that guide or affect the choices that one makes.

Obviously, this definition applies as well to communities and organizations as it does to individuals. Organizational values are therefore shared ideals among people that guide decisions and actions. These ideals can, of course, be either explicit or implicit.

It does not make much sense to try to identify and discuss every value that might be of some relevance to an organization's culture; there are simply too many values to do so. However, the values that people share, the ones that make up an organization's value system, tend to fall into two categories: performance and people.

Performance Values

Performance-related values concern the orientation of the organization to productivity. Maximum attention to customer service, long held to be the hallmark of Nordstrom, is another.

In their work on organizational values, Barry Z. Posner and Warren H. Schmidt found that several values relate to organizational effectiveness.[42] *Competency* refers to an idea that excellent performance—not just getting the job done—is the goal of all employees, from the shop floor up to mahogany row.

Determination refers to an end-goal orientation. Posner and Schmidt found that managers especially value other managers who exhibit an unfaltering focus on accomplishing the firm's objectives. This focus, we may imagine, allows such managers to make choices that further goal accomplishment, such as to make decisions about which department will be able to hire a new staff member.

Leadership qualities were a third major value that managers embrace. Well-managed organizations seem to recognize that performance depends on how effective their leaders are.

3M prides itself on encouraging everyone in its employ to think and act like an entrepreneur. To lead current thinking into new paths seems to be a performance value of the highest order in well-managed organizations.

People Values

People-related values have to do with the social and personal qualities of the enterprise. Peters and Waterman's point that people are important as individuals is an example.

For example, when one financial services company we know is forced to eliminate jobs, their response is usually to put the affected workers through retraining. Note that this "people" value has performance connotations as well. For one thing, retraining may be more efficient than replacement. Moreover, both managers and workers are continually reminded that they need to keep themselves well trained and up-to-date. GE's Jack Welch believed that employees could not be promised lifetime employment; however, through constant education and training, he believed that GE could guarantee them lifetime employability.[43]

Posner and Schmidt, referred to earlier, have identified several people-related values. They found that values relating to cooperation, supportiveness, and dependability are especially important to managers at various levels. *Cooperation* refers to a manager's sharing of time, resources, and information with another. It also means a natural willingness to work together for some joint goal.

Supportiveness was found to be especially valued in superiors—that is, managers especially appreciate organizations in which their bosses act as supporters rather than as judge, jury, or obstacle. "The best boss is the one who views his or her job as helping me get my job done" is the sort of sentiment expressed by the supportiveness value.

Dependability means being reliable and trustworthy. This value is especially appreciated in subordinates. Managers strongly approve of a corporate value system in which dependability is a major element.

It is obvious that these three people values are mutually supportive. A culture that fosters cooperation, supportiveness, and dependability seems a pretty consistent one. Moreover, Posner and Schmidt discovered, their managers held especially high esteem for another value, one that cuts across the performance/people distinction: *integrity.* This is the single most admired value in peers, superiors, and subordinates.

This is not an unusual discovery. Rokeach and others have consistently found the value of *honesty* to rank highest of all values that they have measured, even across different national boundaries.[44] It seems clear, in short, that people prefer organizational cultures in which such attributes as honesty and integrity are valued and promoted.

Basic Assumptions

At the core of figure 3.4's cultural onion are fundamental assumptions and perceptions, probably not even directly known or acknowledged by people in the organization.[45] They reflect how organizational members perceive, think, and feel about things. Since they are hidden so deeply, these assumptions tend to be immune from confrontation or debate, and thus possibly change. There are five major sets of assumptions, which fall into the following categories:

- *Nature of human nature.* What does it mean to be "human," and what attributes are assumed to be intrinsic? Is human nature fundamentally evil or good? Or is it a mixture? Are human beings perfectible if they exercise enough control and discipline? Which is more valid, theory X or theory Y?
- *Organization's relationship to its environment.* To what extent do the people in the organization, especially key members, see the relationship between the organization and its environment as one of dominance, submission, or harmony? Is it the job of humans, through their organizations, to exert mastery over nature, to yield to its power, or to coexist in some kind of accord or even unity? Does management "manage" its environment or acquiesce to it?
- *Nature of reality, truth, time, and space.* What are the rules that define what is real and what is not; what constitutes facts or data? Is truth something simply "known," or can it be discovered (and by whom)? Are organizational members future oriented, past oriented, or here-and-now oriented? Is property individual or communal?
- *Nature of human activity.* What is the "right" thing for humans to do: Should they be active or passive, achieving or accepting, self-developing or fatalistic? What is work and what is play?
- *Nature of human relationships.* Finally, what is the "right" way for individuals to relate to each other, especially with regard to power and love? Is life essentially competitive or cooperative; individualistic or collectivistic? Should relationships be based on traditional legal-rational authority, on personality, on knowledge and skills, or what?

The peeled-onion model of organizational culture depicted in figure 3.4 is useful for a couple of reasons. First, it helps us understand how cultures form, continue, and change. Clearly, the outer layers are easier to change than the inner ones. Second, it reminds us that various aspects of an organization's culture are linked. Taken as a whole, the figure helps us realize that assumptions at the organization's core are reflected in members' basic values, which in turn show up in their rules about proper behavior. And clues to all of this can be found in organizational stories, rites, language, and symbols.

Before we turn our attention to the *how* of change in chapters 4 and 5, it is helpful to note one final assumption with respect to organizations and the *what* of change. Organizations are complex systems, and consequently change is rarely isolated to one object—be it task behavior, organizational processes, strategic direction, or organizational culture. Globalization has been a focus for many companies over the past twenty years, and changing from a national to a global company would have been impossible if any firm had focused on just one object of change.

NOTES

1. L. G. Bolman & T. E. Deal (1997), *Reframing organizations: Artistry, choice, and leadership* (2d Ed.)., San Francisco: Jossey-Bass, 1997. Thanks to Professor Ken S. Keleman for suggesting this point.

2. W. Bridges (1994), *Job shift: How to prosper in a workplace without jobs,* Reading, MA: Addison-Wesley.

3. R. L. Kahn (1974), The work module: A proposal for the humanization of work, in James O'Toole (Ed.), *Work and the quality of life,* Cambridge, MA: MIT Press, p. 199.

4. F. W. Taylor (1923), *The principles of scientific management,* New York: Harper.

5. J. M. Juran & F. M. Gryna, Jr. (1980), *Quality planning and analysis,* New York: McGraw-Hill; W. E. Deming (1982), *Quality, productivity, and competitive position,* Cambridge, MA: MIT Center for Advanced Engineering Study; L. Dobyns & C. Crawford-Mason (1991), *Quality or else,* Boston: Houghton Mifflin; P. B. Crosby (1979), *Quality is free: The art of making quality certain,* New York: New American Library; and P. B. Crosby (1991), *Completeness: Quality for the 21st century,* New York: Penguin.

6. Adapted from P. E. Connor (1984), *Organization structure and design* (Modules in Management series, J. E. Rosenzweig & F. E. Kast, Eds.), Chicago: Science Research Associates; R. L. Cherry (1989), Stages of work redesign, *Journal of Quality and Participation,* Special Supplement (December), p. 54.

7. J. R. Hackman & G. R. Oldham (1980), *Work redesign,* Reading, MA: Addison-Wesley.

8. M. Buckingham & C. Coffman (1999), *First, break all the rules,* New York: Simon & Schuster.

9. J. R. Hackman (1977), Work design, in J. R. Hackman & J. L. Suttle (Eds.), *Improving life at work: Behavioral science approaches to organizational change,* Santa Monica, CA: Goodyear, p. 244.

10. T. S. Bateman & S. A. Snell (2002), *Management* (5th ed.), New York: McGraw-Hill, pp. 508–511.

11. J. Stitt (1990), *Managing for excellence,* Milwaukee, WI: Quality Press.

12. J. R. Gordon (1993), *A diagnostic approach to organizational behavior* (4th ed.), Boston: Allyn and Bacon, pp. 617–618.

13. D. Katz & R. L. Kahn (1978), *The social psychology of organizations* (2d ed.), New York: Wiley, p. 697.

14. E. J. Harrick (1981), A contingency theory of pay, *Topics in Total Compensation,* 4, pp. 148–152; E. E. Lawler (1981), *Pay and organization development,* Reading, MA: Addison-Wesley; Gordon, p. 152.

15. Book excerpt from *Jack: Straight from the gut* by J. Welch & J. A. Byrne. Excerpt titled "Jack and the people factory" ran September 11, 2001, *Fortune,* pp. 75–86.

16. Katz & Kahn, p. 682; P. E. Connor (1992), Decision making participation patterns: The role of organizational context, *Academy of Management Journal,* 35, pp. 218–231.

17. M. Moch, C. Cammann, & R. A. Cooke (1983), Organizational structure: Measuring the distribution of influence, in S. E. Seashore, E. E. Lawler III, P. H. Mirvis, & C. Cammann (Eds.), *Assessing organizational change,* New York: Wiley, pp. 177–201.

18. N. Morse & E. Reimer (1956), The experimental change of a major organizational variable, *Journal of Abnormal and Social Psychology,* 52, pp. 120–129. For an extensive discussion of this experiment, refer to Katz & Kahn, pp. 683–697.

19. Katz & Kahn, p. 683.

20. J. H. Davis, N. L. Kerr, R. S. Atkin, R. Holt, & D. Meek (1975), The decision processes of 6- and 12-person mock juries assigned unanimous and two-thirds majority rules, *Journal of Personality and Social Psychology,* 32, pp. 1–14.

21. J. D. Thompson (1967), *Organizations in action,* New York: McGraw-Hill, p. 26.

22. Ibid.

23. D. A. Gioia & J. B. Thomas (1996), Identity, image, and issue interpretation: Sensemaking during strategic change in academia, *Administrative Science Quarterly,* 41, pp. 370–403.

24. A. D. Brown & K. Starkey (2000), Organizational identity: A psychodynamic perspective, *Academy of Management Review,* 25, pp. 102–120.

25. Thanks are extended to the late Professor Charles M. Gudger for his assistance with this and the following example. See "Phillip Morris, Inc.," in A. J. Strickland III & A. A. Thompson, Jr. (Eds.) (1982), *Cases in strategy and policy.* Plano, TX: Business Publications.

26. http://www.activemedia-guide.com/beermakers.htm

27. See "La Plant-Choate Manufacturing Co.," Case #BP435, Harvard Case File, 1947.

28. T. J. Peters & R. H. Waterman, Jr. (1982), *In search of excellence: Lessons from America's best-run companies,* New York: Harper and Row. It should be noted that the authors have received recent unflattering press with respect to their methodology—the falsification of the underlying data—used in writing the book. See J. A. Byrne (2001), The real confessions of Tom Peters, *Business Week,* December 2, 46.

29. Based on P. Plessinger Craig (1993), Effective organizational change: Pushing the right levers, *Planning Forum Network,* 6 (January), p. 5.

30. R. L. Daft (2001), *Organization theory and design* (6th ed.), St. Paul, MN: West, pp. 314–315.

31. J. G. Hunt (1991), *Leadership: A new synthesis,* Newbury Park, CA: Sage, pp. 220–224.

32. For a thorough treatment of this and other aspects of organizational culture, see H. M. Trice & J. M. Beyer (1993), *The cultures of work organizations,* Englewood Cliffs, NJ: Prentice-Hall, pp. 77–128.

33. *American Heritage Dictionary,* s.v. "Story."

34. J. Martin, M. S. Feldman, M. J. Hatch, & S. B. Sitkin (1983), The uniqueness paradox in organizational stories, *Administrative Science Quarterly,* 28, pp. 438–453.

35. For a wonderful example of this rite, see B. Rosen (1985), Breakfast at Spiro's: Dramaturgy and dominance, *Journal of Management,* 11, pp. 31–48.

36. Adapted by Trice and Beyer, p. 148, from R. Evered (1983), The language of organizations: The case of the navy (pp. 125–143), in L. R. Pondy, P. J. Frost, & T. C. Dandridge (Eds.), *Organizational symbolism,* Greenwich, CT: JAI Press.

37. R. H. Kilmann & M. J. Saxton (1983), *The Kilmann-Saxton Culture-Gap survey,* Pittsburgh, Pa.: Organizational Design Consultants; R. H. Kilmann (1985), *Beyond the quick fix: Managing five tracks to organizational success,* San Francisco: Jossey-Bass; and R. H. Kilmann (1989), *Managing beyond the quick fix,* San Francisco: Jossey-Bass.

38. R. Mitchell (1989), Master of innovation: How 3M keeps its new products coming, *Business Week,* April 10, pp. 58–63.

39. M. Arndt (2002), 3M: A lab for growth? *Business Week,* January 21, pp. 50–51.

40. C. Kluckhohn et al. (1951), Values and value–orientations in the theory of action, in T. Parsons & E. A. Shils (Eds.), *Toward a general theory of action,* Boston: Harvard University Press, p. 390.

41. M. Rokeach (1968), *Beliefs, attitudes, and values,* San Francisco: Jossey-Bass, pp. 124, 160.

42. B. Z. Posner & W. H. Schmidt (1992), Values and the American manager: An update updated, *California Management Review,* 34, pp. 80–94.

43. "Jack Welch's lessons for success" (1993), *Business Week,* January 25, pp. 86–90.

44. M. Rokeach (1979), *Understanding human values,* New York: Free Press; M. Rokeach & S. J. Ball-Rokeach (1990), Stability and change in American value priorities: 1968–1989, *American Psychologist,* 44, pp. 775–784; and P. E. Connor, B. W. Becker, T. Kakuyama, & L. F. Moore (1993), A cross-national comparative study of managerial values: U.S., Canada, and Japan, *Advances in International Comparative Management,* 8, pp. 3–29.

45. This section follows Hunt, pp. 222–223. See also E. H. Schein (1983), The role of the founder in creating an organizational culture, *Organizational dynamics,* 12, pp. 13–28; and F. Kluckhohn & F. L. Strodbeck, *Variations in value orientation,* Evanston, IL: Row, Peterson.

4

Technological and Structural Methods of Change

In the last chapter we examined the objects of change efforts. The purpose of this chapter and the following one is to discuss the how, or methods of change. As we noted, four distinct approaches are covered. First, management may want to effect a change by altering production or service-related processes; this is a *technological* method. Or second, they may decide that the best way is by modifying certain roles or relationships; this is a *structural* method. These form the content of this chapter. In chapter 5 we discuss two additional methods, *managerial* and *human.*

TECHNOLOGICAL METHOD

> Cap'n says to John Henry,
> "Gonna bring me a steam drill 'round,
> Gonna take dat steam drill out on de job,
> Gonna whop dat steel on down,
> Lawd, Lawd, gonna whop dat steel on down."[1] ©

Thus marks the classic description of new technology introduced into the workplace. Directly to our point, however, the Cap'n used a new technology to change the organization's output. This exactly fits our definition: The technological method of change pertains to the organization's production process with respect to the products produced or services provided. It is aimed at improving either the organization's quality or quantity of output. Such change typically involves new equipment or techniques.

In general, changing technology means changing the way in which the organization's output is produced or supplied. Over the past decade, for example, many organizations have embraced a total quality management (TQM) approach to improving their productivity. TQM attempts to effect continuous organizational, product, and service improvement by using both process- and product-control techniques. Unlike other strategies, this approach takes a systemwide focus that includes not only the organization but also its customers and suppliers.[2] TQM and its comparison process, ISO 9000, have been adopted in various forms by hundreds of organizations, ranging from producers of exotic electronic gear to providers of banking services to city governments.[3] Table 4.1 identifies a representative sample of such enterprises.

Computers obviously play a major role in enabling organizations to adopt TQM practices effectively. At a more personal level, computers have also affected many of us who work in organizations. For instance, though this book was written on our personal computers, the final product was produced directly from a disk mailed to the publisher. Before completing the book, the authors exchanged the various chapters for review and editing via e-mail accounts and the use of modems. Just twenty years ago, this book would likely have been written with a typewriter, and likely much secretarial support.

The introduction of computers in grocery stores is another example of a technological change that we have all experienced. Inventory control, pricing, and checkout are three of the more obvious store functions affected. Additionally, however, it is interesting to observe the interactions of clerks and customers at the checkout counters. Have these interactions also changed? Our casual observation is that there is markedly less conversation between customer and clerk, owing to the speed with which the clerk passes the packages over the scanner, listening for the beep that signals another item has been recorded. In any event, the point is clear: computers play an enormous role in changing the way in which a lot of us do business.

Table 4.1
A Sample of Organizations That Use TQM-Based Systems

Boise Cascade	City of Madison, Wisconsin
Ashton Photo	Ford Motor Company
US Bank	Whistler Corp.
Xerox	Hilltop Steak House
Florida Power and Light	Digital Equipment Corp.
USAA	American Express
Oregon Cutting Systems	Corning, Inc.
Kaiser Permanente	Motorola, Inc.
American Airlines	The Boeing Company
Kodak	Texas Instruments, Inc.
Federal Express Corporation	Ritz-Carlton Hotel Company

For all the press they have received, computerization and its companion, automation, are examples of only one type of technological change. On a more comprehensive level, the major approach to such change is through *job design*. The term job design refers to diagnosing the task, breaking it down into smaller elements before possibly adding functions or responsibilities to the job or changing the job's social nature.

Job Diagnosis

In chapter 3 we identified five principal core job characteristics: skill variety, task identity, task significance, autonomy, and feedback. *Job diagnosis* refers to the examination of a task with a view toward identifying and changing one or more of those characteristics.

Probably the most widely cited and used method of job diagnosis is the job diagnostic survey (JDS), based on the job characteristics model introduced in the last chapter.[4] The JDS is intended to do two things: first, to diagnose existing jobs before they are redesigned; and second, to evaluate the effects of a redesign. This evaluation is critical and is conducted to determine which task characteristics changed and which did not, and to assess the impact of those changes on employees' motivation, desire for growth, satisfaction, and effectiveness (refer back to figure 3.2).

In brief, the JDS is used to answer the following questions.[5]

Are there problems with employee motivation and satisfaction? Sometimes management may believe, based on little or no real evidence other than instinct, that employees are not performing their current job at a satisfactory level because they are not sufficiently motivated. It could be that physical conditions or outmoded equipment may be at the source of the problem; however, motivational concerns could still remain after adjustments are made to the work environment or new equipment is acquired that would lead management to embark on a program of job redesign. The JDS attempts to gauge the level of employee motivation and satisfaction early in the redesign process. If the level is low, the evaluator is advised to examine other aspects of the work situation that are perhaps contributing, such as the machinery, facilities, workflow, office layout, and so forth. If levels are adequately high, the JDS moves the evaluator to the next question.

Is the job low in motivating potential? Sometimes the job has no intrinsic motivating potential. The JDS allows the evaluator to make such an assessment. If the job turns out not to be inherently low, other sources of motivational difficulties (e.g., supervisor-subordinate conflict) should be explored. If the motivation potential is low, the evaluator moves to the next question.

What specific aspects of the job are causing the difficulty? In this step, the JDS directs the evaluator's attention to the core job characteristics. The intent here is to pinpoint the specific strengths and weaknesses of the job as it is currently designed. At this point the evaluator needs to have an idea of what the ideal profile of the job should be. In turn, this idea needs to be based on an understanding of how the job characteristics relate to employee and performance outcomes.

Skill variety, task identity, and task significance seem to be positively related to the degree of meaningfulness that the worker experiences. Autonomy enhances the worker's sense of responsibility for the job and its effects, especially its human effects, as we discussed in the last chapter. And feedback contributes to the worker's understanding of what performance effectiveness entails. To the extent that the evaluator wants any of those *outcomes* increased, the JDS indicates which task characteristics to change.

How ready are the employees for change? Once it has been determined that one or more job characteristics need to be changed, the JDS asks if the affected parties are ready and willing. Central to the instrument's evaluation are the knowledge and skills employees bring to the job, their satisfaction with the physical and administrative aspects of the work, and their need for growth—their interest in and desire for improvement and change. The JDS thus helps identify those particular employees who are especially open to change, and therefore are likely candidates for having their jobs redesigned first.

What special problems and opportunities are present in the existing work system? This final question surveys the current situation; it gets the lay of the land, so to speak. By lay of the land, we mean there may be other factors (e.g., outmoded equipment or poor employee training) that could attenuate the impact of job redesign changes if not addressed. Moreover, there may be positive factors (e.g., high satisfaction with supervisors) that should be retained, as best as possible, during the stages of job redesign.

In short, job diagnosis is the initial step in a systematic, managed job-redesign effort. Once the diagnosis of present conditions has been made, a change toward future and desired conditions can be implemented. This implementation can take place through several means. The following are the most usual: job engineering, job rotation, job enlargement, job enrichment, and changing job relationships. Table 4.2 illustrates how these methods—except for job engineering—affect important task characteristics.

Job Engineering

In Frederick W. Taylor's *Scientific Management*, job design was a matter of engineering the tasks to maximize efficiency:

> Perhaps the most prominent single element in modern scientific management is the task idea. The work of every workman is fully planned out by the management at least one day in advance, and each man receives in most cases complete written instructions describing in detail the task which he is to accomplish . . . The task specifies not only what is to be done but how it should be done and the exact time allowed for doing it.[6]

Table 4.2
Methods of Work Design

1. Job rotation
   (Task characteristics affected: task variety)
2. Job enlargement
   (Task characteristics affected: task simplification, task cycle time)
3. Job enrichment
   (Task characteristics affected: task difficulty, task discretion)
   Flextime
4. Job relationships
   (Task characteristics affected: identity, task significance, skill variety, autonomy, feedback)
   Task clusters
   Client relationships
   Feedback channels

In Taylor's management system, rest was also a key component of the job, and of course, benefits accrued not only to the firm but to the employee as well. Taylor: "And whenever the workman succeeds in doing his task right, and within the time unit specified, he receives an addition of from 30 percent to 100 percent of his ordinary wages."[7]

Modern production and operations management experts follow Taylor's lead. Today, job engineering is concerned with three things: (1) physical conditions of work—plant layout, tool design, process design, product design; (2) planning and control of production—operations methods, statistical process control; and (3) precise valuation of the process and its output—work measurement.

As Donald D. Warrick has pointed out, the primary job-engineering methods used to improve motivation and productivity are the following:[8]

- Define the specific duties of the job.
- Define and design the job's work methods and work flow.
- Design the layout of the workplace.
- Establish performance standards.
- Use time and motion studies to determine the most efficient way to perform the work.
- Train workers to be highly specialized in their work abilities.

The typical results of following such methods were documented years ago in C. R. Walker and Robert H. Guest's classic study of workers on assembly lines.[9] They found that job engineering produced jobs with these characteristics:

- mechanical pacing, in which the line or conveyor belt determined the pace of their work;
- repetitiveness, in which employees performed the same task over and over again;
- low skill requirements, whereby low training costs were incurred;
- narrow job scope, in which the worker concentrated on only a small fraction of the total job;
- limited social interaction, caused by a noisy workplace and physical separation of the workers along a moving line; and
- predetermined equipment and methods, by which the worker performs a task using tools and techniques decided in advance by staff specialists.

It is obvious that job engineering has had a long and popular history. In fact, it has dominated manufacturing operations for years. Moreover, its principles frequently have been used in non-manufacturing jobs in service-oriented operations such as credit card call centers where tasks can be broken down into small, specialized units. For a variety of reasons, however—especially pressure from better-educated employees and from foreign competition—job engineering seems to be giving way to other design methods. Job rotation, job enlargement, and job enrichment are three of the most widely used.

Job Rotation

If management wants to increase variety in the worker's job, they may decide to do so by rotating jobs. At its simplest level, job rotation merely involves two or more workers exchanging jobs on some regular basis. Recall the railroad section gang example from the last chapter: The supervisor could have practiced job rotation by having people switch off from carrying the ties to digging up the old bed, setting the ties into place, and so on. In an office, the office manager can rotate secretaries among various sets of tasks—from memoranda and letters to monthly financial reports to weekly staff-meeting minutes.

The reasoning behind this method is straightforward: Performing several jobs, even if they are simple and routine, will add to workers' task variety, reduce boredom, and enlarge their skill repertoires. Additionally, the cross-training that job rotation provides allows workers to develop a broader perspective on the total production process. Many companies apply job rotation to the management-development process. GE is but one example of a company that rotates its managers among major product groups in order to develop senior executive talent.

Having said this, however, we need to note that the reasoning behind job rotation is seriously flawed with respect to nonmanagers. In point of fact, practical experience with job rotation shows little positive impact on the task characteristics in question. It is as easy to become bored with several simple, routine—boring—jobs as it is with one. As Warrick puts it, "Rotating from one boring job to another will not reduce boredom."[10] The best that probably can happen is that monotony and boredom may be relieved for a short time. Still, if all management wants to do is increase the variety of tasks that a worker is exposed to and knows about, then job rotation is a device that can work to a limited degree. It is a short-term technological method for change.

Job Enlargement

If management wants to change the scope of a particular worker's tasks, then more than a mere exchange of routine jobs is necessary. Instead, more tasks of a similar type are added to the original set of tasks. This method of redesign is called job enlargement. For example, instead of putting one gear into a transmission box, a worker assembles the entire transmission. In this way, task behavior is changed: Skill variety is enhanced, repetition is reduced, and the challenge of the task is increased. In addition, job enlargement can increase the complexity of a worker's overall job; it also increases cycle time, or the time it takes a worker to complete a set of tasks and start over.

Another term for job enlargement is "horizontal job loading."[11] Essentially, it is a method of combining similar tasks into a single worker's job. The reasoning behind job enlargement is that it can improve both skill variety and task identity.

Whether one calls the method job enlargement or horizontal job loading, the problem is the same: As with job rotation, this method of technological change is essentially limited. Moving from one routine and monotonous task to a different routine and monotonous task is still not likely to add much true variety and stimulation to the work.

Job Enrichment

Job engineering, rotation, and enlargement have all been criticized as not adding to worker satisfaction and productivity as much as has been claimed. We can best understand their failings by referring to Frederick Herzberg's two-factor theory of satisfaction and motivation.[12]

According to the theory, factors intrinsic to work are the primary determinants of employee motivation. These factors, called *motivators,* include such things as achievement, recognition, responsibility, advancement, and personal growth in competence. However, other factors external to the work itself contribute to employee *dis*satisfaction. Company policies, supervisory practices, salaries and wages, and interpersonal relations on the job are *hygiene factors* that cause workers to be dissatisfied if they are negative or otherwise onerous.

Job engineering, rotation, and enlargement are change methods that do not seem to treat Herzberg's motivators. Increasing or otherwise varying essentially routine and boring jobs will not inherently improve recognition, achievement, advancement, and the like. The idea behind job enrichment, however, is to change the way that work is done in such a manner that these motivating factors are enhanced. Such enhancement may have its origin from ideas and input from the very employees who are performing the work.

Job enrichment is a change method that gives workers more involvement in and control over the planning and evaluation of the job, not just the performance of it. If a worker can plan the job, can perform it in some manner that he or she has determined is best, and has an opportunity to evaluate the results—instead of all these things being done by separate staff or supervisory people—it is likely that this worker's sense of identification with the job will increase.

Another term for this method is *vertical job loading,* suggesting that those tasks usually reserved for people higher up in the hierarchy are now being performed by the worker. Organizations have several ways of achieving vertical job loading:[13]

- Giving workers responsibility for advising or training less-experienced personnel. For instance, bank tellers take new hires through the procedures, providing both a learning opportunity for the new employees and a guiding or coaching experience for the experienced tellers.
- Providing workers increased freedom to manage their own time, including deciding when to start and stop work, when to take breaks, and how to assign work priorities. One example of this idea is flextime, which simply involves suspending regular hours of work attendance in favor of individualizing workers' schedules.
- Encouraging workers to do their own troubleshooting and to handle work crises. By encouraging, for example, the motor pool maintenance supervisor to resolve her own assignment problems—one of the mechanics is unexpectedly out sick—management affords this shop employee an opportunity to put her own stamp on the day's work.
- Providing workers increased control over budgetary matters that affect their own work. For instance, allowing a manager to assign employees as he or she sees fit, as long as all of the work gets done correctly, on time, and within budget, gives the manager both responsibility and accountability.

Thirty years ago journalist/commentator Studs Terkel published his account of what working for a living in America entails.[14] *Working* is a collection of interviews with people in a wide variety of occupations. A strong theme running through the book is that people feel they do not have a chance to extract enough meaning from their work; they feel underutilized. One blue-collar worker, for example, laments: "I have a gallon capacity, but I'm stuck in a quart-size job." Job enrichment is a method of changing the way that people work so they are able to get more meaning from their work. A main effect of job enrichment should be increased feelings of personal commitment to and responsibility for the work and its outcomes, notably increased productivity, customer satisfaction, or both.

Changing Job Relationships

The final technological method of change involves various relationships that the worker experiences. In particular, this method concerns the relationship of the worker to his or her range of job activities, to the job's customer or client, and to the evaluation of the work.

One of the ways to organize an employee's work is to *form meaningful task clusters.* The intent here is to give a worker a "whole" job rather than an isolated part of one. For example, service-station attendants may be assigned individual duties, whereby one fills customers' tanks, another cleans the windshields, and another handles all the charge cards. A more meaningful task cluster might be to assign all the duties for a single customer to a single attendant. Thus the attendant would perform all three functions (fill the tank, do the windshield, and take care of the payment).

To be sure, clustering the tasks in this way causes the station to lose efficiency—note that race-car teams perform individual duties when the driver comes into the pit. However, the attendants do gain a degree of task identity. Moreover, they also increase their task significance, or sense of ownership for the job, since they see directly the impact of their work.

Other examples can show essentially the same results: Rather than specializing in the sale of only one product line to a large number of customers, sales personnel represent all of the company's products to a smaller number of customers. Rather than taking whatever task randomly comes into the pool, typists are assigned all of the work that comes in from a particular department or from a particular group of people who are doing similar work. In all cases, the impact is an enhancement of both task identity and task significance.

Another method of changing the work is to *establish client relationships* for the employee. The intent here is to give the people who produce a product contact with those who use it. In this way the employee can develop an enhanced view of what part his or her work plays in the organization, how that work is used by someone else, and how that work is being assessed by those who do use it.

Thus, for example, the shipping supervisor of a manufacturer can deal directly with the customer's receiving supervisor. By so doing, the two of them can discuss loading procedures, the state of the product when it arrives at the customer's receiving dock, and so forth.

On balance, this method of changing jobs is useful for increasing people's

- skill variety, because of the need to develop and exercise interpersonal skills in managing and maintaining the relationship with the client;
- autonomy, at least to the extent that workers are given real responsibility for managing the relationships with those who receive and use the outputs of their work; and
- feedback, because additional opportunities are created for workers to receive direct praise or criticism of their work outputs.

Finally, jobs can be changed by *opening feedback channels.* This means changing the information flow of the work. Specifically, it means giving the employee better data—more direct, more comprehensive, and more timely—about his or her performance. In this way the worker can see directly whether that performance is improving, worsening, or holding even.

The idea behind this change method is to give the worker a more direct opportunity to assess his or her own work, and to do something about it.

> Job-provided feedback is more immediate and private than supervisor-supplied feedback, and it increases workers' feelings of personal control over their work. Moreover, it avoids many of the potentially disruptive interpersonal problems that can develop when a worker can find out how he is doing only from direct messages or subtle cues from the boss.[15]

With widespread use of personal computers in the workplace, such immediate and private data can be easily provided. Even noncomputerized tasks can be changed in this way, so long as the employee is given the opportunity, and information, to perform his or her own performance-level calculations.

Of course, there are limits to a worker's ability to make changes to how she performs her job. Changes, for the most part, should result from the diagnostic approach outlined in chapter 2. Taylor in *Scientific Management* cautioned against giving workers the ability to change their jobs as they saw fit.[16] Foreshadowing the importance of organizational learning, Taylor argued that it was management's role to ensure that workers not repeat unsuccessful job changes of the past.

Changing the way in which production processes are conducted is, of course, a complex (and sometimes costly) task. The impacts are equally complex. This seems universally true, regardless of the particular circumstance:

- An accounting department changes from entering accounts-receivable data by hand to recording them on a networked desktop personal computer.
- A brokerage house replaces its telephone switchboard with a companywide voice-mail system.
- An office converts to an integrated system in which its telephone, fax machines, and cellular communicators are all controlled through personal computers.

Not only may the physical characteristics of workstations be altered, but the people themselves can also be affected. The task of change managers is to make that effect as positive as possible given the centrality of work to people's lives and self-concepts. We began this section with an extract from the folk classic "John Henry." We are well advised to remember one of its lessons:[17]

John Henry was hammerin' on de mountain,
An' his hammer was strikin' fire,
He drove so hard till he broke his pore heart,
An' he lied down his hammer an' he died,
Lawd, Lawd, he lied down his hammer an' he died. ©

STRUCTURAL METHOD

As we have already noted, management may decide that the best way to accomplish their change purpose is by modifying certain roles or relationships. This is a structural method. One may wonder if changing the organization's structure is not an objective; after all, managers frequently decide to reorganize in some fashion. Doesn't that decision set a change effort in motion, and isn't that effort aimed at restructuring the enterprise? And isn't restructuring therefore an object *of* change, rather than a method *for* change?

After thinking about these questions, we realized that the answer has to be no. Managers do not reorganize for the purpose of reorganizing. They do so because they want to group two department's tasks more closely; or because they want people whose work closely affects each other's to be better coordinated; or because they need decisions to be made by different people, at different levels of the organization. Reorganizing is a means by which these and similar changes can be made. The structural method of change pertains to dividing and coordinating an organization's labor. Such change typically involves creating new roles, new work units, or new reporting relationships.

Basically, an organization's structure is a pattern of relationships that govern the performance of organizational roles. Effecting change structurally therefore involves altering various organizational *dimensions.* It also entails the creation of specific *structural mechanisms.*

Changing Structural Dimensions

Organizational structure concerns the way that labor is divided into its component tasks, the degree to which formal rules govern the performance of those tasks, and how authority is concentrated or distributed in the enterprise.[18] Effecting a change by structural means can involve any of the following dimensions: complexity, formalization, centralization, and coordination. General Electric (see "Focus On: General Electric") is illustrative of an expansive organization that continually effects change.

Focus On: General Electric

Jack Welch sees change as something not to be feared but to be relished. When appointed chairman and CEO in 1981, he inherited a profitable company and quickly earned the nickname "Neutron Jack" as he went about chopping 117 businesses and 100,000 jobs. That was only the beginning.

During Welch's tenure as CEO and chairman, General Electric's yearly revenues grew from $28 billion in 1981 to $130 billion in 1991. This "multibusiness" once known for lighting and appliances is a leader in such industries as medical systems, aircraft engines, power generation, capital markets, and television. There are now ten expansive product groups, and one of these, GE Capital, has twenty-eight separate businesses.

According to Welch, change has no constituency; people like the status quo, the way things are. From the outset Welch was prepared for massive resistance to growing GE. Along the way GE embraced "Six Sigma" and created "boundarylessness" and "Work-Outs."

Six Sigma. A highly disciplined process that helps GE focus on developing and delivering perfect products and services. GE believes that customers value consistent, predictable business processes that deliver world-class levels of quality. The goal of Six Sigma is total customer satisfaction.

Boundarylessness. Welch's term for breaking down barriers—such as hierarchy, job function, and geography—that divide employees and distance companies from suppliers and customers. Boundarylessness is created through willingness to listen, debate, and then take the best ideas from any source and put them into action. By virtue of a boundaryless organization, management talent, capital and ideas are efficiently moved to where they are most needed in the company.

Work-Outs. Meetings that can be called by anybody to address any problem—from small to huge—with no boss in the room. When the participants have a plan—kill a form, replace a machine—the boss is called in and must say yes or no on the spot. GE copyrighted the term "Work-Out" following its implementation in 1989 to provide people with better jobs. Work-Outs have become so common that they occur almost daily in each GE facility without management knowing about them until someone goes to the boss with a plan.

Today, GE is one of the world's most admired companies; it has been named America's most admired company by *Fortune* for five years running. GE's fundamental values—meritocracy, dignity, simplicity, speed, and hatred of bureaucracy—are evident to employees, customers, and competitors alike. Welch retired in September 2001, turning GE over to Jeff Immelt.[1] Immelt's plans for GE include driving Welch's initiatives—

globalization, movement from production to services, digitization, and quality—broader and deeper. Change at GE is not dead or on hold by any means. For example, 40 percent of the company is focused on administration, finance, and backroom functions; Immelt wants to shrink that by 75 percent through digitizing or outsourcing the parts of each business that don't directly touch the consumer. Finally, in the aftermath of the Enron collapse, Immelt is faced with increased demands to provide more hard data to investors on how GE generates its annual double-digit earnings growth.

Sources: A talk with Jeff Immelt (2002), *Business Week,* Jan. 28, pp. 102–104; General Electric: The house that Jack built (1999), *The Economist,* Sept. 18, pp. 23–26; Jack Welch's lessons for success (1993), *Fortune,* Jan. 25, pp. 86–90; M. Boyle (2002), America's most admired companies: The right stuff, *Fortune,* March 4, pp. 85–86; D. Brady (2002), How does G.E. grow?, *Fortune,* April 8, pp. 28–30; P. L. Moore (2000), The man who would be Welch, *Business Week,* Dec. 11, pp. 94–97; P. L. Moore (2000), Running the house that Jack built, *Business Week,* Oct. 2, pp. 130–138; T. A. Stewart (1999), See Jack. See Jack run Europe, *Fortune,* Sept. 27, pp. 124–129; J. Useem (2001), It's all yours, Jeff. Now what? *Fortune,* Sept. 11, pp. 64–68; J. Welch & J. A. Byrne (2001), Jack and the people factory (book excerpt adapted from *Jack: Straight from the Gut*), *Fortune,* Sept. 11, pp. 75–86.

NOTES

1. For a full discussion of GE's CEO succession process, see G. Colvin (2001), Changing of the guard, *Fortune,* January 8, pp. 84–99.

Complexity

The complexity of an organization's structure is reflected in the number of departments, different occupational groups, highly trained specialists, and managerial levels that it has. Usually, it is described in terms of the organization's *horizontal* and *vertical differentiation.*

Horizontal differentiation concerns the degree to which technical labor is divided. Technical labor, which refers to the labor that is used to produce the organization's output, is usually divided into specialties, departments, divisions, and the like.

Vertical differentiation refers to administrative labor; that is, organizations divide their managerial work into different levels. In this way a hierarchy of positions is created. This hierarchy presumes that authority and managerial responsibilities are graded, from lower to higher officials.

Changing an organization's complexity is a common method for changing its ability to innovate. In general, the greater the complexity, the more flexible, adaptive, and innovative the organization can be. In their classic study of three industries, Paul R. Lawrence and Jay W. Lorsch found that an organization's ability to change was clearly related to complexity.[19] Specifically, they found that the more uncertain and changing the industry, the greater the companies' complexity. Therefore, firms in the plastics industry had many more departments and more varied roles than did firms in the cardboard container industry. It should be noted that increased complexity does not necessarily mean greater bureaucracy.

Formalization

Formalization is the degree to which rules and regulations govern people's behavior. It is the means by which people determine which tasks are performed, how, when, and by whom. High formalization means lots of rules and regulations; low formalization means that the organization relies on general guidelines to guide people in the performance of their work.

A traditional assembly-line fabricator, a bank teller, and a maximum-security prison guard will all operate according to fairly detailed rules, procedures, and codes. When an aircraft or space shuttle is checked out before flight, the worker doing the checking responds to a large number of highly specific questions and instructions. (We would hardly want it otherwise; we would not want someone to say, "Uh-oh—departure is in ten minutes; you two run up to the cockpit and see if everything looks OK." There is a time to be casual and a time to be precise.)

In contrast, a basic-research scientist, a university professor, and a skilled cabinetmaker operate under a set of more general guidelines, covering working hours (more or less), budgetary limits, expected output, and so forth.

Generally, high formalization impedes adaptability and innovation. An organization that operates under a large number of specific rules will have difficulty changing. The other side of that coin, therefore, is this: If an organization faces conditions that require a measure of responsiveness, adaptability, or innovation—a measure of changeability, in other words—management would be wise to have as low a degree of formalization as possible. This does not mean, however, that controls are not in place; accountability at some level must still exist.

Centralization

Put simply, centralization is the degree to which members participate in making decisions. The concept refers to the extent that decision making is distributed throughout the firm or agency. A totally centralized company would have all its decisions concentrated in one place, presumably at the top. A perfectly decentralized firm would have all decisions made in concert by all members.

In general, decentralized decision making has a positive impact on innovation, adaptability, and the like. Highly centralized organizations tend to be more rigid, less innovative. The reason for this is that decentralized decision making increases the total amount of information available throughout the enterprise.

In turn, as more people are involved, decisions can then be based on more knowledge, a greater variety of perspectives, and a wider divergence of ideas.

An indirect effect of decentralization is that decisions move out of the hands of a dominant clique or coalition of powerful people. This not only opens those decisions to more and different input, as we said, but also opens up channels of influence to people outside that coalition. New ideas, concepts, and proposals now stand a better chance of getting a favorable hearing. And the organization's ability to change is enhanced.[20]

Coordination

We began this discussion of structural components by identifying one of the most important features of organized activity: complexity. As we said, complexity concerns how labor is divided in the organization. Ultimately, however, that divided-up labor has to come back together to produce a pyramid, a college graduate, or a pair of shoes. Coordination is the process of integrating differentiated resources and activities in a unity of effort.

Organizations use a variety of coordination methods. One way to coordinate is to use the *hierarchy.* By virtue of his or her position in the organizational hierarchy, the boss can collect information concerning a variety of subordinates' work, put that information together, and form a coherent work plan that will tie it all together in a sensible fashion.

Management can also design a variety of *administrative processes* for coordination purposes. Rules, schedules, plans, and policies are all devices that can serve to connect different functions. If the metal shop and the paint shop both use the same schedule for the company's aluminum door product, management can be more comfortable that the door will come out of production on time—and painted—than if no such schedule exists.

Finally, management can establish one or more specific *coordinating roles.* Liaisons, either individual or departmental; committees; task forces; project groups; and the like are all examples of structural coordinating devices.

In general, an organization's ability to respond, adapt, innovate—to change—depends on the extent to which it has built coordinating mechanisms into its system. Lawrence and Lorsch's study produced similar results for coordination as for differentiation. The authors found that successful firms in the high-change plastics industry used a wide range of coordinating devices. In contrast, firms in the container industry paid only minor attention to coordination. Table 4.3 summarizes these results.

To summarize, an organization can be described with respect to its degree of complexity, formalization, centralization, and coordination. Moreover, we in no way want to imply that there is one "right" mix across all four structural means for any given organization. Organizations are continually tweaking, and thus changing, the degree to which they are formalized or centralized, for example.

Table 4.3
Environmental Factors and Organizational Design Characteristics of Effective Organizations

Integrative Devices

Industry	*Environmental diversity*	*Actual differentiation*	*Actual integration*	*Types of integrative devices*
Plastics	High	High	High	Teams, roles, departments, hierarchy, plans and procedures
Foods	Moderate	Moderate	High	Roles, hierarchy, plans and procedures
Container	Low	Low	High	Hierarchy, plans and procedures

Source: Adapted from J. W. Lorsch (1970), Introduction to the structural design of organizations, in G. W. Dalton & P. R. Lawrence (Eds.), J. W. Lorsch (Collab.), *Organization structure and design*, Homewood, IL: Richard D. Irwin, p. 13.

Creating Structural Mechanisms

How do organizations use the structure to effect change? What sorts of mechanisms are available to managers? We can identify two basic modes by which the structure becomes an instrument of change: specifically designed work groups and separate organizational units.

Work Groups

Based on its survey of more than 150 companies, the Conference Board has identified the major approaches to innovation and change taken by organizations in the United States.[21] The report distinguished three methods that use specific work groups.

The *problem-solving group* is established to identify and analyze problems, and then to recommend solutions and plans for implementation to management for approval. Such groups are made up of eight to ten workers, usually from the same department, who join the group voluntarily.

Before the group is able to be effective, the members must undergo training in various problem-solving techniques. Brainstorming, cause-and-effect analysis, and data gathering and analysis are a few of the techniques they learn. The report emphasizes the importance of consensus discussion to this type of effort. If the group can reach collective agreement on definitions, interpretations, and solutions, problem solving becomes a reality rather than a hope.

Problem-solving groups are found in virtually all types of industry. Their use has increased as the popularity of ISO 9000–type approaches has grown.

Both manufacturing and nonmanufacturing companies employ this technique. Inland Steel and Xerox, for example, have used such groups in both blue- and white-collar units. This technique travels under many labels: quality teams, quality circles, worker circles, employee-participation groups, and employee-involvement teams.

What sorts of problems do such groups address? The Conference Board found a wide variety of problems coming under their domain. Safety, tool redesign and placement, parts delivery, and physical working conditions (lighting, ventilation, and the like) were typical issues dealt with. In all cases, the result was some sort of change:

> Work-process solutions included efforts to minimize down-time, reduce scrap, decrease defects, reduce inventory, eliminate bottlenecks in the work flow, and improve product quality. Success in these efforts is attributed to the group's ability to change processes by such actions as altering the rate of machine speed, reorganizing an assembly system, and relabeling or renumbering equipment and storage areas to improve visibility and accessibility.[22]

Managing such a work-group approach to change is not a trivial matter, nor is it simple. It is, however, fairly straightforward. Most companies develop steering committees, usually at the plant level, to coordinate the groups; training, leader selection, methods of funding, and procedures for reward usually fall under the purview of these committees. In some cases, employees undergo extensive training as facilitators, which then allows them to function as group trainers and consultants. Facilitators also serve as liaison between the plant's steering committee and the individual groups.

Probably the most famous structural form for change that modern organizations have adopted is that termed *autonomous work teams* (also known as *self-managed work teams*). Similar to problem-solving groups, autonomous work teams have considerably more responsibility and greater opportunity for managing themselves. In general, such teams have the ability to implement solutions, not merely recommend them.

How is this ability exercised? Typically, work schedules, selection of new team members, and even reward and punishment standards are determined and controlled by the team rather than by supervisors. The result, of course, is that such teams develop a high degree of self-reliance, confidence, and ability to respond to changing requirements in a responsible way.

The General Foods Corporation's pet-food plant in Topeka, Kansas, provides one of the most comprehensive U.S. examples of autonomous work teams in action.[23] Not only did the design of the plant enjoy immediate success, but it has continued to do so. The design was comprehensive:

> The total workforce of approximately seventy employees was organized into six teams. A processing team and a packaging team operated during each shift. The processing team's jurisdiction included unloading, storage of materials, drawing ingredients from

storage, mixing, and then performing the series of steps that transform ingredients into a pet-food product. The packaging team's responsibilities included the finishing stages of product manufacturing-packaging operations, warehousing, and shipping.[24]

As we noted earlier about such groups, the Topeka teams exercised considerable autonomy. Task assignments were based on group consensus; in fact, tasks could even be redefined or restructured to more closely correspond to the skills and interests of the team members. Teams were also responsible for reassigning tasks to cover for absent employees; selecting representatives to plant-wide committees; screening and selecting new employees; and counseling those members whose performance was below acceptable standards.

The Topeka experience was successful for a number of reasons:

- The plant was new.
- It was geographically isolated from the parent organization and thus did not have to combat entrenched values and methods as much as it might have.
- It was small, allowing extensive face-to-face interaction among the employees.
- Time was spent training new employees in the technical and interpersonal competencies they would need to make the team system work.
- A great deal of careful planning went into the construction and design of the plant.
- The plant's new technology was compatible with the development of the teams.
- Finally, new employees were carefully screened before they were hired.

With regard to this last point, it was critical to select people whose skills, interests, and styles were compatible with the autonomous work team requirements. In fact, the notices of job openings emphasized the nontraditional nature of the work setting, even using the titles of "team leader" for first-line supervisor and "team member" for rank-and-file worker.

General Food's success can be contrasted with that of Levi-Strauss, the jeans manufacturer. In the early 1990s Levi-Strauss introduced modular manufacturing production—a team-based structure used to increase the meaningfulness and autonomy that workers felt—only to suspend its use by 1998. Where Levi-Strauss failed, others—Dundee Milles, Rifkin Co., the New Maryland Clothing Factory, and Datrek, to name a few—have thrived.[25] Modular manufacturing has resulted in increased capacity with no increased facility space, reduced labor costs (including lower turnover and worker compensation claims), increased wages, and improved quality.[26]

Where did Levi-Strauss fail? Postmortems don't blame the concept; implementation was the culprit.[27] First, small teams were not adopted. Team size at Levi-Strauss was as high as forty members, not the eight to ten employees considered optimal. Consequently, the teams didn't feel like teams, and they broke up into subgroups and cliques. Second, and more important, was the lack of corporate guidelines and a supportive culture. Many managers implemented modular manufacturing because they were told to, not because they believed in the approach. In changing from a piecework environment to one of empowerment and autonomy, managers freely experimented with differing team structures; pay plans; team sizes; and levels of empowerment and training for workers, supervisors, and support staff.

By no means was the Topeka structure perfect, either. A number of features remain to be improved. In general, though, it has enabled that organization to be adaptable, responsive to change, and innovative. Its characteristics have been adopted at several more General Foods plants and by other companies across the nation, as illustrated in table 4.4. The companies in table 4.4 are not alone. It is estimated that one in five U.S. employees use self-managed teams, and moreover, it is predicted that by the turn of the century 40 to 50 percent of all U.S. workers could be members of such teams.[28]

Separate Units

We observed that one of the Topeka plant's features that allowed it to succeed was its separation from the parent organization. This seems to be a sound principle in general: "If one wants to stimulate new ideas, the odds are better if early efforts to perfect and test new 'crazy' ideas are differentiated—that is, separated—from the functions of the operating organization."[29]

Separation of units that are especially involved in change and innovation is a second major way that structure can be used in managing change. Separation can be physical, as in the case of the Topeka plant, or it can be financial or organizational. Thus aerospace firms typically house their major research efforts in separate research laboratories rather than in their operating depart-

Table 4.4
Examples of Autonomous Work Teams

General Mills: In a cereal plant in Lodi, California, teams schedule, operate, and maintain machinery so effectively that the factory runs with no managers present during the night shift.

Federal Express: At a weekly meeting, a team of clerks spotted and eventually solved a billing problem that was costing the company $2.1 million a year.

Chaparral Steel: A team of mill workers traveled the world to evaluate new production machinery. The machines they selected and installed have helped make their mill one of the world's most efficient.

3M: Cross-functional teams tripled the number of new products in one division.

Aetna Life and Casualty: After organizing its home office operations into so-called superteams, Aetna reduced the ratio of middle managers to workers—from 1 to 7 down to 1 to 30—while improving customer service.

Johnsonville Foods: In Sheboygan, Wisconsin, teams of blue-collar workers helped the CEO make the decision to proceed with a major plant expansion. They told him that they could produce more sausage faster than he would have ever dared to ask. Since 1986, productivity has risen at least 50 percent.

Source: B. Dumaine (1990), Who needs a boss?, *Fortune*, May 7, pp. 52–53.

ments. In an attempt to create more autonomy among its product divisions—commercial airlines, military/defense, and space/communications—Boeing physically moved its headquarters from Seattle to Chicago.

Reservations are units specifically devoted to creating and developing new ideas for future business.[30] They are intended to allow their members to explore, experiment, and innovate in a relatively nonthreatening environment. In general,

- they can be either internal, such as R&D units, or external, such as universities or consulting agencies;
- they can be permanent—most R&D labs are fairly permanent—or temporary, such as a task force set up to develop a new program, process, or product; or
- they can be located either in a division or at the corporate level.

Sometimes, as with General Foods, management decides to start a new work culture, essentially from scratch. *Greenfield plants* (so called because of the rural settings in which they tend to be located) provide such an opportunity.[31] The idea is to construct a new plant that will be especially tailored to encourage innovation and change and that relies heavily on self-managed work teams rather than formal supervision.

This thorough separation of the new plant from the parent organization greatly facilitates the growing of a change-oriented workforce, one that is relatively free from traditional reluctance and resistance to change. Greenfield plants tend to be relatively small and have broad job classifications, a great deal of job rotation, relatively autonomous work teams, and minimal status distinctions among blue- and white-collar workers.

Separation of change-oriented operations from the mainstream organization, whether by reservations or Greenfield plants, is a double-edged sword. It is a useful method to establish a new change-oriented workforce. However, by its nature separation reduces the ability of a new idea to work its way into the larger organization. Indeed, the more isolated the work unit, the less impact it is likely to have on the parent organization. Transferring original ideas, innovative processes, and new products to the operating organization is seldom easy. It is even more difficult if the originating unit is separate and apart. Still, this structural approach can prove to be a highly successful method for introducing, testing, and ultimately managing change.

> Many organizations are reshaping and reorganizing departments to find ways of accomplishing work more effectively. The frequency with which reorganizations occur appears to be accelerating; [they are] essential, if companies are to survive in a tough environment. Making a transition from one organizational structure to another can be a period of intense creativity and progress or it can be one of disruption, anxiety, and low productivity. The ease with which a transition can be made depends to a great extent on management.[32]

We began this section by stating that to modify an organization's structure is to modify the roles that people perform in it. Changing an organization by changing its structure therefore means changing those roles. Change managers will likely find themselves creating and nurturing a whole new set of roles (see chapter 7). Someone, for example, will stimulate or catalyze a new idea; someone else will provide possible ways to solve the new problem or set the new idea into motion. Yet another party may serve as a sort of grand orchestrator of the idea, helping the process of implementation along. Finally, someone may serve to link the needed resources together, bringing the new idea to fruition as an accomplished change event. In short, structural methods of change are not mechanical; in fact, they are extremely complex and, at bottom, human.

NOTES

1. "John Henry," in J. A. Lomax & A. Lomax (Eds.) (1934), *American Ballads and Folk Songs,* New York: Macmillan, p. 6.

2. J. M. Juran & F. M. Gryna, Jr. (1980), *Quality planning and analysis,* New York: McGraw-Hill, 1980; W. Edwards Deming (1982), *Quality, productivity, and competitive position,* Cambridge, MA: MIT Center for Advanced Engineering Study; L. Dobyns & C. Crawford-Mason (1991), *Quality or else,* Boston: Houghton Mifflin; P. B. Crosby (1979), *Quality is free: The art of making quality certain,* New York: New American Library; and his (1992), *Completeness: Quality for the 21st century,* New York: Penguin; B. Creech (1995), *The 5 pillars of TQM: How to make total quality management work for you,* New York: Plume.

3. For information on ISO 9000 (as well as newer programs such as ISO 14000), see the International Organization for Standardization's web page: http://www.iso.ch.

4. J. R. Hackman & G. R. Oldham (1979), Development of the job diagnostic survey, *Journal of Applied Psychology,* 60, pp. 159–170.

5. J. R. Hackman (1977), Work design, in J. R. Hackman & J. L. Suttle (Eds.), *Improving life at work: Behavioral science approaches to organizational change,* Santa Monica, CA: Goodyear, p. 244; J. R. Hackman & Greg R. Oldham (1980), *Work redesign,* Reading, MA: Addison-Wesley.

6. F. W. Taylor (1949), *The principles of scientific management,* New York: Harper & Row, p. 59.

7. Ibid.

8. D. D. Warrick (1984), Managing organization change and development, in J. E. Rosenzweig & F. E. Kast (Eds.), *Modules in management,* Chicago: Science Research Associates, p. 38.

9. C. R. Walker & R. H. Guest (1952), *The man in the assembly line,* Cambridge, MA: Harvard University Press.

10. Warrick, p. 38.

11. Hackman, Work design; Hackman & Oldham, *Work redesign.*

12. F. Herzberg, B. Mausner, & B. Snyderman (1959), *The motivation to work,* New York: Wiley; F. Herzberg (1966), *Work and the nature of man,* Cleveland, IL: World.

13. Adapted from R. H. Miles (1980), *Macro organizational behavior,* Santa Monica, CA: Goodyear, p. 452.

14. S. Terkel (1972), *Working,* New York: Avon.

15. Hackman, Work design, p. 139.

16. Taylor, *Principles of scientific management.*

17. Lomax & Lomax, *American ballads,* p. 8.

18. P. E. Connor (1984), *Organization structure and design* (Modules in Management series, J. E. Rosenzweig & F. E. Kast, Eds.), Chicago: Science Research Associates.

19. P. R. Lawrence & J. W. Lorsch (1967), Differentiation and integration in complex organizations, *Administrative Science Quarterly,* 12 (June), pp. 1–47. See also their (1969), *Organization and environment: Managing differentiation and integration,* Homewood, IL: Irwin.

20. For an empirical treatment of centralization see P. E. Connor (1992), Decision making participation patterns: The role of organizational context, *Academy of Management Journal,* 35, pp. 218–231.

21. H. Gorlin & L. Schein (1984), *Innovations in managing human resources,* New York: The Conference Board.

22. Ibid., p. 5.

23. This discussion relies on the excellent treatment by Miles, *Macro organizational behavior,* pp. 453–466. See also R. E. Walton (1972), How to counter alienation in the plant, *Harvard Business Review,* November–December , pp. 70–81. Similar approaches are popular with the makers Volvo and Saab automobiles; see J. Kapstein (1989), Volvo's radical new plant: "The death of the assembly line"? *Business Week,* August 28, pp. 92–93.

24. Walton, How to counter alienation, p. 74.

25. C. Gilbert (1998), Did modules fail Levi's or did Levi's fail modules? *Apparel Industry Magazine,* September , pp. 88–92.

26. Ibid.

27. Ibid., and J. Abend (1999), Modular manufacturing: The line between success and failure," *Bobbin,* January, pp. 48–52.

28. J. S. Lublin (1992), Trying to increase worker productivity, more employers alter management style, *Wall Street Journal,* February 13, p. B1.

29. J. R. Galbraith (1982), Designing the innovating organization, *Organizational Dynamics,* Winter, p. 11.

30. Ibid., p. 14.

31. Gorlin & Schein, *Innovations,* pp. 9–10.

32. J. M. Kaplan & E. E. Kaplan (1984), Organizational restructuring: How managers can actively assist in shaping a firm's new architecture, *Management Review,* January, p. 15.

5

Managerial and Human Methods of Change

We continue here the discussion of change methods begun in chapter 4. As noted earlier, we first describe the idea that administrative actions can be taken; this is a *managerial* method. Second, we discuss how the *human* element can be used; people can be educated, trained, coached, counseled, or removed.

MANAGERIAL METHODS

Managers do not have to rely solely on technological or structural mechanisms to effect change. There are at least two forms of action they can take themselves. First, they can employ the *reward system* to promote a move from the status quo to a new state (of course, it can also be used to discourage such a move). Second, *labor-management cooperation* can provide a means for change to occur in a positive and constructive manner.

Reward System

Rewards are an important, tangible part of organizational life. It is difficult to imagine participating in an organization if there were no rewards for doing so. As Amitai Etzioni has proposed, there are a number of bases on which people involve themselves in organizations:[1]

- Sometimes the relationship is essentially hostile or *alienative*, such as that between a convict and warden.
- In other organizations, especially business firms and government agencies, members relate to the enterprise in a *utilitarian* way; their relationship is essentially rational, usually in a financial sense.
- Finally, organizations such as churches, schools, convents, and political parties encourage and rely on an involvement that can best be described as *moral.*

How are people rewarded in organizations dominated by such relationships? In alienative organizations, the major reward, if one can call it that, is a relatively lower degree of coercion; in utilitarian enterprises, the reward is in the form of some tangible remuneration—salary or promotion, for example; and in moral organizations the main form of reward is a normative sanctioning or approval of one's actions. This reward is given by both one's managers and one's peers.

Our concern here is with the use of an organization's reward system as a managerial method of change. By *organizational reward system* we mean the "formal and informal mechanisms by which employee performance is defined, evaluated, and rewarded. The primary rewards in most work organizations are compensation, promotions, benefits, and status."[2] Using the reward system as a means for effecting change is based on a straightforward assumption, namely, that people are motivated to behave in ways that are rewarded. Michael LeBoeuf calls this assumption "The Greatest Management Principle in the World": *What gets rewarded gets done.*[3] In general, pay and promotion are especially effective as means for influencing behavior because they tend to be fairly important to people. Therefore, such rewards can be effective for changing people's behavior. For example, offering individuals bonuses for successfully and rapidly implementing organizational change can speed change; and when individuals perceive that a change will lead to a better pay system, change is encouraged.[4]

Theories of Motivation

Just how do rewards contribute to changed behavior? There are as many answers to this question as there are theories of motivation. Two types of motivation theories, *content* and *process*, merit our attention. Content theories are based on the idea that people are motivated by their needs to act in certain ways. Which needs are important depends on which theory is invoked: Abraham Maslow's hierarchy of needs, from physiological to self-actualization; David McClelland's needs for achievement, affiliation, and power; or Frederick Herzberg's satisfiers and hygiene factors.[5]

In contrast to content theories' focus on unconscious need satisfaction, process theories assume that people make conscious decisions about their behavior. One basis for such decisions is equity, and another is expectancies. Equity theory argues that people want fairness and justice in their social relationships. This includes their relationships in organizations, both horizontal and vertical. The theory suggests a three-step process: First, as individuals we evaluate a given social relationship, much as we would an economic transaction, by measuring contribution (investment) against results (returns). Second, we compare that evaluation against other people. We want to know not only what we got in return for what we gave, but also how that compares with what others got. And third, we make a conscious decision to act. We evaluate, we compare, and we behave accordingly.

When we perceive that a relationship is equitable, we respond positively; when it is inequitable, we respond negatively. In short, we make a rational decision to behave in a way that's consistent with our perceived investment and return.

Basing a change effort on the organization's reward system is especially consistent with the other major process theory of motivation: expectancy theory. This idea suggests that a person's motivation to perform depends on the effort that it takes to produce a given set of outcomes and on the outcomes themselves. Four assumptions are at the heart of the theory:[6]

- Behavior is determined by a combination of forces in both the individual and the environment that provides the context in which the person is acting.
- People make conscious decisions about their behavior.
- Different people have different types of needs, desires, and goals.
- People make choices from a number of alternative behaviors. These choices are based on the perceptions of the extent to which a given behavior will lead to desired outcomes.

In short, the theory says that people are motivated when they expect their efforts will be successful (however they define "successful"). Each of us calculates the probability that a given effort will result in a particular performance, which in turn will yield a desired outcome.

Figure 5.1 illustrates the expectancy model of motivation. As the figure indicates, the model argues that an individual's motivation leads him or her to exert effort. That effort, when combined with his or her ability and the organization's working conditions (context), leads to a certain level of performance. As a result of that performance, the individual receives a set of outcomes (rewards) that in turn leads to a level of satisfaction. Underlying this whole process is the idea of expectancies: The individual expects that effort will lead to high performance, that performance will result in certain outcomes, and that those outcomes will be valued.

Motivation, Rewards, and Change

Although expectancy theory focuses on the individual, it is also instructive for thinking about the whole organization. The organizational reward system is doing its job when[7]

- rewards are tied to performance,
- rewards are awarded in a timely manner,
- there are a sufficient number and diversity of rewards,
- criteria for allocating rewards are clear and complete,
- rewards are distributed equitably, and
- rewards compare favorably with those in similar organizations.

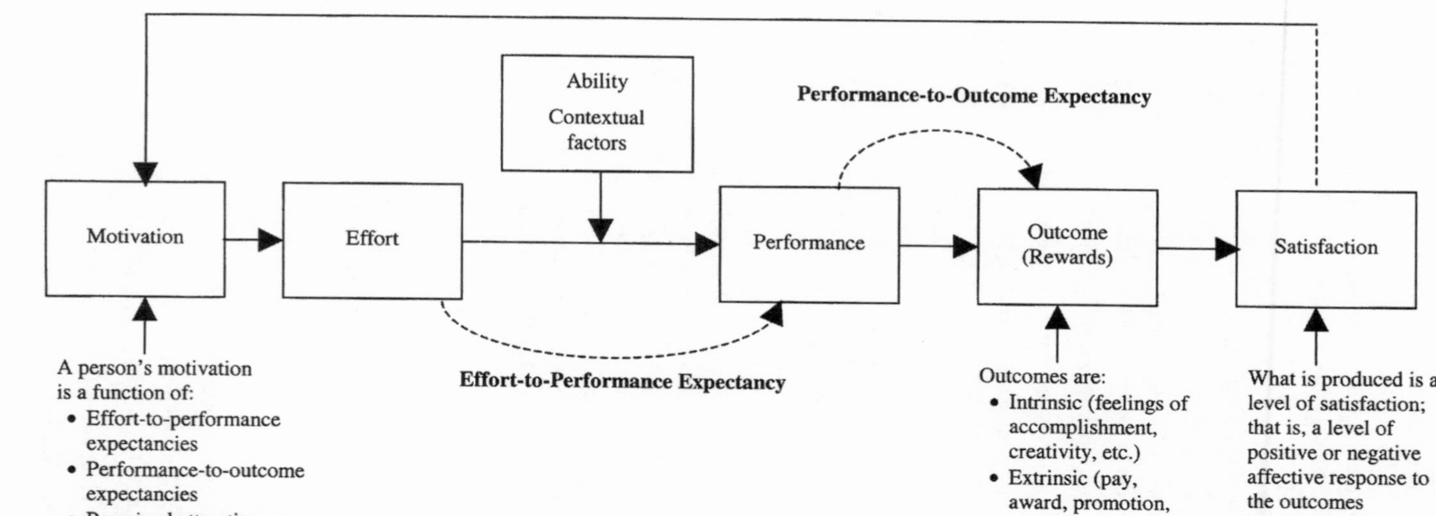

Figure 5.1 The Expectancy-Theory Model of Motivation

Source: Adapted from E. W. Lawler III (1981), *Pay and organization development*, Reading, MA: Addison-Wesley, pp. 21, 232, 235. *Pay and Organization Development* by Lawler. © Reprinted by permission of Pearson Education, Inc., Upper Saddle River, NJ.

Because of the interrelationships between motivation and rewards, the organization's reward system often is a good place to begin a change effort. This is true for several reasons.[8] First, as noted previously, pay, bonuses, and promotions generally are important to managers and nonmanagers alike. If a change involves issues with which people are unfamiliar, such as creating self-managing teams, response may be slow or unfocused. Tying a change effort to the reward system gets people's attention.

Second, beginning a change effort with the reward system gives a clear indication that the organization is committed to that effort. Too often, change programs begin with trivial or at best superficially symbolic actions. It seems, for example, that every time a college football coach is fired and a new one is hired, the replacement begins his reign by painting the weight room. Restriping the company parking lot and installing bright new banners in the cafeteria fall into the same cosmetic category, as does the creation of new corporate taglines used for motivational and marketing purposes (e.g., Ford's "Quality Is Job One" or Nike's "Just Do It"). Beginning the effort with the reward system, however, signals a managerial intention to deal with serious matters, not just superficial ones.

Third, problems often exist with any organization's reward system. Perceptions of inequity, salary compression at the top of various scales, poor administration, and rewards based on factors other than performance are problems many organizations suffer. Revising or even overhauling the reward system lays helpful groundwork for change; however, it is oftentimes easier said than done effectively. In a seminal article, Steven Kerr documents how organizations or managers think they are rewarding one behavior only to have other behaviors reinforced—as the article's title indicates: "On the folly of rewarding A, while hoping for B."[9] Examples include managers who hope to foster teamwork but provide individual performance rewards, or universities that seek the highest-quality instruction for students but grant tenure based solely on the professors' research records. Kerr's lesson is simple: Managers who find that their workers are not motivated or not performing as desired should consider the possibility that the reward system(s) in place are paying for behaviors other than those being sought.

Fourth, beginning with something held near and dear to the hearts of most organizational members can pave the way for changing or dealing with other problems. Successful changing of the pay and promotion system can serve as a model for the way other changes can be managed.

Fifth, reward systems tend to be tied fairly closely to other organizational programs and procedures; beginning with the former can help identify problems with the latter. Performance appraisal, information flow, control, job design, accounting, decision responsibilities, and communication are all examples of the sorts of issues that can be highlighted by attempts to change the reward system. In fact, the need for such changes may not become apparent until changes in pay, promotion, and other rewards have been put in place.

In general, managers tend to rely on a number of approaches in using the reward system as a means of change; these approaches range from the simple to the complex. Among the more straightforward are piecework systems, commission plans, and merit bonuses, all of which tie rewards to performance. As we will see, *gainsharing* plans and *job posting* programs are more complicated approaches.

Gainsharing Plans

Gainsharing plans, which are again experiencing increased popularity,[10] link people's rewards to their performance in complex ways. In general, gainsharing allows organizational members to share in productivity improvements by earning bonuses based on group performance.[11] Several plans are fairly popular, at least in North America. Six of them are outlined in table 5.1.[12] As an illustration of the way in which gainsharing plans tend to work, let's look at the most famous—the Scanlon plan:

In the 1930s a union leader developed an organization-wide incentive plan. Joe Scanlon's idea was to reward both workers and management for improvements in efficiency:

> Simply put, the Scanlon plan uses historical experience in a plant in establishing labor costs as a percentage of sales. A base ratio is determined by dividing payroll by sales, plus or minus inventory. A bonus is earned in any month in which actual labor costs are less than this ratio.[13]

After a part of the cost savings is set aside as a contribution to company capital expenditures, the rest is distributed to employees. This is usually done on a monthly basis, and the amount is determined as a percentage of employees' wages. Committees composed of managers and workers meet regularly to develop ideas for cost savings. Ideas that are adopted can be implemented only through a vote of organization members—production workers, service personnel, and senior executives alike.

Scanlon plans have been effective not only because they directly relate to the compensation system, but because they also promote a system of involvement by everyone in the effective accomplishment of organizational goals—a system of empowerment, in more current terms. Thus, it is much more than a pay incentive plan:

> As originally conceived by Joe Scanlon, it was supposed to create a climate that stressed common goals, participation, joint problem solving, and open communication. The plan involves extensive joint worker-management committees that are charged with finding opportunities for cost savings and reviewing the payment of the plan. The power of the plan lies in the congruence between the pay system and the philosophy of participation it was designed to enhance. The philosophy is further reinforced by the committee structure and a consultative process.[14]

Table 5.1
Comparative Analysis of Six Gainsharing Plans

Program Dimensions	Scanlon	Rucker	Improshare	Productivity/Waste Bonus	Group/Plant	DARCOM
Philosophy/theory	Organization or single unit; share improvements; people capable and willing to make suggestions, want to generate ideas	Primarily economic incentive; some reliance on employee participation	Economic incentives increase performance	Economic incentives increase performance	Economic incentives increase performance	Economic incentives increase performance
Primary goal	Improved productivity	Improved productivity	Improved productivity	Improved productivity and quality	Improved productivity	Improved productivity
Subsidiary goals	Improved attitudes, communication, work behaviors, quality, reduced costs	Improved attitudes, communication, work behaviors, quality; reduced costs	Improved attitudes, work behaviors	Improved attitudes, work behaviors	Improved attitudes, work behaviors	Improved attitudes, work behaviors
Worker participation	Two levels of committees: screening (1), production (many)	Screening (1) production (1) (sometimes)	Bonus committee	Bonus committee	Bonus committee	Bonus committee
Suggestion making	Formal system	Formal system	None	None	None	None
Role of supervisor	Chair, production committee	None	None	None	None	None
Role of managers	Direct participation in bonus committee assignments	Idea coordinator; evaluate suggestions, committee assignments	None	None	None	None
Bonus formula	Payroll / Sales	Bargaining-unit payroll / Production value	Engineering std. X BPF*; / total hours worked	Output per hour ± waste	Output per hour	Earned hours / Direct labor hours
Frequency of payout	Monthly	Monthly	Weekly	Monthly/weekly	Quarterly	Quarterly
Role of union	Negotiated provisions; screening committee membership	Negotiated provisions; screening committee membership	Negotiated provisions	Negotiated provisions	Negotiated provisions	Negotiated provisions
Impact on management style	Substantial	Slight	None	None	None	None

*BPF = base productivity factor

Source: Adapted from C. S. Miller & M. H. Schuster (1987), Gainsharing plans: A comparative analysis, *Organizational Dynamics*, 16 (Summer) p. 48. Copyright 1987, with permission of Elsevier Science.

Focus On: Health-Care Industry Gainsharing

With a change in policy by the U.S. Department of Health and Human Services Office of Inspector General permitting the use of gainsharing arrangements, hospitals were provided a significant opportunity beginning in 2001 to reduce operating costs and thus increase profits. Following more than a decade of soaring costs and falling profits, hospitals can now reinvest these savings into equipment purchases, facility renovations or expansions, service-line development, clinician recruitment and retention, or any combination of these.

Hospitals are now free to contract with participating consultants or physicians regarding current operational practices within the various clinical specialties. The process works something like this:

- Physicians are expected to comply with standard policies, procedures, and protocols.
- The best practices are reviewed and revised to ensure consistent, quality care.
- Operating cost reductions are documented by the hospital over a specified period after the best practices are implemented.
- Participating physicians are monitored with respect to mutually agreed upon objective benchmarks called quality safeguards.
- If quality safeguards are met, participating physicians are paid a fixed percentage of the reduction in operating costs.

Additionally, the gainsharing programs have to be structured to conform to all federal laws. They must also (1) be transparent (cost-saving initiatives must be clearly and separately identified), (2) document medical propriety (patient care is not adversely affected), (3) be open to ongoing medical review of outcomes, and (4) place thresholds (or limits) on cost reductions.

Two hospitals—St. Joseph Mercy in Ann Arbor, Michigan, and St. Joseph's Hospital in Atlanta—were part of a four-hospital project in their coronary artery bypass departments from 1991 to 1996. In that time, St. Joseph's reduced operating costs by $15 million and St. Joseph Mercy by $10 million. The two other hospitals that did not employ gainsharing arrangements reduced operating costs by only $5 million to $7 million. More important, patient outcomes improved at the participating hospitals with inpatient and post-bypass mortality rates declining an average of 8 percent annually.

Source: M. Reynolds (2002), Gainshairing: A cost-reduction strategy that may be back, *Healthcare Financial Management,* 56, January, pp. 58–64.

Scanlon plans have been implemented in both unionized and non-unionized plants as well as in service centers and hospitals (see "Focus On: Health-Care Industry Gainsharing"). In the unionized setting, the plan's terms are developed by a joint labor-management committee; these terms are then kept separate from the collective bargaining agreement. Scanlon plans have proven to be a popular means of effecting productive change because when they work, they produce the following types of outcomes:[15]

- They enhance coordination, teamwork, and sharing knowledge at a lower level.
- Social needs are recognized via participation and mutually reinforcing group behavior.
- Attention is focused on cost savings, not just quantity of production.
- Acceptance of change, whether in technology, market, or methods, is greater because higher efficiency leads to bonuses.
- Attitudinal change occurs among workers, and they demand more efficient management and better planning.
- Workers try to reduce overtime; they try to work smarter, not harder or faster.
- Workers produce ideas as well as effort.
- More flexible administration of union-management relations occurs.
- The union is strengthened because it is responsible for a better work situation and higher pay.

In short, Scanlon plans are one form of gainsharing that enables management to use the pay system as a means to effect important change in an organization. Actually, gainsharing plans can stimulate a climate of employee participation that goes beyond pay and promotion: they can change the heart of the workplace itself.

Open Job Posting

While gainsharing plans speak to issues of pay and monetary compensation, they do not directly relate to another major part of a reward system—promotion opportunities. Promotion is one of the most important rewards that an organization can offer, yet promotion decisions are often made in secrecy. Even the criteria for promotion are not always spelled out; it is therefore difficult for employees to know what behaviors lead to that reward.

Changing the promotion process (and the perks associated with higher-level positions) is an important way to use the reward system as a method of change. In particular, managers can bring that process out into the open. Doing so improves employees' sense of having some involvement in determining their organizational destinies when organizations are not seeking to bring "new blood" into the organization. Posting available jobs in an open and public manner is a useful way to accomplish this objective.

What does announcing job openings and inviting employees to nominate themselves do? The following effects can result:[16]

- Employees gain authority and control previously held by management over their careers.
- Employees obtain open feedback from employers about their performance as they are accepted or rejected for jobs.
- Internal trouble spots can be pinpointed, since supervisors who provide a poor work climate will have trouble keeping and attracting employees.

The premise of open job posting is that the practice will change—that is, improve—employees' chances for receiving promotions. The success of the practice depends, of course, on management's willingness and ability to communicate the opportunities available and the criteria used in assessing candidates.

As with gainsharing plans, open job posting does more than change the overall compensation system. It is also a method of changing—opening up, so to speak—the administrative climate of the organization.

Labor-Management Cooperation

The second principal managerial method of change is based on cooperation between management and labor. Since the mid-1980s, a new collective bargaining paradigm has emerged—especially in the private sector—that embraces an equal partnership between labor and management.[17] In a study that included over 1,000 private-sector contracts covering 1,000 or more employees,[18] researchers identified 485 contracts that contained one or more cooperative clauses; 286 contracts had explicit language addressing the desire or intent to cooperate.

A participation agreement does not replace or get around the basic collective-bargaining agreement between the union and company. Rather, it is concerned with such matters as improving employee morale, solving production and work-technology problems, developing training programs, and the like. For example, following is an excerpt from the letter of understanding between Ford and the United Automobile Workers (UAW):[19]

> Constructive efforts to involve employees to a greater degree in relevant workplace matters may . . . enhance employee creativity, contribute to improvements in the workplace, support goals of achieving the highest quality products, heighten efficiency, and reduce unwarranted absenteeism.
>
> The parties agreed to provide joint management and union leadership and support to increase levels of employee involvement. Accordingly, a National Joint Committee on Employee Involvement is established, composed of three (3) members appointed by the Vice President, Director of the UAW National Ford Department, and three (3) members appointed by the Vice President-Labor Relations, Ford Motor Company. . . . [This Committee will] have responsibility for:
>
> (a) Reviewing and evaluating existing programs which involve improving the work environment of Ford employees represented by the UAW.

(b) Developing new concepts and pilot projects including:

- Actions which encourage voluntary employee participation in identifying and solving work-related problems. Autonomous work groups, team building and quality circles are examples of matters for joint consideration.
- Actions directed at minimizing the disruptive effects of unwarranted absenteeism on employees and on operations. . . .
- Examination of alternative work schedules designed to improve the work climate, to increase the utilization of facilities and to reduce absenteeism and its effects.

This excerpt indicates a desire by both the union and the company to benefit from cooperative efforts. With mutually understood and desired objectives, they hope to improve the climate for change. Not incidentally, they also hope to reduce the pressures for taking on the adversarial posture that characterizes so many union-management relationships. Table 5.2 illustrates the sorts of benefits sought by both parties.

Some agreements, however, go beyond focusing on improving the labor-management relationship. In a 1997 resolution, the AFL-CIO Executive Council called for increased worker influence over the success of the companies they work for in order to create stronger futures for both the union and the companies.[20] Moreover, in the aforementioned labor agreement study, the researchers differentiated between "full partnership" (27 in total) and "extensive partnership" (54 in total) agreements. In a full partnership agreement, the union shares decision making with management and participates in dealing with the strategic issues the firm faces. In other words, labor and management participate in the formation and implementation of the company's business plan and in its financial planning. Companies with full partnership agreements

Table 5.2
Benefits Sought by Ford Motor Company and the United Automobile Workers of America

To Company	To Union
Employee training and development	Employee training and development
Employee involvement	Guaranteed income stream
Increased work time	Pilot employment projects
Comparable contributions	Plant-closing provisions
Economic and benefit adjustments	Seniority recall rights
Improved competitiveness	Redundancy program
Mutual growth	

Source: E. J. Savoie (1982), The new Ford-UAW agreement: Its worklife aspects, *Work Life Review*, 1.

included Alcoa, Harley-Davidson, Ford, and Chrysler. With extensive partnership agreements—at such companies as Lucent, Scott Paper, and Kimberly-Clark, and between the United Mine Workers and independent mining companies—worker participation starts after the development of the firm's business plan; labor does not participate in investment planning. Table 5.3 lists the common elements for building increased labor-management cooperation and partnership.

"PEOPLE" METHODS

The fourth major method of organizational change is people. By "people" methods, we mean methods of effecting change through the people who work in the organization rather than through procedures, structural relationships, or other impersonal ways. We can identify three principal methods by which people are the major instrument of change: selection and attrition, education and training, and organizational development (OD) interventions.

Selection and Attrition

Ben Schneider argues that the attributes of people, not the nature of the external environment, organizational technology, or organizational structure, are the fundamental determinants of organizational behavior.[21] In effect, the environment is a function of people and their behaviors; an organization as a system emerges initially from the kind of person or persons who establish it. Over time, behaviors in a given organization are the result of people being attracted to the company and selected by the company, and then staying with the company. Different kinds of organizations attract, select, and retain different kinds of people. Schneider calls this the attraction-selection-attrition (ASA) model.

Table 5.3
Top 10 Common Elements for Increased Labor-Management Cooperation and Partnership

1. Leaders on each side have to be willing to take risks.
2. Proceed in the absence of trust—build it as you go along.
3. Cooperation is not a bargaining chip.
4. Let go of past baggage.
5. Commit to a long-term process.
6. Plan for changes in leadership.
7. Learn from others and do what seems right to you.
8. Respect the needs of both institutions: labor and the company.
9. Make decisions together.
10. Look at the bottom line.

Source: B. Stump, From adversaries to allies: Labor-management cooperation, *Journal for Quality and Participation,* vol. 22, 1999, pp. 44–47.

The ASA model, as outlined, has major implications for change initiatives in organizations when the focus is on the people. First, Schneider argues that changes in structures or processes are not likely to be useful; such changes will occur only when the behaviors of people change. If the current people won't change, then those employed by the company will have to change. Second, during an organization's life, people who do not fit the environment will tend to leave; thus those who remain will tend to be more similar, constituting a more homogeneous group. They think and behave in like ways. And, as a collective, they become a dominant force (and often one that is resistant to change) in the company.

When faced with an altered competitive landscape, where does a company then turn in order to ensure survivability? To individuals internal or external to the organization? Schneider provides powerful arguments why *both* internal and external change agents have difficulty effecting change in organizations. On the one hand, the in-house change agent's thoughts and actions are similar to everyone else's in the organization. Can such a person be expected to champion a new and/or radical strategy? On the other hand, a "newcomer" will likely face resistance from the established workforce unless the agent is seen as "similar" enough with respect to the key attributes of the already established employees.

Focus On: Xerox

After dubbing itself "The Document Company" in the early 1990s under CEO and chairman Paul A. Allaire, Xerox was faced with reinventing itself by 1997 to ensure growth and profitability.

Over the years, Xerox had not capitalized on breakthroughs at its Palo Alto Research Center. Such inventions included the personal computer in the 1970s followed by the fax machine, the laser printer, and the Ethernet. In all cases, Xerox underestimated the potential of the inventions and watched as other companies created hugely profitable businesses from Xerox ideas. In 1997, Xerox was seen as a high-tech company that was failing to cash in on the high-tech boom, as it faced consumers' shifting tastes from copiers to desktop printers as well as harsh competition within the digital copier arena.

In 1997 Allaire brought in G. Richard Thoman from IBM as president and COO, selecting him for his intellectual energy and outsider's perspective. Thoman's plan was to create new growth by entering new businesses. Xerox was to become a digital-document company. Thoman, who before coming to Xerox had worked his entire career with Louis Gerstner at such companies as McKinsey & Co., American Express, RJR Nabisco, and eventually IBM, was named CEO at Xerox in 1999 only to be ousted a mere thirteen months later.

Reasons for Thoman's undoing are many, but primarily he failed in the execution of his strategy thanks to the pace of his change initiatives and resistance from the company's entrenched "Xeriods," as the employees like to call themselves. Thoman had attempted to change the structure before training the people; this resulted in acute dissatisfaction among the sales staff and customers. By the time of Thoman's ouster, Xerox, the company with the household name, was fighting for its very survival. The first quarterly loss in sixteen years (reported in October 2000), foreign-currency losses in excess of $1 billion, crippling corporate debt of $17 billion, and a stock price languishing at or below $10 further highlighted Xerox's woes. In total, Xerox lost $20 billion in stock market value during Thoman's tenure.

Enter Anne M. Mulcahy, a Xerox lifer and former vice president of human resources, as the new president and CEO-in-waiting. Mulcahy's first challenge will be improving Xerox's balance sheet and income statement *before* making real strategic changes. As one consultant put it: "The good news or the bad news is she has the soul of Xerox. The risk is, maybe she's too close to it." Luckily, early on, no one doubts her motives.

Sources: A. Bianco & P. L. Moore (2001), Downfall: The inside story of the management fiasco at Xerox, *Business Week,* March 5, pp. 82–92; A. Kupfer (2000), Xerox jam is too much for Thoman, *Fortune,* May 29, pp. 42–43; P. L. Moore (2001), She's here to fix the Xerox, *Business Week,* Aug. 6, pp. 47–48; P. L. Moore (2000), How Xerox ran short of black ink, *Business Week,* Oct. 30, p. 56; P. L. Moore (2000), Xerox: Rick Thoman speaks up for himself, *Business Week,* May 29, p. 51.

The business literature is rife with examples of companies that have attempted to effect dramatic change by bringing in someone from the outside to spearhead the change effort. Naturally, the unsuccessful attempts are the most visible—notably Xerox and G. Richard Thoman (see "Focus On: Xerox"). Chrysler (and Lee Iacocca in the late 1970s) and IBM (and Louis Gerstner in the early 1990s) best represent the most visible successful examples.

Education and Training

For many organizations, however, bringing in an external agent or making wholesale personnel changes is not an option. Rather, they must rely on the less spectacular method of education and training to serve their change-management needs. Education and training have become probably the most widespread form of intervention into organizational life today. Rare is the organization that does not have a training officer, and many have a full-fledged education and training department (e.g., GE's Crotonville Training Centre).

Education and Training Programs

In essence, education and training refer to activities that are aimed at upgrading people's knowledge, skills, abilities, and even beliefs. Probably the earliest form of such activities was known as "human relations training." Following the research known as the Hawthorne Studies, so-called human relations programs were designed by and for managers.[22] The intent of such programs was to make managers more sympathetic to and considerate of workers' needs and wants. Usually a program would involve discussion of hypothetical cases that described some problem between a manager and a work group. Participants in the program were then helped to see that the workers had reasons for behaving the way they did, and frequently those reasons were rooted in the manager's interpersonal incompetence. The managers were then helped to understand general concepts of worker needs and motivations as well as to develop listening, communication, and counseling skills.

Although education and training are still organizationally important, the frequently manipulative qualities of the human relations movement has led to a modification of method. Previously, many programs were merely thinly disguised attempts to train managers in effective ways to manipulate workers' attitudes or beliefs. The goal was to bring the workers into conformity with those attitudes and beliefs desired by management.

Today, education and training programs cover everything from managing stress to improving communications skills. For example, here is a list of programs offered in one year by one firm, a large financial services company: sexual harassment, effective listening, total customer service, speed reading, managing in a changing environment, managing to affirmative action, coping with stress, presentation skills, time management, cultural diversity in the workplace, training for trainers, situation leadership, working with the media, and the planning process. As the list suggests, the programs range from the immediately practical to the conceptual, almost philosophical. And, in fact, according to the training director, this is the intent of the offerings. The programs are intended to give a variety of educational experiences, at different conceptual levels and for different levels of experience, to both company management and nonmanagement people.

Management Development

A more general method of education and training is known as management development. In essence, management development is aimed at preparing senior and middle managers to participate in change. The guiding objective of most management-development efforts is to bring managers more fully into the organization's culture. Typically, such efforts attempt to improve management concepts and styles; they can range from classroom courses on decision-making techniques to a program of systematic job rotation among a group of managers.

As reported in a Conference Board study, management-development programs were used frequently to effect new thrusts in corporate strategy. Such programs were described as basically strategic plans "to manage change through the [managers]."[23] Examples cited included the following:

- Hewlett-Packard's "Managing Managers" program is designed to improve the counseling, coaching, and team-building skills of senior managers.
- Fireman's Fund Insurance Companies conducted research to identify successful management practices. Based on this research a training program was developed to develop skills based on these practices.
- Prudential Insurance Company of America conducts a confidential survey of middle managers and a sample of their subordinates. Workshops are then held to inform the managers of the results and help them respond to their implications.
- Lear Siegler, Inc. conducts what it calls a "resource management" program for middle and first-line managers. Training emphasizes ways to improve productivity through increased employee participation. Additionally, each manager is "sponsored" by another manager, typically from a different functional area, who serves as a resource, advisor, coach, and so forth. This "sponsorship" program is designed to encourage new ideas and to provide ways around traditional chains of command.

The actions taken by these companies all reflect a desire to develop people who are prepared to cope with and sustain a changing managerial environment.[24] How does this process work? Basically, the organization has two choices in developing its managerial corps: Do nothing or do something. Figure 5.2 represents the do-nothing choice, illustrating what may be called a "natural" management development process. The process is natural in the sense that if left alone, it would proceed on its own to some conclusion, regardless of whether any action is taken by management.

Following the figure from the top down, the idea is that somehow, for whatever reasons, as individuals go along in their professional lives they undergo various combinations of education, training, and experience. As a result, they acquire knowledge and abilities. And since the organization needs new managers from time to time, someone gets selected.

Figure 5.2 is not good enough. In the "natural" scenario the effectiveness of the process—the quality and appropriateness of the knowledge and abilities acquired—is essentially left to chance. The chance is that at least one individual will somehow figure out what he or she needs to do to be selected as a manager.

Figure 5.3 is figure 5.2 with a simple management overlay imposed. While the figure does not show all the complexities involved in developing management people, it is still helpful. In particular, the management side of figure 5.3 shows that "managed" management development requires the organization to do three things:

1. Conduct an ongoing examination of what its managerial *requirements* are for the future. The guiding question should be this: What knowledge and abilities will the organization need? At the same time an assessment of the knowledge and abilities currently available should be conducted.
2. Offer a number of developmental *methods* to help its employees meet those requirements. Education, training, job rotation, and on-the-job experience constitute the

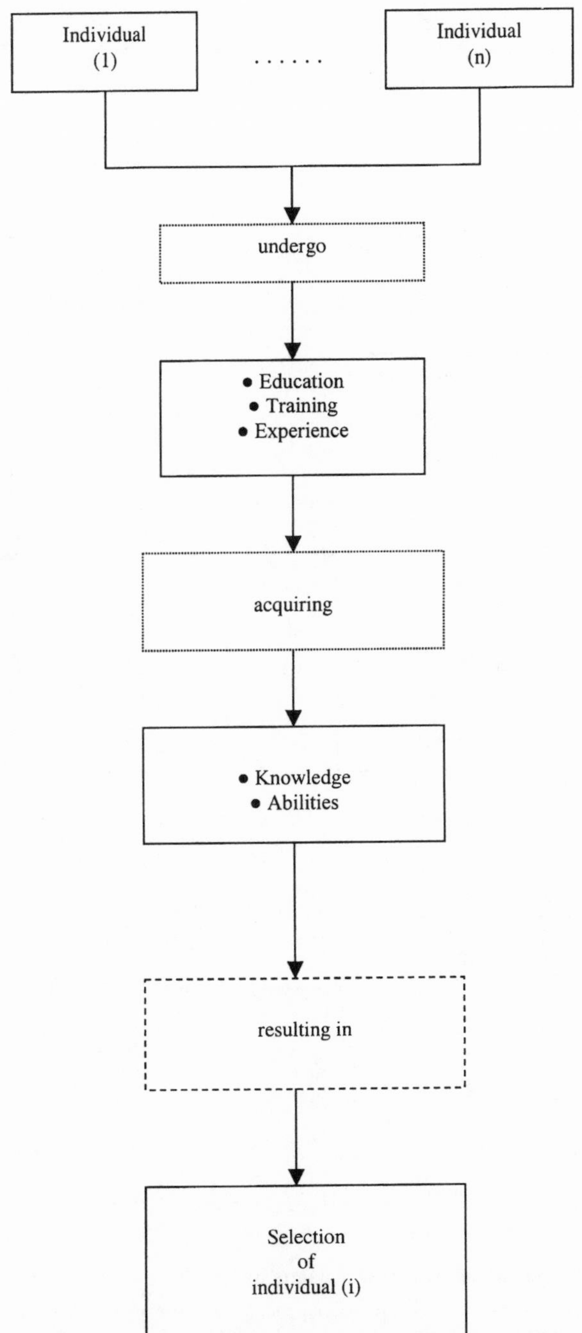

Figure 5.2 "Natural" Management Development

Source: Patrick E. Connor, "Developing Managers: A Case Study in Laying the Groundwork," *Journal of Management Development* 10, no. 3 (1991): 65.

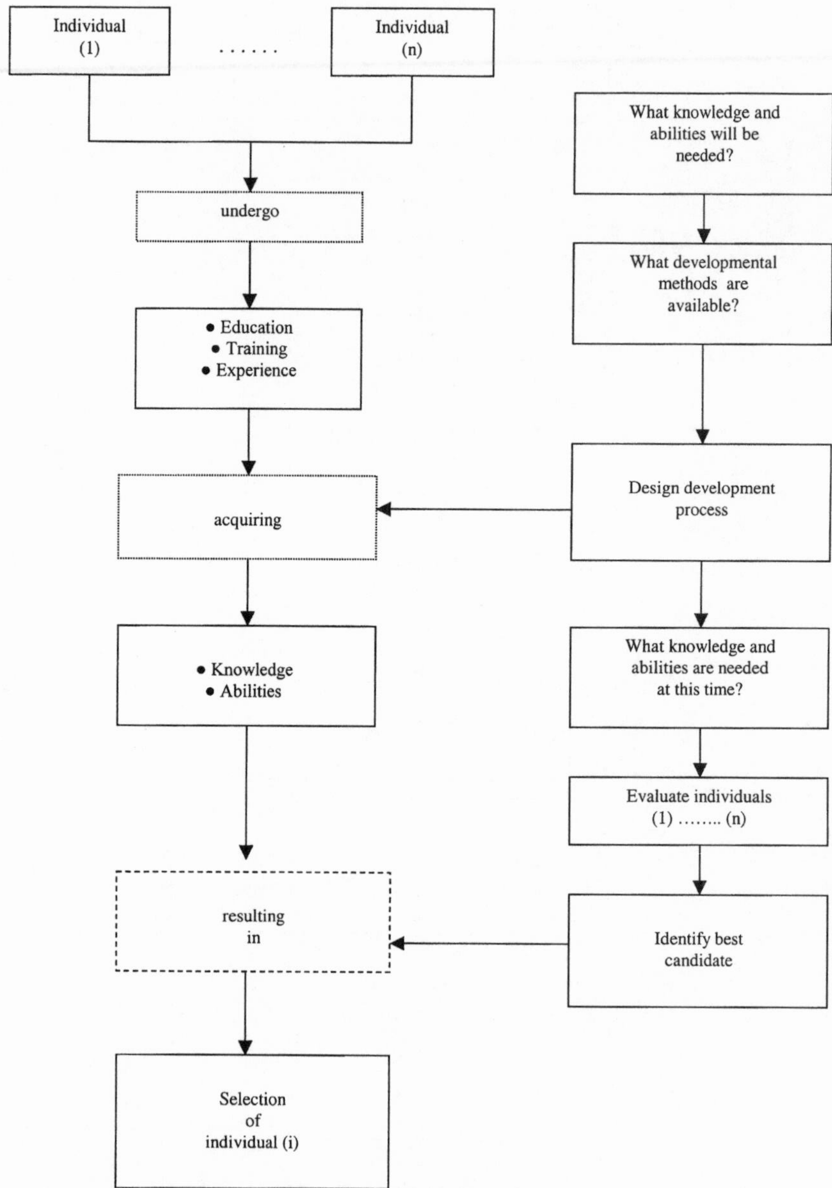

Figure 5.3 Managed Management Development

Source: Patrick E. Connor, "Developing Managers: A Case Study in Laying the Groundwork," *Journal of Management Development* 10, no. 3 (1991): 65.

major methods available. A comprehensive management-development program will have a number of activities for each method available to its people.

3. Commit to a *process* that will not leave the development of managers to chance.

As Kenneth Wexley and Timothy Baldwin have argued, developing managers means, simply, enabling people to learn, grow, and improve their competence in performing professional management tasks.[25] And as figure 5.3 showed, it is not something that an organization can leave to the individual acting alone—leave to luck, as it were. Certainly, people are ultimately responsible for their own growth and development. Still, it is clear what management development requires of an organization:

> a conscious effort to provide its managers (and potential managers) with opportunities to learn, grow, and change, in hopes of producing over the long term a cadre of managers with the [competence] necessary to function effectively in that organization.[26]

When such an effort is expended, the organization's ability to succeed and prosper under changing circumstances is greatly enhanced. This "people" method of change can be a powerful one.

Organizational Development

Organizational development, known generally as OD, is a set of concepts and techniques designed to bring about organizational change in service of improved productivity. Whether its conceptual emphasis is on the approach used, the organizational task focused upon, or the time frame for making the change happen, the hallmark of OD is its emphasis on planned interventions into various aspects of organizational life.[27] OD practitioners intervene into individual, group, and systemwide processes and practices. For example, a team of OD consultants was called in to help a large city bus system.[28] Their interventions included extensive data gathering, organizational diagnosis exercises, feedback sessions, and behavior-modeling training. The object of these interventions, and OD interventions in general, is to improve organizational and employee climate, health, functioning, and well-being.

OD Assumptions, Values, and Objectives

Organizational-development change methods are rooted in a number of assumptions and values pertaining to people, organizations, and performance. The central ones were articulated several years ago by French and Bell:[29]

- Most individuals have drives toward personal growth and development.
- Most people want to make, and are capable of making, a higher level of contribution to the attainment of organizational goals than most organizational environments will permit.

- Most people want to be accepted and to interact cooperatively with at least one small group of peers and other coworkers, and usually with more than one group.
- All group members, not just the leader, are critical to group effectiveness.
- Suppressed feelings adversely affect problem solving, personal growth, and job satisfaction.
- The level of trust, support, and cooperation is lower in most organizations than is necessary or desirable.
- Win-lose conflict strategies are ultimately deleterious to overall organizational effectiveness.
- If they are to succeed, OD interventions must be reinforced by the organization's total human resources system.

As this list suggests, OD programs are based on a conception of people and their organizations as employee and client centered. They emphasize flexibility, openness, and clarity; and they value competence, compassion, and performance. The aim of such programs is to bring the organization, through its people, to that conception. In fact, a survey of 1,000 OD practitioners revealed five key desires that drive their work:[30]

- Increasing effectiveness and efficiency
- Creating openness in communication
- Empowering employees to act
- Enhancing productivity
- Promoting organizational participation

By combining these assumptions, values, and desires, we can see the sorts of change that OD attempts to effect. This is illustrated in table 5.4.

The change objectives identified in table 5.4 are broadly framed. Slightly more specific objectives, addressed to the organization as a whole, have also been developed by OD practitioners. When met, those objectives enable an organization to become "healthy" (in OD parlance): strong, viable, self-renewing, and productive. Some of the major characteristics of so-called healthy organizations have been identified by Don Warrick, an OD consultant; they are listed in table 5.5.

OD Intervention Methods

We noted earlier that OD practitioners intervene into individual, group, and systemwide processes and practices.[31] OD interventions that focus on the *individual* range from personal coaching and counseling to broad Gestalt training. Coaching and counseling are designed to encourage personal changes in cognitive skills, behavior, and habits. Gestalt methods focus on the whole person, helping individuals know, acknowledge, and be themselves. Such methods may involve training programs in which individuals identify their own training

Table 5.4
Change Objectives of Organizational-Development Programs

Away From:	Toward:
1. A view of people as essentially bad	1. A view of people as essentially good
2. Resisting individual differences	2. Accepting and utilizing individual differences
3. Walling off personal feelings	3. Expressing feelings
4. Game playing	4. Authentic behavior
5. Distrust	5. Trust
6. Avoiding risk taking	6. Willingness to take risks
7. Emphasis on competition	7. Emphasis on collaboration

Source: Adapted and abridged from R. Tannenbaum & S. A. Davis (1969), Values, man, and organizations, *Industrial Management Review*, Winter, pp. 67–86.

needs and then design a program to satisfy them. Programs may include such elements as formal training, within or without the organization; reading schedules; or management-sanctioned experiments in new ways of doing things on the job.

Other OD interventions emphasize *group* relationships. The most popular methods range from survey-feedback activities to T-groups. In survey feedback, data are collected on some issue facing a group or work unit. Data concern employees' perceptions and attitudes (for example, satisfaction and supervisory style), and usually questionnaires and interviews are the major methods used to collect the data. The results are presented to the group, which then discusses the implications and attempts to form a plan for dealing with the issues raised.

Team building is another popular OD group method. Team-building activities aim to do two things: enhance the effectiveness and satisfaction of individuals who work in groups or teams, and promote overall group or team effectiveness. All aspects of the team—its structure, health, performance, role relationships among its members, and so forth—are examined and evaluated. Ideally, team building is an organization-wide activity, beginning at the top and fanning down through the enterprise. Typically, the process attempts the following:

- Build a climate for enhanced performance
- Evaluate the group's structure and processes
- Solve problems the group is experiencing
- Set goals and form plans for achieving them

Table 5.5
Characteristics of "Healthy" Organizations

Key Criteria	Characteristics
Organizational philosophies (explicit and implicit)	Strong employee-centered orientation that values, respects, and treats employees fairly regardless of position or status Strong client-centered orientation that is shared throughout the organization Long-term perspective that values both results and quality of work life Innovation and creativity encouraged and rewarded
Leadership	Top leader competent, respected, effective, people centered: inspires people to action Top management functions as team, has big-picture perspective, and is skilled in teamwork and developing and accomplishing worthwhile goals and policies
Management	Managers get results in terms of both high performance and satisfaction High level of competence in management skills Managers view management as profession requiring continuous study and upgrading
Human resource management	Competent and compatible employees with positive attitudes recruited, trained, and retrained Personnel policies and practices designed to help employees excel and develop quality work life High performance, healthy behavior, growth, and collaboration encouraged and rewarded
Capital resources	Strong financial planning and resources Excellent facilities and equipment Technologically advanced

(continued)

- Provide to group members training in individual, group, and/or technical skills (depending on what the group needs, of course).

T-groups are among the original methods employed by OD practitioners. They typically involve unstructured meetings, usually lasting from a few days to several weeks, with little in the way of an agenda, except to help members learn about themselves and each other. A trained leader, called a trainer, is

Table 5.5
(Continued)

Key Criteria	Characteristics
Structure	Lean, flexible, nonbureaucratic, and results-oriented structure designed to achieve and reward high performance, healthy behavior, innovation, and entrepreneurship
	Clear and worthwhile goals, policies, and responsibilities
	Minimal but effective controls for managing resources and performance
	Excellent working conditions
	Formal and informal structures reasonably congruent
Processes	Communication open and straightforward
	Effective planning keeps organization vital
	Decision making results oriented, decentralized, and participative when appropriate
	Problems and conflicts confronted openly and constructively
	Meetings productive and evaluated for process as well as content issues
	Relationships between individuals and within and between groups supportive, productive, and developed by design
Growth and development	Continuous growth and development fostered on an individual, group, intergroup, and whole-organization level
	Managerial, technical, and personal development training encouraged and sponsored
Work climate	Work culture characterized by openness, trust, support, teamwork, fairness, results orientation, and fun
Performance	High productivity and work quality
	High employee satisfaction
	Success in terms of both goal attainment and quality of work life

Source: Donald D. Warrick, *Managing organization change and development* (Chicago: Science Research Associates, 1984), pp. 4–5. *Managing Organizational Change and Development* by Warrick. © Reprinted by permission of Pearson Education, Inc., Upper Saddle River, NJ.

present to provide some limited technical expertise and to prevent harmful experiences from developing. Members of the group (about a dozen or so) gain feedback about how their own behavior affects others; in addition, they learn about group dynamics. T-groups were especially popular in the 1960s and early 1970s; they seem to have declined significantly since then, however, probably because of a number of unsuccessful experiences and the apparent difficulty of transferring the learning back into the organization.

Process consultation focuses on interpersonal relations and social dynamics occurring in work groups. A process consultant observes groups in action so as to develop an understanding of their decision-making and leadership processes, how their members communicate, how cooperation is enhanced, and how conflict is resolved. The consultant then gives feedback to the group members on these observations, with the objective being to help them develop the skills and understanding necessary to identify and solve their problems themselves.

Finally, a number of OD interventions function at the organizational, or *systemwide,* level.[32] The search conference, for example, is an organization-wide meeting to clarify organizational values, explore innovative ways to look at problems and opportunities, and even to set a new course for the enterprise. As a result of this intervention, organizational members can find themselves working much more in concert than ever before.

An organization confrontation meeting has objectives similar to those of the search conference but is usually employed when the organization is experiencing stress. The intent is immediate: to get management and employees to work on solving problems and taking action.

Another set of interventions is aimed at improving intergroup relations, that is, relations among departments or different groups within the organization. Usually a consultant is employed to help two groups understand the nature of their conflicts and to develop methods for resolving them.

Some interventions are deliberately normative in their approach. The consultant offers a specific OD package for identifying problems and suggesting solutions. Two examples of this approach are the Likert System 4 Management and the Blake and Mouton Grid Organization Development.[33] Both are packaged OD programs containing standardized instruments for measuring organizational practices, methods for analyzing the results, and procedures for helping the organization achieve its desired results.

OD practitioners use a number of other methods as well, too many to discuss here. Fishbowling, role analysis, ideal-norm building, conflict-resolution meetings, third-party interventions, and problem-solving meetings are all methods aimed at helping people effect change through group relationships.[34]

NOTES

1. A. Etzioni (1961), *A comparative analysis of complex organizations,* New York: Free Press, pp. 8–11.

2. J. B. Barney & R. W. Griffin (1992), *The management of organizations: Strategy, structure, and behavior,* Boston: Houghton Mifflin, p. 571.

3. M. LeBoeuf (1985), *The greatest management principle in the world,* New York: Putnam.

4. E. E. Lawler III (1981), *Pay and organization development,* Reading, MA: Addison–Wesley, p. 27.

5. A. H. Maslow (1943), A theory of human motivation, *Psychological Review,* 50, pp. 370–396; D. C. McClelland et al. (1953), *The achievement motive,* New York: Appleton-Century-Crofts; F. Herzberg (1962), New approaches in management organization and job design, *Industrial Medicine and Surgery,* 31, pp. 477–481.

6. Barney & Griffin, *The management of organizations,* p. 561; D. A. Nadler & E. E. Lawler III (1983), Motivation: A diagnostic approach (pp. 67–78), in J. R. Hackman, E. E. Lawler III, & L. W. Porter (Eds.), *Perspectives on behavior in organizations* (2d ed.), New York: McGraw-Hill.

7. J. R. Gordon (2001), *A diagnostic approach to organizational behavior* (7th ed.), Upper Saddle River, NJ: Prentice-Hall; T. G. Cummings & C. G. Worley (2001), *Organization development and change* (7th ed.), Cincinnati: SouthWestern, p. 392.

8. Lawler, *Pay and organization development,* pp. 197–199.

9. S. Kerr (1975), "On the folly of rewarding A, while hoping for B," *Academy of Management Journal,* 18, pp. 769–783.

10. J. B. Arthur & L. Aiman-Smith (2001), Gainsharing and organizational learning: An analysis of employee suggestions over time, *Academy of Management Journal,* 44, pp. 737–754.

11. Cummings & Worley, *Organization development and change,* pp. 401–404.

12. E. J. Harrick (1990), A contingency theory of pay, *Topics in total compensation,* Vol. 4; C. S. Miller & M. H. Schuster (1987), Gainsharing plans: A comparative analysis, *Organizational Dynamics,* 16, 1987, pp. 44–67.

13. H. Gorlin & L. Schein (1984), *Innovations in managing human resources,* New York: The Conference Board, p. 10.

14. M. Beer (1980), *Organization change and development,* Santa Monica, CA: Goodyear, p. 176.

15. B. E. Moore & P. S. Goodman (1973), Factors affecting the impact of a companywide incentive program on productivity, Report submitted to the National Commission on Productivity, January. Cited in Lawler, *Pay and organization development,* pp. 148–149.

16. T. M. Alfred (1967), Checkers or choice in manpower management, *Harvard Business Review,* 45, pp. 157–167. Cited in Beer, *Organization change and development,* p. 177.

17. The following discussion is based on G. R. Gray, D. W. Myers, & P. S. Myers (1999), Cooperative provisions in labor agreements: A new paradigm?, *Monthly Labor Review,* 122, January, pp. 29–45.

18. Ibid. The 1,041 contracts covered 4,545,478 employees and expired between September 1, 1997, and September 30, 2007.

19. Letter from Mr. S. F. McKenna, Vice President–Labor Relations, Ford Motor Company, to Mr. K. Bannon, Vice President, Director–National Ford Department, International Union, UAW, October 4, 1979. Source: N. L. Badore et al. (1984), Cultural change within a large system, Ford Motor Company presentation to annual meetings of the Academy of Management, Boston: August 12–15, pp. IV B1–IV B2.

20. B. Stump (1999), From adversaries to allies: Labor-management cooperation, *Journal for Quality and Participation,* 22, pp. 44–47.

21. The following discussion is based on B. Schneider (1987), The people make the place, *Personal Psychology,* 40, pp. 437–453.

22. H. M. Parson (1974), What happened at Hawthorne, *Science,* 183, pp. 922–932.

23. Gorlin & Schein, *Innovations in managing human resources,* p. 13.

24. The following discussion is based on P. E. Connor (1991), Developing managers: A case study in laying the groundwork, *Journal of Management Development,* 10, pp. 64–76.

25. K. N. Wexley & T. T. Baldwin (1986), Management development, *Journal of Management,* 12, p. 277.

26. M. W. McCall, Jr., M. M. Lombardo, & A. M. Morrison (1988), *The lessons of experience: How successful executives develop on the job,* Lexington, MA: D.C. Heath and Company, p. 147.

27. Cummings & Worley, *Organization development and change,* pp. 1–3.

28. I. A. Miners, M. L. Moore, J. E. Champoux, & J. Martocchio (1992), Effects of OD intervention on absence and other time-uses: A multi-year time-serial investigation (pp. 196–200), in J. L. Wall & L. R. Jauch (Eds.), *Best Papers Proceedings,* Las Vegas, NV: 52nd Annual Meeting of the Academy of Management, August 9–12, 1992.

29. W. L. French & C. H. Bell, Jr. (1973), *Organization development,* Englewood Cliffs, NJ: Prentice-Hall, Inc., pp. 65–73.

30. A. H. Church & W. Burke (1993), What are the basic values of OD? *Academy of Management ODC Newsletter,* Winter, pp. 1, 7–12.

31. D. D. Warrick (1984), *Managing organization change and development* (Modules in Management series, J. E. Rosenzweig and F. E. Kast, Eds.), Chicago: Science Research Associates, pp. 28–38; Cummings and Worley, *Organization development and change.*

32. This section relies on Cummings and Worley, *Organization development and change,* pp. 244–265.

33. R. Likert (1975), *The human organization,* New York: McGraw-Hill; R. Blake & J. Mouton (1964), *The managerial grid,* Houston: Gulf; R. Blake, J. Mouton, L. Barnes, & L. Greiner (1964), Breakthrough in organization development, *Harvard Business Review,* 42, pp. 133–155; R. Blake & A. McCanse (1991), *Leadership dilemmas—grid solution,* Houston: Gulf.

34. See Cummings and Worley, *Organizational development and change,* for an excellent compendium of OD interventions.

6
Strategies for Change

During what is considered the formative years of organizational behavior theory, Kurt Lewin set forth what has been called a field theory of motivation.[1] Lewin's idea was derived from physicists' concept of magnetic fields. Humans are thought of as operating in a kind of field of various forces, and human behavior is seen as the product of those forces. Management scholars have since applied this field concept to the analysis of problem solving, decision making, and change management.

The elegance of Lewin's idea is its simplicity. As figure 6.1 indicates, the concept is that a change situation involves moving from a current state to a desired future state. The force-field view of change management assumes that most situations are held in equilibrium by two sets of forces: those that facilitate movement to a new situation and those that restrain such movement. Under this condition the organization will maintain the status quo. When forces in one direction exceed those in the opposite one, the organization will move in the direction of the greater forces. If the facilitating forces (forces for change) exceed the restraining forces (those against change), then change will likely occur.

An example of this relationship was seen by one of the authors. In a western state a particular division of state government decided to introduce total quality management to all of its operations.[2] At the outset Ron, the person in charge of implementing the program, saw his division as being suspended in equilibrium between two sets of forces:

- Facilitating forces, including a desire by employees for greater involvement and training, a unanimous aspiration for a TQM workplace, and the support of both top management and union officials.
- Restraining forces, including an organizational culture of "cover your backside" rather than serving the customer; a history of failure in implementing the management fad-of-the-month; a lack of change elsewhere in state government; and fear—of failure, of ridicule, and of reprisal.

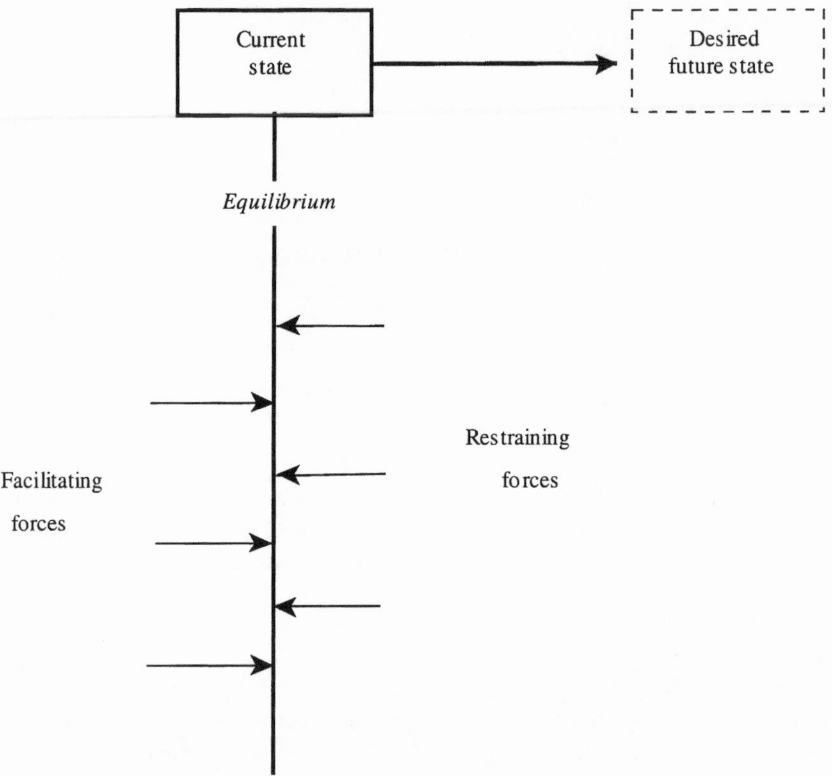

Figure 6.1 Force-Field Analysis of Change

The force-field concept is useful because it suggests that identifying and understanding facilitating and restraining forces can help answer the question of how best to go about managing a change. As a senior executive told one of us, "My philosophy is that I will cause change each day. And I learned at the beginning of my career to find out early where the roadblocks and opportunities are." This executive has learned to ask the questions that force-field analysis calls for: Should we concentrate our efforts on reducing certain restraining forces? Should we give one or more facilitating forces added emphasis? Should we introduce new facilitating forces? Can we somehow transform a restraining force into a facilitating force?

In the state government example just cited, Ron felt that for change to occur, the division could do little to reduce the restraining forces: It would be extremely difficult and time-consuming to change an entrenched culture; similarly, it would probably be a waste of everyone's time to try to change people's perceptions of history; and it would be nearly impossible to affect all of state government. Therefore, their best bet was to try to strengthen the facilitating forces. Resources and other emphases were applied, especially to employee training and to increasing employees' involvement in implementing the new program. As a result, life has changed for those who work in that division. Examples of how life is different include the following:

- Much more openness in discussing feelings and emotions
- A willingness to suggest changes to processes and procedures
- Less tendency to believe that things will never change
- A belief that staff are part of the process, playing an active role
- An understanding that it is not just management that is responsible for making things happen

The force-field questions cited previously reflect management's need to develop a general plan of attack, or a strategy for managing change. But how is that selection made most effectively? What criteria are important in such a choice? Some have argued that there is essentially only one choice to be made in selecting a strategy: whether the change should be conducted from the bottom of the organization up, or whether it should begin at the top and be pushed downward. This choice seems simple, but even so, at least four criteria have to be considered in making it: distribution of power, participation, speed, and uniformity. If equal power distribution and high employee participation are important, then a bottom-up strategy is suggested. If, however, a change has to be implemented quickly, and with uniform results throughout the organization, then a top-down approach is indicated.

More criteria than the four identified here are important, however, and change managers have more than two strategies from which to choose. Therefore, the purpose of this chapter is twofold: to describe the criteria used in selecting strategies, and to identify the set of strategies available to change managers.

CRITERIA

What criteria should be used to determine the most appropriate strategy? Although we could identify many—one treatment describes no fewer than fourteen criteria, for instance[3]—we suggest that the key aspects to consider are the following four: time available to effect the change, extensiveness of the proposed change, characteristics of the recipients of change, and characteristics of the change agent.

Tempo and Time Available

How much time is available to make the change? Must it be executed very quickly, or is there time for its gradual accomplishment? Change agents must understand the interrelatedness of time with what is changing. Often, different organizational elements undergoing change must change at different rates.[4] This is an important consideration because, as we shall see, some strategies simply require more time—with respect to the rate, rhythm, and pattern of change[5]—to implement than others.

Focus On: Episodic versus Continuous Change

One could argue that implicit throughout our discussion of change in this book has been a model of change that is more episodic, in contrast to continuous, in nature. By episodic we mean changes that can be portrayed as infrequent, discontinuous, intentional, or any combination of these. Episodic change—invariably driven by inertia and the inability of organizations to keep up—is considered more strategic in its content and more deliberate and formal than emergent change. As a result, it is driven by the sequence of unfreeze—transition (moving)—refreeze.

For many organizations, changes can be ongoing, evolving, and cumulative. The distinctive quality of continuous change is the idea that small continuous adjustments, created simultaneously across units, can accumulate and eventually create substantial change. With continuous change any semblance of stability is an accomplishment. The alert organization is unable to remain stable as it reactively and proactively modifies itself on a continuous basis. The challenge for the change managers and change agents is directing—or more likely redirecting—those changes that are under way. Consequently, a more plausible sequence would be freeze—rebalance—unfreeze.

As Weick and Quinn outline, to freeze continuous change is to make sequences visible and to show patterns of what is happening. With respect to rebalancing, patterns are reinterpreted, relabeled, and resequenced so that they unfold with fewer blockages. This is accomplished, for example, by reframing issues as opportunities, or reinterpreting history, or both. Finally, to unfreeze after rebalancing is to resume improvisation, translation, and learning in the hope that people are more mindful of sequences, more resilient to anomalies, and more flexible to execution in the future.

Source: K. E. Weick & R. E. Quinn (1999), Organizational change and development, *Annual Review of Psychology*, 50, 1999, pp. 361–386.

Extent of the Change

The second criterion to consider in selecting a strategy is the extensiveness of the advocated change (see "Focus On: Episodic versus Continuous Change").

What are the *scope* and *depth* of the change? Scope means the number of individuals and organizational units that will be affected by the change. Limited-scope changes could be as minor as a revision of job titles, whereas changes of great scope might involve choosing new long-range corporate strategies or implementing sweeping reorganization plans.

Depth refers to the number of behaviors that need to change and the importance of the changes to the individuals involved. For instance, using team building and T-groups seeks deeper, more emotionally involved change than mere adjustments in behavior. In other words, it is important to see that some strategies are intended to make very deep changes within a wide group of individuals, whereas others are intended to produce relatively minor surface changes in a limited number of people. It is obviously inappropriate to select a strategy that goes too deep, or is wider in scope, than the change requires.

The extent of change can also be evaluated with respect to whether first-order or second-order change is planned.[6] First-order change is incremental and convergent, meaning it does not involve fundamental change in an organization's strategy, core values, or corporate identity. Under such circumstances, change recipient learning is routine, incremental, and oriented to the status quo. Second-order change, however, is transformational, at times radical, and it fundamentally alters the organization at its core. Such change is difficult and risky. The change recipients must develop new patterns of thought and behavior.

Favorableness of the Change Recipient

The first two criteria, time and extensiveness, concern the context within which the change occurs. The third considers the set of people who are the recipients of the change. These are the people on whom the change will be visited, the ones who will find that their jobs have taken on new activities, that their reporting relationships have been rearranged, and so forth.

Recipients of change are discussed more extensively in chapter 7; for now, however, we can say that recipient favorability toward change means the following:

- *Recipient awareness,* or the degree to which recipient members perceive the need for change
- *Belief in the need for change,* or the degree to which members accept the idea that change should occur
- *Degree of commitment,* or the degree to which members are dedicated to making the proposed change work

In addition to these attributes, a recipient group is considered favorable if its members generally have a high degree of competence in dealing with the change at hand, and are knowledgeable about the situation and their own abilities.

Favorableness of the Change Agent

Finally, the strategy that is most appropriate depends on the characteristics of the person(s) who have operational responsibilities to conduct a particular change. These people are called change agents, and they also are discussed in chapter 7.

The favorableness of a potential change agent to effect change is determined by such features as his or her position- and person-based abilities and the resources tied to each. In particular are the agent's

- *positional authority;*
- *knowledge* of the change plans, rationale, and strategies and tactics available for conducting the proposed change;
- *ability to conceptualize* goals, obstacles, and intended outcomes; and
- *adeptness* at cooperating with and directing others.

If the change agent does not have the appropriate resources or technical and interpersonal skills, or access to them, the change cannot be effected without somehow going back and restructuring the change situation—or selecting a new agent.

In addition to possessing such attributes, the effective agent is able to endow members of the recipient group similarly. According to a study by Anthony Buono and Aaron Nurick, two keys to being an effective change agent are to help members of a recipient group (1) conceptualize and understand the nature of their situation, and (2) assess the potential opportunities for them that exist in change situations.[7]

CHANGE STRATEGIES

One might think that change-management strategies have been dealt with extensively in the organization and management literature. To be sure, many authors seem to have discussed the subject, virtually to exhaustion.[8]

However, despite the fact that these authors all use the term strategy, the majority of them then proceed to describe what are more accurately called techniques, tactics, or procedures. That the word strategy is often used incorrectly reveals the prevalent confusion over the concept; in general, the term is left undefined. Moreover, little substantial rationale is offered for lists of so-called strategies or for the various classification systems by which they are organized.

Robert H. Lauer is one of the exceptions.[9] He suggests that a clear distinction exists between change strategies and tactics. For him—and for us—a strategy is "the general design or plan of action," whereas tactics are "the concrete and specific actions that flow from the strategy." While strategies evolve over time, tactics can change quickly, being added or dropped as the strategy for change is implemented. Moreover, as will be discussed in chapter 7, change managers focus on strategies, change agents on tactics.

For example, imagine that the corporate vice president for underwriting at Global Insurance Company of Delaware has decided to change the computer system the firm's underwriters use. Imagine further that the underwriters want the new system; they just need help adopting it. This circumstance calls for a facilitation strategy (discussed later). However, the VP still has another decision to make: whether to employ self-study, instructional movies and tapes, classroom instruction, or a program of on-the-job training. These are all tactics that can be used to carry out the overall strategy.

Were this distinction applied to most of the change-management literature, the lists of so-called strategies would disappear. In their place we would find numerous lists of correctly identified tactics.

In any event, we offer here four types of strategies as generally available for effecting change; these we label facilitative, informational, attitudinal, and political. Although the strategies are discussed separately, several strategies—but not necessarily all of them—can be utilized simultaneously or in a planned pattern for a given organizational change effort.

Facilitative Strategies

Years ago, Larry E. Greiner suggested that strategies for managing change can be conveniently arrayed along a power continuum.[10] In the middle of the continuum, between what he called unilateral and delegated approaches, lies the "shared" approach. This approach involves the use of managerial authority, but with a concomitant sharing of power and with significant interaction between the manager and the recipient group.

A strategy of shared responsibility and involvement in change management is necessarily based on an assumption that the members of a recipient group have some willingness and ability to participate. This assumption led Zaltman and Duncan to define a more descriptive strategy, one that they and we call *facilitative.*[11]

Facilitative strategies assist the members of a change-recipient group in making the change or using their abilities or resources in conducting the change. Basically, such strategies make it easier for the change recipient to accomplish a given change program. For example, change recipients may be offered a critical resource that will aid them in making the change.

Criteria for Facilitative Strategies

In general, facilitative strategies are best in situations in which members of the recipient group have some sense of what they want to do but do not have all of the means to do it. Thus, facilitative strategies are called for when management can make the following assumptions regarding our four criteria:

Tempo and time.

The amount of time required for facilitation strategies to be effective can vary—especially if first- or second-order change is planned. If the strategy is used to provide a single, crucial link in a change process that is well under way, the change can be rapidly completed. On the other hand, if a facilitation strategy is being used to supply a large variety of resources to change recipients who need a great deal of training, assistance, or both, then the facilitation strategy will require a considerable amount of time.

Extensiveness.

Facilitative strategies are especially important when the proposed change is extensive and may involve more than one department or organization. However, members of the recipient group (or groups) must have a high level of commitment to accomplishing the change. Even without such a commitment, though, facilitation can be used as an initial part of an overall strategy—a starting point, as it were.

Recipient favorableness: Awareness.

A change program can be conducted in a facilitative way when members of a change-recipient group recognize that a change is needed. In particular, the recipient person or group realizes that something needs to be changed, is aware of what the various options may be, knows where help can be found to implement the needed change, and is ready to embrace that help. In short, a facilitative strategy is used when the members of a recipient group simply need a helping hand to do what they want to do.

Such an attitude does not come about by accident, of course. It is engendered by involving members of the recipient group(s) in the change manager's decision process. The reason that such involvement is helpful is that it serves to lower feelings of distance, even alienation. Moreover, it usually stimulates and assists communication among recipient-group members—and this further stimulates their interest in and openness to change.

A slightly cynical view suggests that when a manager involves a recipient group in the decision process, the group members frequently leave the meeting(s) with the manager's point of view firmly implanted in their heads. In other words, being involved can be a socializing experience, one that increases the members' openness to the managers' contemplated change.

Recipient favorableness: Belief in the need for change.

It is not enough that recipient-group members are merely aware that a change is indicated. A change can be facilitated even more appropriately when they *believe* that they must change.

Recipient favorableness: Degree of commitment.

Finally, as we noted briefly earlier, facilitative strategies are useful when the recipient members are not only aware that a change is needed and believe that the indicated change should take place, but are also committed to the change. We mentioned earlier the Global Insurance Company's underwriting vice president's desire to implement a companywide change in the underwriting computer system. It will be much easier for her to install a new computer system if her underwriters believe that such a change is necessary and are committed to it. Such commitment is helped by the fact that top management—in this case the VP—is also perceived to be strongly committed to the change. If the underwriters' commitment is low, she will have to link her facilitative efforts to some educational activities. The purpose of these activities would be to demonstrate the ways in which the proposed change will help underwriters do their job more effectively.

In brief, then, the Global VP's strategy of facilitation will be made easier when her underwriters (1) perceive the presence of the problems, (2) are willing to work to remedy those problems, and (3) have the commitment and ability to do so.

Agent favorableness.

To facilitate people's willingness to change requires that the change agent make available the necessary knowledge, dollars, or other resources the group needs. This is not as straightforward as it seems, however. In most instances change agents have competing demands on their time and energies; therefore, they have to be careful about getting involved in a long-term facilitation effort. A typical procedure deals with this issue by having the facilitating agent operate for a specified length of time, after which the recipient group is expected to be self-sustaining.[12]

Example

Management in one rapidly growing electronics company devised a way to help people adjust to frequent organizational changes. First, it staffed its human resource department with four counselors who spent most of their time talking to people who were feeling "burnt out" or who were having difficulty adjusting to new jobs. Second, on a selective basis, they offered people four-week mini-sabbaticals that involved some reflective or educational activity away from work. And finally, the company spent a great deal of money on in-house education and training programs.[13]

As this example shows, facilitation is not an especially efficient change strategy. In fact, its basic drawback is that it can be time-consuming, expensive (particularly in labor costs), and still unsuccessful. Even so, when recipient-group members essentially want the change but are hesitant for reasons that are either psycho-emotional (such as of fear and anxiety over the prospect) or technical (such as lack of the necessary knowledge or skills), change managers are well advised to provide some facilitative support.

Informational Strategies

Probably the method managers use most frequently to overcome resistance to change is educating people about the change. Such education works best when it anticipates and defuses particular points of resistance. This method can involve plant, departmental, or "town" meetings; one-on-one conferences; memoranda or newsletters to work groups; or even notices posted on the lunchroom bulletin board.

Such education efforts reflect an *informational* strategy. When using informational strategies, those responsible for managing a change effort offer knowledge, facts, and opinions so that change recipients can make rational decisions and take the indicated action.

Criteria for Informational Strategies

Informational strategies are based on a simple assumption: members of recipient groups will act rationally in the face of factual information; moreover, given adequate information, they will recognize the problem and come to a mutually agreeable solution because the facts are so compelling. In short, if management believes that members of the recipient group simply need information to understand why the change is necessary, and how they should relate to it—either in action or in feelings—then an informational strategy is indicated.

Tempo and time.

Informational strategies vary in the amount of time they require to prepare and implement, depending on the condition of the change recipients when the strategies are first applied. If members of the recipient groups are highly favorable to the proposed change, implementation may take place in a relatively short time. If not, an exclusively informational strategy will require a much longer time to accomplish the desired change objectives.

Extensiveness.

Informational strategies are especially important when the recipient group needs an extensive amount of information. If, however, the change is intended to be implemented over a short time, and recipient members' motivation is low, then a strictly informational strategy will undoubtedly prove ineffective. On balance, such a strategy is valuable for an extensive change because of its short-term influence; it can serve to provide a small number of interested individuals with information that enables them to serve as models for the rest of the group.[14]

Recipient favorableness: Awareness.

Transmitting information is an especially important part of an overall change strategy if members of the recipient group are generally unaware that a change situation is in the offing. Such an effort is also called for if management wants to arouse a concern about a problem, one not yet perceived by members of the recipient group. Finally, if management assumes that those members don't know what actions need to be taken in implementing the change, then an informational strategy is also indicated.

Recipient favorableness: Belief in need for change.

Members of a recipient group may be aware of a problem without believing that a particular change—or any change at all, for that matter—is needed. Informational strategies can then be used to develop perceptions of that need. Thus, informational strategies are indicated when it can be assumed that there is a need to connect causes and symptoms, to create awareness that a problem exists, and that the problem can be remedied.

Survey feedback is one of the most popular methods by which informational strategies can be implemented. As we noted in chapter 5, the technique consists of collecting data from an organization by means of a questionnaire or interviews. The data are then summarized, reported back to the members of the organization, and used by them to diagnose and articulate their problem. The collection of data highlights the two-way communication that occurs before actions to be taken are developed.

Following are some guidelines that have been developed to ensure that the survey-feedback technique is employed effectively:[15]

1. All members of the organization, including those at the top, should be involved in preliminary planning of the survey, usually with the assistance of an external, independent consultant.
2. The survey instrument is administered to all members of the organization involved.
3. Usually, an external consultant analyzes the survey data, tabulates the results, suggests approaches to diagnosis, trains internal resource people, and provides help in analyzing the data.
4. Data reporting ("feedback") usually begins at the top of the organization, distributed to either the top manager, the executive team, or members of a special task force.
5. If or when the initial reporting back is given only to the top manager, that manager holds a meeting with immediate subordinates as soon as possible to review and interpret the data.
6. Frequently, especially in large organizations, data are reported to successively lower hierarchical levels of managers and their work groups. This is sometimes known as a *waterfall* or *cascading* reporting approach.

Recipient favorableness: Degree of commitment.

An informational strategy assumes a fairly high level of commitment on the part of recipient-group members. If that commitment is missing or quite low, the members will not assimilate the information effectively enough to prepare them for involvement in a change program. Multiple information-providing methods applied over an extended period may be necessary to build commitment among the change recipients.

There is more than one way by which recipient-group members may express commitment, of course: working overtime without pay, providing services not spelled out in budget or goal statements, distributing or signing a petition, or simply complying with the basic ideas of the advocated change.

Agent favorableness.

An informational strategy relies on the agent's possessing and transmitting pertinent—and valid—knowledge, facts, and opinions. Obviously, these resources have to be available to the agent if the strategy is to be effective.

Moreover, as we noted previously, if the recipient group is not ready to change, an exclusively informational strategy will require a relatively long time to accomplish the desired change objectives. In such cases change agents will need to provide the pertinent information over an extended period. Needless to say, such a commitment will not be made lightly.

Example

Corporate management of a large service organization has decided to drastically change its spousal-assistance program. The company's officers believe that their ability to compete successfully in the labor market for highly qualified employees will be significantly improved by aggressively helping candidates' spouses to relocate; find employment; and identify desirable housing, schools, medical services, and the like. Now another decision has had to be made: how to make certain that some 9,500 management people (nationwide) fully understand the ramifications of the new program for their own regions, divisions, and departments. After weighing a number of options, company management has decided to have its personnel officers travel the country, giving personal, face-to-face presentations to management groups. Slide-show presentations are planned, complete with extensive question-and-answer sessions. In addition, videotapes of company executives addressing a variety of questions and issues about the program are being sent to each of the company's twenty-nine regional offices around North America.

In general, then, informational strategies are indicated when it can be accurately assumed that recipient-group members lack the information they need or possess information that is incorrect or misleading. It is further assumed under such circumstances that once informed, people will help with the change program's implementation. On the other hand, providing information in a meaningful and useful way can be time-consuming, especially if a large number of people and units are involved.

Attitudinal Strategies

We opened this chapter with a discussion of Lewin's field theory of motivation. At that time we pointed out the essence of the theory: the dynamic tension between forces working to facilitate movement to a desired condition and forces restraining such movement. Lewin went further, however. He suggested that modifying the restraining forces involves less tension and resistance than trying to increase the facilitating forces and therefore is a more effective way to bring about change.

Lewin's model[16] is applicable specifically to attitude change as well as more generally to organizational change. A three-stage process describes the means by which attitudes are modified (see figure 6.2):[17]

1. *Unfreezing.* To change, old attitudes must be "loosened" from their locked position. The analogy is to thawing something fairly frozen. This step usually involves removing support for old attitudes, communicating information in support of new attitudes, and reinforcing new attitudes.
2. *Moving.* This step involves moving toward acquisition of the new attitudes. Frequently, elaborate rites are conducted, as in a military boot camp, a church convent, or a bank boardroom. The intent of the rites is to help the person(s) convert to the new attitudes.
3. *Refreezing.* Finally, the attitudes are stabilized in their new equilibrium. This step usually involves providing support for the new attitudes, communicating supporting information, and reinforcing the new attitudes.

Attitude change is important for the simple reason that people's attitudes underlie and have a determining impact on their behavior. *Attitudinal* strategies for change therefore are based on the premise that a change in attitude will either produce a change in behavior or help maintain a behavior that already has been changed. Such strategies frequently mean that those who favor the change—change agents, for example—attempt to send persuasive messages. A great deal of research has been conducted on the characteristics of persuasive communications. This research has produced a number of guidelines, presented in table 6.1.

Criteria for Attitudinal Strategies

The intent of attitudinal strategies is to change attitudes, and thereby change behavior. In general, such strategies are most appropriate when the intended change is to be nonsuperficial and long-lasting. Such impacts clearly do not occur quickly.

Tempo and time.

If management believes it needs to effect a change at the attitude level, then it will have to be committed to an extended period of effort. It is simply in-

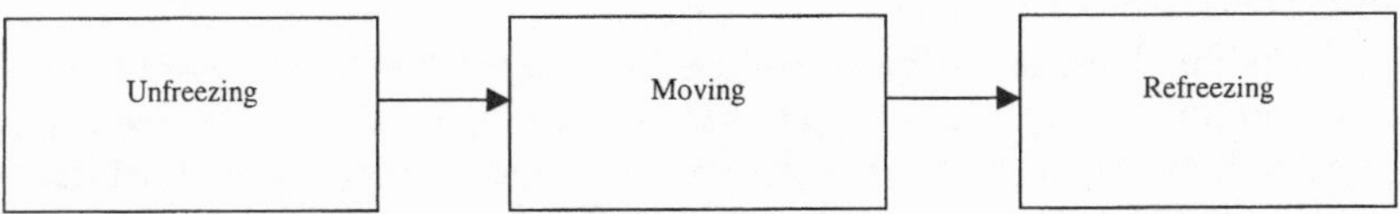

Figure 6.2 A Three-Step Change Model

Table 6.1
Changing Attitudes through Persuasive Messages: Some Guidelines

- *Establish your credibility.* Nothing undermines persuasive efforts more than lack of credibility. People don't want to listen to a person they don't trust or believe. Credibility is developed through demonstrating competence, objectivity, and high ethical standards.

- *Use a positive, tactful tone.* Assume the person you are trying to persuade is intelligent and mature. Don't talk down to that person. Be respectful, direct, sincere, and tactful.

- *Make your presentation clear.* Before you can convincingly articulate your view to someone else, you need to be clear about what it is you want to say. Once your objective is clear, you should present your argument one idea at a time. Don't jump from issue to issue, and do avoid unrelated topics. Focus on your end objective, and then present your ideas in a straight path that will lead the person to the conclusion you want and the objective you set.

- *Present strong evidence to support your position.* You need to explain why what you want is important. Merely saying your viewpoint is not enough.

- *Tailor your argument to the listener.* Effective persuasion demands flexibility. You have to select your argument for your specific target. Whom are you talking to? What are his or her goals, needs, interests, fears, and aspirations? How much does the target know about the subject you're discussing? What are his or her preconceived attitudes on this subject? How entrenched are those attitudes?

- *Use logic.* While a logical, reasoned argument is not guaranteed to change another's attitudes, if you lack facts and reasons to support your argument, your persuasiveness will almost certainly be undermined.

Source: S. P. Robbins (2001), *Organizational behavior* (9th ed.), Englewood Cliffs, NJ: Prentice-Hall, p. 188. *Organizational Behavior* by Robbins. © Reprinted by permission of Pearson Education, Inc., Upper Saddle River, NJ.

feasible for organizations to conduct a successful program of deep and abiding attitude change in a short time.

Extensiveness.

Attitudinal strategies are not appropriate for producing relatively minor surface changes. Instead, we are talking about second-order learning and change; thus, attitudinal strategies are particularly important when the proposed change is intended to be extensive. For one thing, extensive changes are more likely to be perceived as risky, confusing, and threatening than are narrow, surface changes. In such cases recipient-group resistance is likely to be higher. An attitudinal strategy can be effective by laying the perceptual and attitudinal groundwork for the change actions.

Recipient favorableness: Awareness.

Means for changing attitudes are less necessary when members of the recipient group already perceive a need for change. In contrast, however, is the situation in which no such perception exists. In such a case an attitudinal strategy may be appropriate, especially if it is designed to create openness to change in general or receptivity to information about a particular change.

Recipient favorableness: Belief in need for change.

If members of the recipient group already believe in the need for the proposed change, obviously there is little requirement for a strategy that intends to affect their attitudes. However, attitudinal strategies may be appropriate if they do not like the change or if they believe that it is too unimportant to bother with.

Recipient favorableness: Degree of commitment.

The essential elements of attitude change—unfreezing, moving, and refreezing—are directly related to increasing commitment. Thus, the lower the recipient-group members' commitment to the change, the more appropriate an attitudinal strategy may be. Moreover, successful attitudinal strategies not only will produce increased commitment, but will do so for an extended length of time.

Agent favorableness.

To be successful at implementing an attitudinal strategy, a change agent obviously needs to be able to understand why recipient-group members hold attitudes that are incompatible with the proposed change, and which elements of those attitudes are most (and least) susceptible to unfreezing. He or she also needs to be skilled at conducting the attitude-change methods that are needed. In other words, the resources the change agent possesses are persuasive abilities rather than budget dollars, data, or capital equipment. As we have said, these latter resources are more relevant to facilitative or informational strategies.

Example

Persuaded of the merits of total quality management, executives of a large, moderately high-tech company decided recently to change thoroughly the way their manufacturing processes would be managed. Customer and vendor relations, materials management, inventory control, and production planning all were to be drastically changed. The first strategy decision was to create and carry out a corporatewide program of attitude change. The intent of this program, as one executive put it, has been "to change the way we think about how we do business." The strategy involves persuasion and education, through which management is advocating and teaching new operating methods and procedures to go along with the new thinking.

On balance, then, attitudinal strategies are indicated when there is no requirement for speed; when the planned change is extensive rather than minor or superficial; when members of the recipient group are not favorably disposed toward the planned change; and when the change agent can bring persuasive, attitude-changing skills to the effort. Attitudinal strategies are especially appropriate for long-run, rather than temporary, change.

Political Strategies

Organizational politics involves those activities taken within organizations to acquire, develop, and use . . . resources to obtain one's preferred outcomes in a situation in which there is uncertainty or dissensus about choices.[18]

We began this chapter by reporting what some people argue—that there is basically only one choice to be made in selecting a strategy: whether the change should be conducted from the bottom of the organization up, or whether it should begin at the top and be pushed downward.

We also began our discussion of strategies by noting that they can be conveniently arrayed along a power continuum. At one extreme of Greiner's continuum is that which he labeled unilateral action.[19] Unfortunately, his definition has a coercive theme to it, as does the idea of a "power" strategy.[20] Our view here is that coercion and unilateral action are aspects of a broader concept: Political strategies are those that conform to Jeffrey Pfeffer's definition that begins this section, and therefore can occur top-down, bottom-up, or in some other direction. They can also occur in a blatant "do-it-or-else" coercive manner, or more subtly, as in "You scratch my back, I'll scratch yours."

Traditionally, political behavior determines who gets how much of what, when. Political strategies therefore are those that depend on giving, withholding, competing, or bargaining for scarce resources so as to accomplish the planned change's objectives.

Criteria for Political Strategies

As noted, political strategies can vary greatly, from unilateral coercion to complex maneuvering. Because of this variability, selection criteria are important in different ways, depending on the nature of the political strategy needed.

Tempo and time.

If time is of the essence and members of the recipient group are generally reluctant to accept the proposed change, then a power-type political strategy (e.g., unilateral, do-it-or-else) will likely be most expedient. However, if the change is to be *sustained* over a long period, then such a strategy will probably not be very fruitful.

On the other hand, what if there is time for the complex maneuvering that a full political process requires? Moreover, what if management knows that the change will have to be maintained over a long period? In this case, a political strategy is indicated. For example, if our underwriting vice president has to secure the cooperation and expertise of the insurance company's data-processing department to both install and maintain the new computer system, she will be well advised to employ elements of a political strategy.

Extensiveness.

The magnitude of a proposed change does not in itself determine whether a political strategy should be selected. It does matter, however, whether a power or maneuvering form of the strategy is likely to be effective. A power-type political strategy will be more effective if a proposed change is either small in magnitude or can be divided into small components. If the change is extensive, however, and cannot be broken down very easily into subparts, then a more complex political process—one combining elements of power, negotiation, compromise, and integration—will be called for.

Recipient favorableness: Awareness.

If members of the recipient group do not perceive the need for change, then a power-type political strategy might be indicated, especially if time is short to implement the proposed change. Otherwise, recipient awareness probably has little to do with the question of whether a political strategy should be selected.

Recipient favorableness: Belief in need for change.

If recipient-group members do not believe that the planned change is needed, *and* if action must be taken quickly, then a power-type political strategy may be effective. If there is a fair amount of time to accomplish the change, then it may be useful to conduct a more complex political strategy—especially if an informational strategy can be brought to bear as well.

Recipient favorableness: Degree of commitment.

In general, power-type political strategies produce compliance rather than commitment. Moreover, such a consequence usually requires that the recipient group be subjected to surveillance so as to maintain the compliance. So if it is important that members of a recipient group be committed to the planned change, then such a strategy will likely prove dysfunctional.

Agent favorableness.

The essence of political change strategies, as noted in the definition quoted earlier, is the use of organizational resources to achieve what one wants to achieve. By this, then, a change agent is able to conduct political strategies to the degree that the agent controls resources that others—especially members of the recipient group—want. Zaltman and Duncan put it succinctly: "The absence of such resources precludes the use of [political] strategies."[21]

Unlike in the case of attitudinal strategies, resources used in political strategies may take any form: budget dollars, machinery that a department may want, opportunities to be placed on a fast-track promotion list, and so forth. Political strategies are indicated to the degree that the change agent controls such resources.

On balance, power-type political strategies are indicated when the proposed change is to be accomplished quickly, the change is not extensive, members of the recipient group are not favorably disposed to the change, and the change agent controls necessary and valued resources. On the other hand, more complex political strategies are indicated when speed is not necessary, the change is relatively extensive, the recipient is more favorable, and again the agent controls the necessary and valued resources.

Example

This section was originally going to be titled "The Manager as Politician." After talking to some manager friends, however, it was learned that such an appellation was taken as an insult. Managers aren't politicians, I was told. They are rational, interested in efficiency and effectiveness, hard-working, and engaged in the serious business of resource allocation and strategy formulation in major enterprises that control vast sums of wealth and energy. They certainly are not politicians, engaged in frivolous conflict and dispute, subject to various pressures and responding to constituencies which could promise them the most votes or money. However, as they talked about their activities during their work, my informants told me about maneuvers which were relevant to their career advancement, such as showing up opponents at meetings, getting access to some critical information, making a point with the boss. I heard about maneuvers to get their subunit's point of view across more effectively, including forming alliances with other units, and about attempts to make decisions in uncertain and complex situations; in short, I heard about a lot of political activity. Fortunately, these associates were quite normal in their selective perception, motivation, and responses to commitments—not at all like the calculating, disinterested, highly motivated, and completely objective paragons I seem to encounter in my books on management and organizations.[22]

Focus On: Advanced Change Theory

The question as to why so many change efforts fail was the impetus for the advanced change theory (ACT) developed by Quinn, Spreitzer, and Brown. The conclusion drawn by Quinn and his coresearchers is simple: Change efforts fail because they do not alter human systems. Where traditional change strategies rely on explanation, persuasiveness, forcing others to comply, and searching for win-win solutions, Quinn et al. argue that "any change that requires changes in ingrained behavior patterns requires a social movement at some level" (p. 156). Thus, change requires changing ourselves first, as evidenced by the lives of Jesus Christ, Martin Luther King, and Gandhi.

The principles of ACT include the following:

- *Seeking to create an emergent system.* In organizations that apply ACT, a community emerges that can learn, adapt, and grow and is based on inclusion, openness, and development.
- *Recognizing hypocrisy and patterns of self-deception.* Human nature is such that we organize our lives around four basic values—remaining in control, winning, suppressing negative feelings, and making a rational pursuit of objectives (Argyris, 1991). We all want progress, but unfortunately we pursue the preservation of our current position.
- *Personal growth through values clarification and alignment of behaviors.* Change agents should consciously seek and choose new frames to ensure that behavior is aligned with key values. Such clarification is necessary if one is to relinquish control, accept short-term defeats, identify and explore negative feelings, and trust the uncontrollable emergent process.

- *Freeing oneself from the system of external sanctions.* Change agents are to do what is right rather than what is prescribed by existing laws, rules, authority, or public opinion. The focus is on living in the present and feeling the needs of others.
- *Developing a vision for the common good.* Real change leadership begins with a compelling vision for the common good for the future. Integrity then attracts others to act on behalf of the change.
- *Taking action to the edge of chaos.* One must continue to act on faith without guarantees as individuals leave the well-structured world of known cause and effect and enact a new order. At times the change agent is placed in possible jeopardy as she actively engages uncertainty.
- *Maintaining reverence for others involved in change.* The freedom and dignity of others does matter when operating for the common good.
- *Inspiring others to enact their best selves.* Here the leader continually models the courage, integrity, competence, and concern expected by all.
- *Modeling counterintuitive, paradoxical behavior.* If existing routines are to change, they must be distorted so that sense making in others occurs. When this takes place, the system does operate at the edge of chaos at times.
- *Changing the self and the system.* In challenging the current system, people are forced to choose between what is expedient and easy and what is the right thing to do.

ACT does not require perfection from change initiatives; instead, it recognizes the dangers inherent in change while embracing the pain, the risk, and the resulting chaos. To that end, it is easier to bring about radical change if the organization has a culture of respect and honor for its employees from the outset.

Sources: C. Argyris (1991), Teaching smart people how to learn, *Harvard Business Review,* May–June, pp. 99–109; R. E. Quinn, G. M. Spreitzer, & M. V. Brown (2000), Changing others through changing ourselves: The transformation of human systems, *Journal of Management Inquiry,* 9, pp. 147–164.

CONCLUSION

Selecting a strategy or applying a mix of strategies for managing change obviously is a matter neither trivial nor easy. We have seen that a number of considerations have to be taken into account, ranging from the amount of time available to conduct a change program to the overall capacities and capabilities of both change recipient and change agent. Change does not come easily even under the best of circumstances, and one recent article advocates a strategy that is less observable and more complex than those outlined here (see "Focus On: Advanced Change Theory").

Strategies differ as to their implications. For example, implementing some may produce a fairly superficial impact, a sort of quick fix, whereas others may have an in-depth effect. Other implications center on a speedy versus a drawn-out rate of implementation, short- versus long-term consequences, and helping versus persuading attempts. Referring to figure 6.3, we can see that implementing the four strategies has implications along the following dimensions:

- Surface versus in-depth impacts: Coercive-type political strategies are effective primarily on the surface, that is, on behavior of a compliance nature. At the other extreme, attitudinal strategies are intended to operate more deeply, at the level of attitude, not merely action. Commitment, rather than simply compliance, is the goal of this type of strategy.
- Fast versus slow implementation rate: Political strategies, especially of the coercive type, and facilitative strategies generally can be implemented quickly, although, as discussed earlier, for different reasons. Informational and attitudinal strategies involve a slower rate of implementation.
- Short-term versus long-term consequences: Political and attitudinal strategies can differ dramatically as to the duration of their effects. Political strategies (especially of the coercive type) tend to produce consequences that last over a relatively short duration. In contrast, successful attitudinal strategies have substantially longer-lasting effects.
- "Helping" versus "persuading": Figure 6.3 shows that facilitative and informational strategies share a common element in that they both are used in an attempt to help members of a recipient group accept, absorb, or adopt a proposed change. Financial resources or information may be provided, for example. On the other hand, political and attitudinal strategies are used to persuade, force, or even manipulate the recipient into adopting the change.
- Negotiation, compromise, bargaining, and integration: Finally, the middle of figure 6.3 indicates the most complex strategic approach that change management can take. This approach can involve a combined program of negotiation, compromise, and bargaining. Most people understand the negotiation-compromise-bargaining process; however, Mary Parker Follett in writings from the 1920s offered another approach—integration.[23] Integration occurs through invention and the creation of a "new way," whereby the desires of all sides are addressed and no side ends up sacrificing. This is in stark contrast to compromise, in which all sides give up something. Integrative solutions are reached when all sides bring issues, including concerns, demands and differences, out into the open so that the significant features (not the dramatic ones) are evaluated with respect to people's desires. In short, regardless of the approach, a comprehensive strategy involves a range of approaches: facilitation, information sharing, political maneuvering—even some attitude affecting.

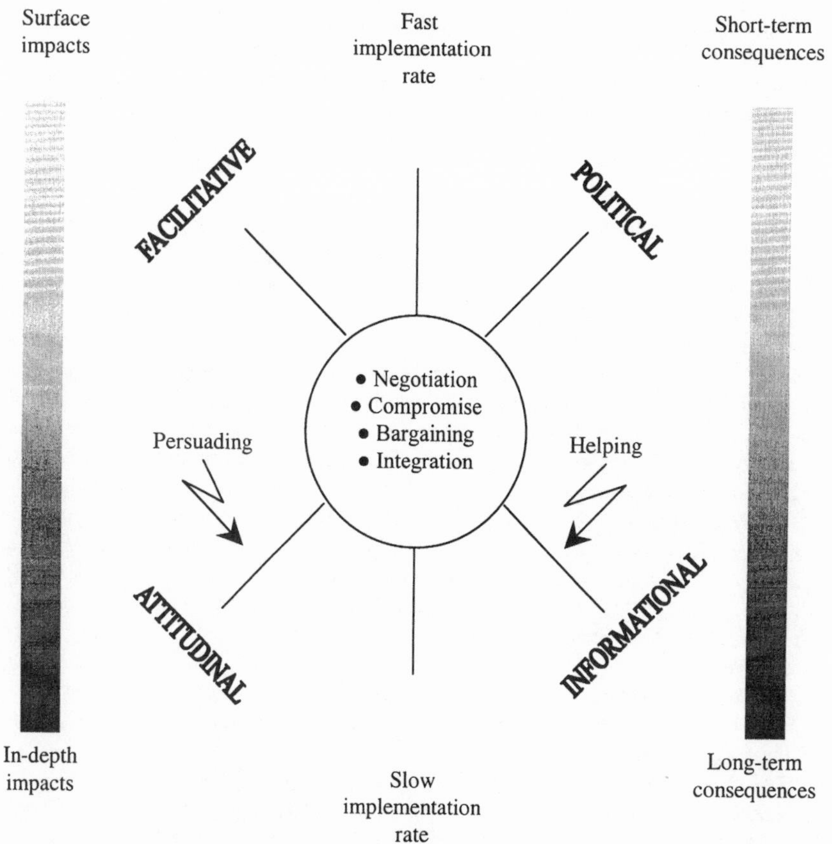

Figure 6.3 Change Strategies and Some Implications

NOTES

1. K. Lewin (1938), *The conceptual representation and the measure of psychological forces*, Durham, NC: Duke University Press; K. Lewin (1951), *Field theory in social science*, New York: Harper & Row.

2. Thanks for this example to Russell P. Allen and James M. Morrell.

3. G. Zaltman & R. Duncan (1977), *Strategies for planned change*, New York: Wiley.

4. Q. N. Huy (2001), Time, temporal capability, and planned change, *Academy of Management Review*, 26, pp. 601–623.

5. K. E. Weick & R. E. Quinn (1999), Organizational change and development, *Annual Review of Psychology*, 50, pp. 361–386.

6. A. M. Pettigrew, R. W. Woodman, & K. S. Cameron (2001), Studying organizational change and development: Challenges for future research, *Academy of Management Journal*, 44, pp. 697–713; A. D. Meyer, J. B. Goes, & G. R. Brooks (1993),

Organizations reacting to hyperturbulence, in G. P. Huber & W. H. Glick (Eds.), *Organizational change and redesign,* New York: Oxford University Press, pp. 66–111; J. Bartunek & M. K. Moch (1987), First-order, second-order, and third-order change and organization development interventions: A cognitive approach, *Journal of Applied Behavioral Science,* 23, pp. 483–500.

7. A. F. Buono & A. J. Nurick (1993), Intervening in the middle: Coping strategies in mergers and acquisitions," *Human Resource Planning,* 15 (2), pp. 19–33.

8. For example, G. N. Jones (1969), *Planned organizational change,* New York: Praeger; D. C. Basil & C. W. Cook (1974), *The management of change,* London: McGraw-Hill,; E. Burack (1975), *Organization analysis: Theory and applications,* Hinsdale, IL: Dryden; R. Lippitt, J. Watson, & B. Westley (1958), *The dynamics of planned change,* New York: Harcourt, Brace; R. Chin & K. Benne (1976), General strategies for effecting changes in human systems, in W. G. Bennis et al. (Eds.), *The planning of change,* New York: Holt, Rinehart; M. Beer & J. W. Driscoll (1977), Strategies for change, in J. R. Hackman & J. L. Suttle (Eds.), *Improving life at work,* Santa Monica, CA: Goodyear; R. H. Lauer (1977), *Perspectives on social change,* Boston: Allyn and Bacon; Zaltman & Duncan, *Strategies for planned change;* J. P. Kotter, L. A. Schlesinger, & Vijay Sathe (1977), *Organization,* Homewood, IL: Irwin; M. Beer (1980), *Organization change and development,* Santa Monica, CA: Goodyear; G. Egan (1988), *Change-agent skills b: Managing innovation and change,* San Diego: University Associates; T. D. Jick (1993), *Managing change,* Homewood, IL: Richard D. Irwin; and T. G. Cummings & C. G. Worley (2001), *Organization development and change* (7th ed.), Cincinnati, OH: South-Western.

9. Lauer, *Perspectives on social change,* especially p. 347.

10. L. E. Greiner (1967), Patterns of organization change, *Harvard Business Review,* 45 (May–June), pp. 119–130.

11. Zaltman & Duncan, *Strategies for planned change,* pp. 90–109.

12. Zaltman & Duncan, *Strategies for planned change;* Egan, *Change-agent skills b: Managing innovation and change;* Cummings & Worley, *Organization development and change;* Jick, *Managing change.*

13. J. P. Kotter & L. A. Schlesinger (1979), Choosing strategies for change, *Harvard Business Review,* March–April, p. 110.

14. Zaltman & Duncan, *Strategies for managing change,* chapter 5.

15. Cummings & Worley, *Organization development and change,* pp. 135–140.

16. Weick & Quinn's "freeze-rebalance-freeze" sequence outlined in their paper "Organizational change and development" provides an alternative perspective to Lewin's "freeze-move-refreeze" model.

17. Lewin, *Field theory in social science.*

18. J. Pfeffer (1981), *Power in organizations,* Marshfield, MA: Pitman, p. 7.

19. Greiner, Patterns of organization change, p. 120.

20. Zaltman & Duncan, *Strategies for planned change,* pp. 152–165.

21. Ibid., p. 156.

22. Pfeffer, *Power in organizations,* pp. 369–370.

23. M. P. Follett (1996), Constructive conflict, in P. Graham (Ed.), *Prophet of management: A celebration of writings from the 1920s,* Boston: Harvard Business Press, pp. 67–95.

7

Who's Who in the Change Process

In the previous chapters we have examined three central elements of organizational change: objects, methods, and strategies. Now we consider a fourth element—and likely the most important: the people involved. Change managers constitute one group involved in change. As we stated in chapter 1, change managers design, oversee, and direct change as part of carrying on their regular duties. They might be responsible for managing a department or an entire company, and as they do this, change is part of what they manage. Change managers—sometimes referred to as change strategists[1] because they lay the foundation and craft the vision for change—anticipate the elements of change, choosing and guiding those who will participate in the change, selecting strategy packages, and assessing the results. Key activities for change managers are outlined in table 7.1.

The topics of this chapter are the three other groups of people involved in change. In the first group are those who create and conduct change. They are the change agents. Change agents (sometimes called change implementers[2]) play a variety of roles in the management of change. A change manager's choice of a particular person as a change agent depends in part on that person's individual and organizational characteristics. The second group consists of those who work in the changing organization and must implement the changes. They are called the change recipients. Change recipients may be primary targets of an organizational change, or they may have to change as a result of other changes made in the organization. Finally, we introduce a third group that we call *change allies.* Change allies are not the primary targets of change, but they play a vital, informal role in helping to sustain and move along change initiatives.

CHANGE AGENTS

Change agents are those people charged with altering the status quo in an organization.[3] Based on instructions from change managers, their intention is to cause parts of an organization to operate differently from the way they have

Table 7.1
Key Activities for Change Managers

- Define and communicate the vision, the purpose(s) and the objectives for change
- Communicate the priority of the project by taking personal ownership.
- Participate in the planning and implementation of the change by developing realistic goals and timelines by attending progress meetings.
- Supply critical resources – including outside resources when needed – for the change management project.
- Protect change agents from attack by opponents to change.
- Provide clear options and clear consequences.
- Provide training to all affected employees, including senior managers. Personally attended training sessions when appropriate.

Sources: R. Axelrod (2000), *Terms of engagement,* San Francisco: Berrett-Koehler; J. Brown & B. Waymire (eds.) (2001), Best practices in change management, *Prosci Benchmarking Report*, www.prosci.com.

operated in the past. Beyond this basic intention, what can be said of change agents? Two things: First, because the term change agent encompasses a number of different roles, one or several people may be filling those roles during a particular change. Second, change agents' organizational and personal characteristics influence their success in initiating and implementing changes.

Change Agent Roles

Organizational change is not a single event but occurs as a series of events. The need for change arises and is recognized, plans are formulated and modified, changes are implemented; each of these steps is a part of the overall change process. At different points in the process, different demands are made on a change agent. The role of change agent requires a temporal capability, which is the ability to comprehend various temporal conceptions (i.e., time perspectives, including clock, inner, and social time) and dimensions (i.e., sequencing, timing, and pacing) of change.[4]

Because the roles they must assume are so diverse, an assortment of people may be called upon to play the necessary role(s) at different points during the change. Change managers exercise their own management obligations by choosing people who can best fill each of the following change agent roles as the need arises.[5]

Catalysts precipitate change by acknowledging, and sometimes encouraging, dissatisfaction with the status quo. If destabilizing forces already exist in the organization, catalysts can make efforts to get others to notice those forces. An analyst reporting the results of a work-flow study that highlights low productivity or antiquated methods can be a catalyst for change. Emotion and zeal can be powerful tools of people in this role. "We just got bad news from the accountants," "We've got to cut inefficiency and waste," "The competition is walking all over us," and "The people at Acme Company make a lot more than we do" are effective examples used by some change agents in this catalytic role. They can use the force of emotion to move others to become discontent.

Focus On: Issue Selling

Issue selling is the process by which individuals attempt to influence others' attention to and understanding of events, developments, and trends that have implications for organizational performance. Managers "sell"—via their persuasive efforts—"issues" that are "bought" by top managers who control the firm's strategic direction.

By actively selling issues, such managers help to determine which change initiatives get activated within the firm; therefore individuals outside the top management team are capable of being potent initiators of change. Of course, at any given time, there can be multiple individuals selling complementary or competing change initiatives in the organization. Being knowledgeable in an organization's context (including rules, routines, values, and norms) and strategy is critical to successful issue selling attempts.

Managers focus on three types of "moves"—process, packaging, and involvement—to sell issues.

- *Process* reflects the formality (e.g., through written methods or orally), preparation (i.e., doing one's homework before proceeding), and timing (i.e., persistence, opportunism, and involving others at the right time) of issues.
- *Packaging* the issue involves the presentation, or how an issue seller goes about actively promoting an issue; and bundling, or sellers' attempts to connect the issue to other issues or goals (e.g., profitability). Sellers also employ the tactic of continuous proposal making.
- *Involving* key organizational members to increase the visibility of the issue, to grow a powerful coalition, and/or to ensure that attention and action are devoted to the issue. This move focuses on the targets, the nature of the targets' involvement, and the timing of their involvement.

Source: J. E. Dutton, S. J. Ashford, R. M. O'Neill, & K. A. Lawrence (2000), Moves that matter: Issue selling and organizational change, *Academy of Management Journal*, 44, pp. 716–736.

Catalysts can also promote dissatisfaction in the status quo by encouraging the destabilizing forces until their existence is impossible to ignore (see "Focus

On: Issue Selling"). A person in the catalyst role may deliberately increase response time at the parts order window until all who request materials begin complaining about delays. Eventually, those who seek parts will demand that changes be made. In another situation, a change agent seeking approval for streamlining reporting relationships may begin following the prescribed—and very slow—routes for all messages and requests. Eventually, everyone is made to feel adequately frustrated, and a change is demanded.

Solution givers offer suggestions about what can be done to solve the problems the catalyst has made obvious. To make useful and appropriate suggestions for solutions, the change agent in this role must understand the intricacies of the organization as it currently stands, and the extent of its available resources. Sometimes committees or task forces are appointed and given the task of giving solutions to the problems that catalysts have caused to be acknowledged. In other cases change managers may not actually choose a solution giver; he or she may arise spontaneously with a solution. In still other settings, the solution is offered by a vendor, as in the case of a large computer software-hardware company or telecommunications system integrator whose products and services solve corporate problems and necessitate significant organizational change.

Process helpers play their part in organizational change by showing change managers and organization members how the process of change works—both generally, and in the specific case at hand. Processes that need explanation and training include definition of needs, diagnosis, and creating and evaluating solutions. Skills in communication, securing cooperation, and persuasion aid in accomplishing these processes. To successfully carry out the role, process helpers must have not only skills but also credibility with the participating individuals and groups.

Change managers often call upon organization development (OD) specialists to assist in understanding change processes. Because of their special knowledge and perspective,[6] they may be brought in for specific phases of a change to assist during that phase only, or they may be available throughout the process to coach and train individuals involved in all roles.

Resource linkers bring together various financial, people, and knowledge resources. Change agents effective in this role know where the necessary resources are and how to make them available to the present case. They also recognize where and when each of the many resources must be applied.

A fifth role is also played in managing change, and it has to do with solidifying the change. Once the change is implemented, the organization must be stabilized around it. *Stabilizer* is not a change agent role, but one of management. Management may appoint stabilizers to work with the recipient group, but they serve as an extension of the manager, not as change agents.

In some organizational changes, there is essentially one major agent of change. This agent recognizes the need for the change and causes others to see it, plans the change, gathers the necessary resources, and finally assists others in making the change. More often, several people play the different roles in the change, or more than one person may perform any one of the four roles. Unfortunately, the role of the change agent is often poorly defined and poorly understood,[7] thus making the change agent's job more difficult given how inadequately recognized, supported, encouraged, and rewarded he or she can be.

Change Agent Characteristics

Selecting people to fill the four major change agent roles is not an easy task. The change manager can benefit, however, by considering both organizational and personal characteristics.

Certain organizational characteristics can greatly influence change agents' effectiveness. These include the source of their designation as change agents,[8] whether they are in staff or line positions, and whether their position is external or internal to the changing organization. In this section we discuss these organizational characteristics, plus the advantages and disadvantages, associated with each.

Organizational Characteristics: Source of Designation as Change Agent

Some change agents take on that role for themselves. It is they who decide they will do something to change the status quo. These people can be termed *spontaneous* change agents. After days of seeing books returned torn or dirty, a librarian may post a notice stating that books are to be returned in good condition or a fine will be levied. Money is then collected from those who return books in poor condition. Over time, fewer and fewer books are returned torn or dirty. Through this act, the librarian has changed a policy of the library and has utilized a coercive means of getting people to comply. Thus the librarian has been the spontaneous agent of a change.[9]

Using spontaneous change agents has its advantages. By taking on the role themselves, spontaneous change agents are likely to have the enthusiasm, commitment, and clear vision required to achieve a new state. As a result, they will provide the necessary energy and drive even if the road of change is difficult.

Interestingly, the major disadvantage in having a spontaneous change agent is the spontaneity itself. It is difficult both to be spontaneous and to have objectivity and a real understanding of short-term results versus long-term consequences. In addition, the spontaneous change agent may be a good person to recognize that change is required but poorly suited for carrying it out because of organizational position, lack of talents and skills, or lack of time.

In other instances, people are *designated* as change agents by someone else—for example, a boss, a committee, or a consultant. Though they can then choose whether or not to accept the role, they are originally called upon by someone else to become a change agent. A shipping department supervisor, for example, may ask an employee to devise and implement a means for clearing up delayed shipments. The subordinate's new role is clearly that of a designated change agent.

Designated agents may also bring to the task the advantage of commitment and vision, of course. Those who have already identified with the new directions into which a particular change is expected to take the company can be an obvious choice as change agents. They will have already demonstrated a certain vision of that new direction, and their commitment can be encouraged.

Whatever motivation they might have to do well as change agents can also be enhanced by the circumstances of their appointment. For instance, the designated agent may be given the task as a chance to prove his or her fitness for other work in the organization. Motivation may be limited for the immediate change agent role but high for obtaining the promised reward.

The designated agent may be at a disadvantage because, as an appointee, he or she may lack drive or the conviction that the change is really necessary. Also, because of other commitments, an appointed agent may not have the time or energy necessary to implement a change, even if firmly committed to its necessity.

Organizational Characteristics: Organizational Position

Change agents may hold either staff or line positions within the organization. Some staff support positions are specifically designed to bring about or facilitate change. These employees may be in human resources, specialize in organization-development activities, or report to the VP of human resources and/or industrial relations.

Agents who hold support positions may have the time to devote to change but may lack the necessary influence or authority to actually accomplish it. It is not enough for upper management to request that a staff change agent work on a particular problem; they must also delegate the appropriate authority to carry it out. In some settings, this would require higher-level managers to make it clear that the change agent has the authority to request certain actions. On the other hand, higher-level managers may also make it clear by their acceptance of the change that the staff agent has adequate authority to request actions of other employees.

In other companies, a staff support person seeking to facilitate certain changes must establish his or her own credibility. In general, the employee does this by displaying exceptional talent or insight. This credibility then carries with it its own authority to compel that certain changes get made. Such is often the case when a technical specialist advocates a technical change. For instance, an engineer may design a more efficient machine component and then advocate for its adoption.

People in line positions also serve as change agents. Their advantage is often that they are already vested with adequate formal authority to require changes in those who work for them. That authority, however, is usually limited to those working directly under them. They may have little or no influence on those in other hierarchical paths or on those whose positions are above them on the corporate ladder.

It is also a disadvantage to those in line positions that they have to add the role of change agent to their already considerable duties. Today's work must be completed even as tomorrow's world is being planned. In addition, being a line manager does not guarantee that the employee has the expertise to properly carry out all the phases of the change.

External or Internal

Change agents are sometimes an ongoing part of the organization's regular membership,[10] and sometimes they are brought in as outsiders, specifically to conduct all or part of the change activities.

External agents are sometimes outside consultants hired for a variety of reasons by the changing organization to lead the efforts. One reason they are brought in is that outside agents can bring a greater degree of objectivity and neutrality to the situation. Such qualities can be particularly valuable when some organizational members are worried about the suggested needs for, or possible outcomes of, the change. External agents may be forced upon the organization by regulatory agencies or financial backers, or by consumer watchdog groups. In these cases, the agents can lose their perceived neutrality if organizational members do not agree with their appointment or actions.

External agents are sometimes viewed negatively because they have little or no stake in the long-term outcomes of their actions and recommendations. Their payoff is from the activities they undertake now. They are not paid according to how those activities affect the company in the future. What's more, they won't be there to suffer or enjoy the organizational consequences.

External agents also are sometimes criticized for not being able to really understand the organization and its members, because they see only a small part of the operation and see it over such a relatively short time. From an organizational-culture perspective, this has some validity, for as cultural observers, external agents begin at a disadvantage. Unaccustomed to the idiosyncrasies of language the culture shapes, outsiders do not understand the organization's common language and symbolic meanings and therefore may not fully understand the significance of what is being said. In fact, the outside agent may not even know the questions to ask or how to ask them. External agents seeking to implement organizational changes may find that cultural barriers[11] are too great to surmount if they have only a short time to work with the organization.

Internal change agents have positions within the organization. As insiders, they have the advantage of an historical perspective on the current problems. They have either heard stories or actually witnessed preceding events. They already know the various organizational relationships between departments and between individuals. Inside agents frequently know where power is vested and where change forces can most efficiently be applied. In attempting to diagnose the situation, they obviously begin at an advantage over an external agent because of the amount of information they have assimilated. Internal agents also have an easier time gathering additional, necessary information. Knowing the culturally special language and having witnessed and interacted with the cultural symbols, they tend to be better able to phrase questions and to know who should be asked those questions.

Finally, internal agents may seem much less threatening than externals. Internal agents are familiar figures. Organizational members are accustomed to seeing them, answering their questions, and sharing opinions with them. They can seem far less menacing than an outside agent brought in for some not-quite-so-well-understood purpose.

There are also disadvantages to using internal agents. Because of their history in the organization, they may be prejudiced for or against a certain view, and so are unable or unwilling to operate objectively as they gather diagnostic information. Because they may have stronger ties to one part of the organization than to others, their neutrality is suspect—and sometimes nonexistent.

Because internal agents sometimes have other organizational duties, they may not have adequate time to devote to the change effort. Also, they may be in influential organizational positions but may not have the knowledge or special skills required to perform the change agent roles of catalyst, solution giver, process helper, or resource linker.

The seeming advantage of knowing the culture and history of an organization can in fact be a disadvantage if it too narrowly restricts the agent's creation of visions of the future or plans for implementation. An internal agent too thoroughly imbued with the current culture may make future plans that look like a replay of the past. In a company culture that dictates a bold approach to solving all problems, more cautious solutions—even if they would work better—are unlikely to be implemented, or even suggested. It may be a question not of an inside agent's hearing just what he wants to hear, but of his hearing only what he *can* hear. He may suggest not what he wants to suggest, but the only action it is conceivable to suggest.

Internal agents often expect to have a new role in the new organization when the change is implemented. But if they cause too much unforgettable damage or disturbance to others who will also have roles in the new organization, their own place may be jeopardized or made uncomfortable. For that reason, they may be unwilling to take certain steps during the change. The external agent can slip away after the change is implemented; the internal agent must live with it, and in it.

There is a third type of agent, a sort of hybrid of the first two. This is the person *recruited* into an organizational position to shake things up, to make some big changes. The recruited change agent's position has some of the ad-

gents' Organizational Characteristics

	Advantages	*Disadvantages*
Designation		
eous	Enthusiasm, commitment, clear vision	Spontaneity and enthusiasm may interfere with objectivity
ated	Commitment and vision can be fostered	May lack commitment to this change Role may be overlaid on an already busy schedule
anizational Position		
ff support	Spontaneity and enthusiasm may interfere with objectivity	May lack necessary influence or authority over change targets
Line	May lack commitment to this change Role may be overlaid on an already busy schedule	May lack time because of existing duties
External or Internal		
External	Greater objectivity and neutrality	No stake in long-term outcomes May not adequately understand culture of organization
Internal	Perspective and knowledge of current problems Less threatening because they are well known	May lack objectivity and neutrality If role is added to other demanding internal roles, it may not be possible to give this role adequate attention May not have skills to perform change agent roles May be overly cautious because of ongoing position in the organization

During an organizational change, people may have to adjust in large or small ways. They may be required to change the way they perform daily tasks, where they report to work, the way they conceptualize problems and opportunities, even what they believe in. In the big picture of a major system or work-group transformation, these changes may look minor, but to the individual confronting them, they are everything. In the face of contrary habits and tradition, employees are asked to alter the entire structure of their days' routines, re-

vantages and disadvantages of both internal and external agents. Like the external change agent, the recruited agent has just arrived in the organization, so he or she knows little organizational history and culture and is not bound by that way of thinking. On the other hand, he or she is unlikely to know the culturally appropriate way of conducting the diagnosis and implementing the indicated changes.

Like the internal agent, the recruited agent intends to remain in the organization after the changes are implemented, and so must either not make enemies of those who will also be there or must have sufficient power to deal with whatever enemies are made.

Personal Characteristics

Not only do change agents seek to alter an organization's status quo, they also must be able to bridge the gap between the status quo and the new state. To get from one place to the other, they must be able to determine what is not right about the current state, imagine a new way, and gather and apply the resources required to arrive at the changed state. Doing this well requires a variety of characteristics, skills, and talents.[12]

Interest in Change

Good change agents have had successful experience with change. They have positive attitudes about change, believing that life is most interesting when it does not stay the same. They also enjoy the careful analysis, planning, and other phases of organizational change.

Vision of the Future

Change agents must be able to envision a new way of doing things. The picture they can make of the future is the goal of the change effort. By picturing a future state, the change agent can more clearly see what must be changed and what its new form will be, and imagine the resources and actions necessary to accomplish it. Without that vision, plans and action steps may lack direction and focus.

Persistence

Because change is met with resistance through people, organizational policy, managerial processes, and habit, change agents must be willing to continue their efforts even in the face of short-term difficulties and setbacks. Change agents must be willing to pursue their goals with persistence. Some changes simply take sustained effort until finally accomplished.

Anticipation of Problems

Problems that are anticipated can be either avoided or moderated. Resistance can be stemmed, and unexpectedly negative results can be sidestepped by those change agents who can anticipate their occurrence. Problems or pitfalls that are not anticipated may spell a halt to an otherwise well-conceived change.

Sense of Timing

Knowing when to push and when to ease back, recognizing when the time is right and when other actions have finally met their goal, are all a part of timing and are important to successful change. All the correct actions can be taken, but if not done at the proper time, they will not have the anticipated results.

Big-Picture and Detail Orientation

The ability to combine a big-picture outlook with attention to detail is a rare combination in a single individual; this reality can dictate the need for several people to serve as change agents in a particular change. The big-picture orientation is important for the conceptualizing and innovative thinking required to imagine a new state. It is equally important to the success of the change effort that the change agent be able to attend to a myriad of details during the implementation and institutionalization phases.

Ability to Secure Cooperation

Recognizing that change is necessary and developing new ways of doing things are futile activities if the agent is unable to secure the cooperation of others. Gaining this cooperation and overcoming resistance to change is discussed later in the chapter.

Change involves both cognitive and emotional responses, and consequently, change agents must be skilled in gaining both information and participation throughout an organizational change. Recent research in emotional intelligence (EQ) addresses several necessary skills. EQ is defined as skills that contribute to the accurate appraisal and expression of emotion in oneself and others.[13] More important, those high in EQ use feelings to motivate, plan, and achieve organizational outcomes. If they are unable to get the cooperation of those who are expected to change, then the changes will never be fully implemented.

Implications for Change Agents

As we have already noted, a single individual may perform one or many of the roles required of a change agent. The point of this discussion is that just as some people are well suited to being change agents, others are not. The change agent roles should not be handed to those people who simply haven't anything better to do. Nor should they automatically be given to people holding certain organizational positions. Who should assume the change agent role is determined by the combination of personal and organizational characteristics that various individuals possess.

People who lack the appropriate person
poor choices as change agents. Someone
is perfectly capable of managing settled, r
to visualize a future, marshal resources, or
state.

In considering spontaneous and designated
that spontaneous agents

- can fan passion in those who are sympathetic to th in others;
- are driven most forcefully by what they believe in an others' direction;
- may lack adequate organizational resources such as p access; and
- may lack personal resources such as tact, sensitivity, and p

Designated change agents, however, can be chosen for

- personal characteristics conducive to successful change; and
- organizational characteristics that facilitate successful change p

The advantages and disadvantages of change agents' vario
characteristics are summarized in table 7.2.

Whether they are taking on the role spontaneously or being
successful agents of change

- must be provided with adequate organizational resources of authority, propriate assistance;
- must believe in the need to change;
- must possess personal resources related to successful change—these are the that cannot be given to them; and
- can be rewarded for their change efforts with other desired assignments.

CHANGE RECIPIENTS

Change recipients are people who are expected to change when the organization changes. As discussed in chapter 5, changing the people in an organization can be a primary method of changing the organization as a whole. Education, training, and organizational-development interventions are the general means of carrying out the people-oriented methods of change.

In other instances, people may be required to change not as the primary method of organizational change, but as a result of other changes being made in the organization. Whatever the route, as the method or as an involved party to a change object (task behavior, process, policy, or culture), people become recipients of change in nearly all instances.

Table 7.2
Change A

Source o
Spontan
Desig
Org
St

quired to give up comfortable work relationships, forced to function in new physical and psychological surroundings.

It is no wonder that in all changes, resistance to change is demonstrated to some extent by at least some change recipients. Because resistance can stymie even the best-considered change efforts, it is the major topic of this section of the chapter.

Resistance to Change

People do not always adjust smoothly and easily to the changes asked of them. Much like people, organizations too are prone to ego defenses in an attempt to maintain collective self-esteem and continuity of the organization's existing identity.[14] Organizations require such an identity for collective action, and attempts to change what has been central, enduring, and/or distinctive to an organization will likely result in resistance. Microsoft's move from a software developer to a service company, as discussed in chapter 3, is but one example of a company attempting to change its identity.

While some respond to an upcoming change by standing their ground and refusing to move (i.e., active rejection), more often their acts of resistance are subtle and less willful (i.e., reinvention or reinterpretation of the change efforts).[15] Faced with a change, they may simply sit as spectators, watching and criticizing but not participating; they may delay their participation in the change;[16] or they may subtly keep others from joining in. People do not always rush to embrace change, and their reluctance can be a major source of concern, even irritation, to change managers. Indeed, resistance is viewed as a primary impediment to implementing change and is typically termed not a response to change but "resistance to change."[17]

Resistance to change is any attempt to maintain the status quo when there is pressure for change.[18] Acts of resistance can slow or stop the organization's transition from its current state to some desired future state. Viewing resistance only as a negative or malicious act puts a manager in a defensive state and leads some to believe he must fight back—to meet force with force. A more constructive, and in the long run more effective, approach is to acknowledge the validity of the class of responses as a whole and respond from a position of understanding and respect.[19] In effect, resistance can *inform* change strategies and tactics.

Change agents who acknowledge the inevitability of resistance to change, recognize both the generalized and personal roots of it, and then develop strategies for dealing with it in a positive way can successfully manage the organization's transition. Change agents who dismiss the topic of resistance or declare war against it will likely be left with an organization caught somewhere between the original and the transition, with more problems created than solved. We discuss resistance to change because (1) it is a universal phenomenon; (2) if it is adequately understood, its characteristics in a particular change can be anticipated; and (3) when it is anticipated, strategies can be developed to deal with it constructively, and the organization can emerge stronger and more effective than before.

Why Resistance to Change?

Some changes may be advantageous to a corporation yet disadvantageous to some of the individuals working in that corporation. When resistance occurs under those conditions, it seems perfectly appropriate. Resistance can be expected when the reasons are obvious: if people once had much freedom and are asked to give it up; if they once made high wages and are asked to cut back; if they once had many benefits and now have few.

It is less obvious why resistance surfaces in response to changes that appear to make organizational life better for the people involved. For instance, shouldn't there be positive responses to the installation of computers, because they make life so much easier? Or eager anticipation of new furniture that has custom-designed spaces for all supplies and equipment? And especially happy responses to new private offices with windows, reduced noise, and increased privacy? When resistance to such apparently positive changes appears, it often surprises those who are attempting to manage the change.

When change managers are confronted by resistance to changes that they view as obviously advantageous, they typically respond in one or more of the following ways. First, they might decide that the change is not worth the difficulties they are encountering and therefore adjust their plans or discontinue implementation. Second, they may decide that the people who work in the organization are narrow-minded, stupid, or ungrateful and therefore must be fired or transferred to another part of the organization. Third, they may decide they have not been forceful enough in making it clear that the change will take place and therefore simply repeat all of their arguments.

Each of these change manager responses has some merit in certain situations. Certainly the first, considering that the change is not a good idea and abandoning it, shows that resistance can in fact signal that there is something significantly inappropriate in the change plans. When change plans are poorly conceived, are produced without adequate information, or propose an unreasonable solution, then resistance is a significant sign to change agents to seriously consider whether this is a good change. Resistance in such a case is an important organizational safeguard against an incorrect course of action.

Considering change recipients stupid or ungrateful if they resist a particular change and repeatedly declaring the change will take place also assumes that the resistance is specific to this change and peculiar to these change recipients. While this may be the case, there is a strong likelihood that those are not the only sources of the resistance. In addition to resisting a specific change, people have generalized reasons for resisting change. Those generalized reasons can be expected in almost any change proposed and so can be anticipated, understood, and dealt with respectfully and effectively.

Generalized Resistance to Change

People tend to resist change or alterations of the status quo. This resistance is broader than simple opposition to a particular change, and more widespread than a particular group's or individual's refusal to accept a specific change. There is simply the wish to maintain the consistency and comfort that the status quo holds.[20] This generalized resistance to change stems from a variety of sources. We have categorized these causes or sources into three groups: barriers to appreciation, barriers to acceptance, and barriers to acting.

Barriers to Appreciation

Some resistance phenomena can be traced to people's failure to appreciate the need for change, the reason for the particular change proposed, the substance and details of the proposed change, or the likely outcomes.

Some of the lack of knowledge or understanding of a change may be intellectual—the information simply has not been communicated. This happens when change managers and change agents are vague in describing the change. Their vagueness may be unintentional; they believe they have conveyed to others precisely what they intend to have happen, but they've actually failed to do so. On the other hand, change managers and/or change agents may intentionally omit details in the belief that there will be less disruption for workers and the work if they postpone full discussion of the change until they have worked out all their plans and are ready to declare that the change is under way. A great deal of time may pass while change recipients resist the changes presented because they have no basis for understanding them.

Some of the lack of appreciation by the change recipients is not intellectual as much as cultural. A change agent may explain the change and plan for it from the point of view of a culture that is foreign to the change recipients. Using words that come from the special language of the change agent's culture will not satisfy the change recipients' needs to know what is taking place. On the other hand, changes explained with the aid of symbols and rituals familiar to the change recipients will convey needs and plans quickly and accurately.

Other barriers to appreciating a proposed change can be caused by inconsistent behavior from executives, managers, or change agents. Sometimes an influential individual or group publicly advocates one course but acts in ways better suited to another. When that happens, change recipients in the organization perceive the equivocal messages and cannot understand what is expected of them. Inconsistency is also seen if rewards are still being given for the old behaviors and are not yet given to encourage new behaviors. An example is provided in "Focus On: Barriers to Appreciation."

Focus On: Barriers to Appreciation

When a fifteen-year-old social service agency faced dwindling contracts and erosion of its client population, drastic changes were needed to save it from financial collapse. The top executive and key members of the board of directors arrived at a plan containing all the changes required to transform the organization. Additional services would be developed to serve an entirely new population of clients. A reorganization would allow the agency to serve the new population while still providing limited services to the traditional client population. Some existing staff would be laid off, and fewer clients would be treated at reduced fees. Finally, existing managers would be replaced with those who had a better understanding of financial management and controls.

The board of directors completed and announced the plans. The board expected dissension and resistance and dealt with these reactions by providing as little information to existing staff as possible. The announcement was brief and lacked detail on why the changes were necessary, when they would take place, and how the transition would be staged. To this point, most staff members had had no idea of changes in state laws, changing client-population demographics, or the recent change in priorities in the county's use of social services funds that led to the changes. They heard only that the people they had always served would be shoved aside in favor of a group whose problems and needs were foreign to them. And as a final blow, they heard that some of the highest positions in the agency would no longer be held by those with credentials in any of the professions important to direct service, but by businesspeople incapable of exercising proper judgment where treatment and services were concerned.

From the moment of the announcement, resistance to the change was obvious. As the existing staff talked, speculated, and worried among themselves, the resistance increased. Soon there were two armed camps—the old staff on one side, and the new staff and board of directors on the other. Policy and procedural changes were argued about or ignored. Virtually everything the new staff tried to do failed. The reputation of the agency suffered when the new service programs were poorly implemented. Rather than solving the original financial problems, the changes—as they were implemented—merely compounded the agency's problems.

This example illustrates several sources of barriers to appreciation. First, recipients had no awareness of the environmental forces necessitating change in the agency. They saw no clear danger to the traditional means of conducting business and providing services. The recipients saw little reason to justify the drastic and uncomfortable changes being made. Second, each day brought additional changes, but the entire plan was never made clear to them in advance. There was no attempt to clearly map the transition so that important players could make their own preparations—emotionally as well as more objectively.

A third barrier to understanding this change was that change recipients quickly found themselves confronted by, and unable to communicate with, a whole new group of people—business managers. These new managers neither understood nor seemed to care about treatment philosophies and how they affected appointment scheduling or group size. Their conversational topics were only revenues, costs, and balance sheets. What information was exchanged was not understood on either side. Finally, because the change recipients were not involved in the planning, nor were they kept well informed of current and upcoming details of the change, they could only speculate what the real outcome could be. Their speculations were very emotional and reflected their fears for their patients and for themselves.

Activities for reducing barriers to appreciation.

What activities can be used in anticipation of these generalized barriers to understanding so that action can be taken to reduce their effect? First, change agents can use resources to make certain that change recipients understand the need for change. Accomplishing this requires relying on some of the change-agent activities described earlier in the chapter as the catalyst role: not only telling people that problems exist, but also letting them see the problems in a variety of ways. Indeed, change recipients will best understand the need for change if they can participate in defining existing problems and creating solutions.

Second, when change agents explain the need for change, it must be told in culturally and organizationally understood terms. Although many proposed changes have a financial motivation, explaining them to change recipients at all organizational levels will not be successful if balance sheets, profit-and-loss statements, and bank credit lines are the only terms used.

Third, change agents can encourage understanding and help avoid misunderstanding by supplying as many details as possible about the vision of the future state of the organization once the changes are implemented. People who know clearly what is going to happen and what the result will be can become partners in the change, not resisters. When change recipients aren't told the truth or are left without adequate information, they will rely on a construed reality based on "rumors, hunches, suspicions, and scattered bits of information."[21] They will seek information from other sources—personal or reported experience in the current company or another—and then treat it as reality. Their resulting actions may appear to be resistance to the proposed change when, given the absence of real information, it is a reasonable way to react to this construed reality.

Finally, telling people about a change a single time is not enough. Repeating the details, using consistent words and phrases to describe what needs changing and what the new system will be, helps change recipients fully understand the course they are embarking upon. An essential part of managing the change is realizing that barriers to appreciation cannot be eradicated one time at the outset and then be expected to stay away. A change agent must be always alert to the possibility of additional or recurring incidents of misunderstanding. The methods for reducing barriers to appreciation are summarized in table 7.3.

Barriers to Acceptance

A second group of resistance phenomena can be categorized as barriers to acceptance. In this type of resistance, change recipients cannot or will not accept the change. Acceptance requires believing the necessity for the change and being willing to follow through in accomplishing it. Barriers to acceptance are more emotionally based than are the barriers to appreciation. Even when a change is well understood and properly communicated and explained, there may be barriers to its being accepted.

A primary barrier to acceptance is people's *need for security.* People gradually gain an understanding of the organization they are in so that they know how to act in that environment. In knowing where to go to get what they need and what is expected of them, they have a sense of control over their organizational lives. At the beginning of a change, often there are numerous unknowns about the details of organizational life in the imagined future organization. The uneasiness is much like that employees experience when first beginning work in a company. In the first few months, new employees must discover which behaviors will be rewarded and which will be punished, and who is helpful and who should be avoided. Most importantly, they learn whether they have the capacity to do the job they were hired to do. As the organization is transformed

Table 7.3
Reducing Barriers to Appreciation

1. Ensure that recipients appreciate the need for change.	• Engage recipients in discovering, defining, or detailing problems relevant to the need to change. • Express the need for change in culturally and organizationally relevant terms. • Repeat the need to change in clear and consistent terms.
2. Ensure that recipients appreciate the vision of the intended future state.	• Explain the big picture of the plan for change and the intended outcome of the change. • Repeat the vision in clear and consistent terms.

into something new, the change recipients are thrust into new roles and conditions, and the result is uneasiness and anxiety.

A *threat to self-confidence* can also pose a barrier to acceptance. If the changed organization is known in advance to require essentially the same responses from change recipients as they give today, they can be confident of meeting the requirements. Acceptance will come with the explanations of what must be done and who must do it. When the new organization is assumed to require radically different actions, then change recipients' speculation about these actions can be destructive. If they do not clearly know what their daily routines, their associations, and other details of their lives will be in the new organization, they begin to speculate about them. The more they speculate, discuss the situation with friends, and possibly build a completely incorrect view, the less able they will be to accept the change as proposed. The anxiety that builds becomes a barrier to accepting the change.

A third barrier to acceptance is *anxiety about a loss of organizational power.* The organizational power that a person finally comes to have is gathered with effort. People who are comfortable with the degree of organizational power they currently hold will not be eager to rush into a new organization in which they do not know how much power they will have.

Such a threat to the power structure creates anxiety. The degree of anxiety about power can vary greatly over different groups of employees. Managers, for instance, may be uncertain about how they will fare in the new environment, yet they believe the period of transition offers them opportunities to improve their own situations. Because the future organization is still being detailed, managers may eagerly anticipate the opportunity to gain rather than lose power in the new organization. They are willing to pay the price in anxiety, ambiguity, and even lost productivity if they believe their group or they themselves will be relatively better off when the change is finally in place than they are in the current situation. An example is provided in "Focus On: Barriers to Acceptance."

Focus On: Barriers to Acceptance

One of the authors observed the various responses of a group of people within a department when a West Coast company reorganized. The department most affected by the change was the information services (IS) department. Within that department was the systems-development group, which designed, constructed, and installed new computer applications for departments all over the company. Systems-development employees are trained as analysts and technicians, and their work involves needs analysis, systems planning, and computer programming. The change recipients in IS were told only that the systems-development functions would be decentralized. Additional details were to be worked out, but essentially most of the staff would eventually be moved out of the IS department and into the business-user groups. A particular development team, composed of programmers, analysts, and a manager, were soon to report to the sales division; another team to construction; a third to corporate finance; and a new team would be assigned miscellaneous special projects.

Executive management portrayed the new situation with this and similar statements: "Don't worry, you'll still be doing the same jobs, designing and writing computer applications for this company. You'll just be reporting to new people—users you've worked with and gotten along with for a long time. It's not going to be all that different." The executives offered little additional guidance or explanation and seemed unaware of the magnitude of the changes being asked of the systems-development teams. It was clear to observers, however, that numerous changes were looming for the systems-development staff.

All of the systems-development staff had worked together in IS for quite some time. They socialized at work and away from work. They often were called in on late-night and weekend emergencies that caused them to work together, and under pressure, for twenty or more hours straight. Although they naturally interacted with people in other areas of the company, it was in this department that they had their primary and most satisfying work relationships. With the decentralization, the group would be dispersed—physically and socially. Their habits, routines, norms, and values—the systems-development culture—were being threatened.

A second change that caused concern was the possibility of greatly altered work rules. IS management in this organization (as in many) believed their employees worked best under different rules from those governing the rest of the organization. IS staff worked flexible hours to accommodate project requirements, generally wore decidedly casual clothes, and periodically launched into esoteric projects that might not pay off for months or years. Could the same management philosophy be expected of managers in more conventional departments, such as finance, accounting, or construction? It was clear those departments operated under far different rules now, so would exceptions be made for the development teams?

The list of questions and concerns was lengthy, although not easily articulated by the change recipients involved. The author spoke to them and eventually arrived at the following list of concerns:

- New bosses
- Change to organizational affiliations rather than professional affiliations
- Trade known status for unknown status or possibly low status
- Lock into work for single functional group rather than do work for a variety of functional groups

- Unknown career ladders in new functional areas
- Unknown physical settings
- Unknown organizational relationships
- Questions of work rules: flextime, dress, formal/informal relationships, strict hierarchical reporting?
- Will funds for projects, additional employees be easy or difficult to obtain in new department?
- What will the development groups' relationships be with their new functional groups—adversarial, neutral, mutually supportive?

The items in the list of concerns related to the change recipients' feelings of security, threats to self-confidence, and anxiety about changes in organizational power. Such concerns were heightened by the fact that change recipients were certain the changes would be major, while management tried to minimize them—not by supplying details about the proposed change, but by delivering unsubstantiated platitudes.

Activities for reducing barriers to acceptance.

What activities can be used in anticipation of these generalized barriers to acceptance? Change agents can include recipients in the planning for a change to occur and in the formulation of the vision of how the new organization will operate. The hope is that such involvement could result in recipients' feeling some sense of control that comes from participation in the process.

When management's "plan" for change is vague and states only the organizational goal, change recipients' anxiety builds. Many of the details recipients are concerned about can be investigated and planned out relatively easily. Questions of the new organization's physical and reporting arrangements can be the first items of discussion and planning either as the change is being formulated or as soon as the change is announced. Change recipients with operational responsibilities can often be the best choices to formulate timelines and transition plans because they know the work flows and people affected.

Change recipients' anxieties about possible differences can be dealt with by replacing supposition with facts. Informational materials, meetings, and discussions can make the new organization or the unit being joined a real entity with known characteristics. Some managers choose not to conduct such activities, believing that time spent in such meetings unnecessarily reduces productivity. In fact, such activities, by containing the anxiety and alleviating it with factual information, damage productivity far less than when people find their thoughts and energies focusing on the change rather than on the jobs they are doing. If a change is announced without details, the amount of productivity lost to speculation and anxiety can be tremendous, decidedly greater than the amounts lost to informational meetings and planning sessions.

Finally, change agents can reduce barriers to acceptance by dealing with the emotional aspects of people's resistance to change. Management's ignoring or denying these aspects frequently increases them. Attempting to diminish or dismiss the effects of change on the change recipients only increases the recipients' resistance. Seeing from their point of view the numerous changes that nearly any change can require helps managers understand the reasons for the anxiety, apprehension, and finally resistance they are witnessing. The methods for reducing barriers to acceptance are summarized in table 7.4.

Barriers to Acting

The third type of resistance to change are the barriers to acting or carrying out the change. These barriers stem from two sources: some from within the change recipients themselves, and others from generalized conditions within the organization or in the larger environment.

A primary barrier to acting upon an understood and accepted change is the change recipient's lack of skills or abilities. The changed organization may require people to use skills they simply do not have. These may be physical skills such as might be required in assembly work or intensive physical labor, communications skills such as those required by new reporting and coordinating arrangements, or new conceptual skills such as those required when a department takes on additional planning and control responsibilities. If the people lack the necessary skills, the change will not be fully accomplished and the status quo will be maintained.

Barriers to acting can also stem from existing conditions within an organization but outside any one individual change recipient. Inadequate resources to conduct the necessary range of change activities can drastically slow the

Table 7.4
Reducing Barriers to Acceptance

1. Ensure that recipients know as much, as possible, about the change and their part in it.	• Solicit participation in making and carrying out plans and activities related to the change as early as possible in the process. • Work hard to convey facts—down to the smallest detail—about the change.
2. Acknowledge recipients' emotional concerns and attend to them.	• Listen to recipients' objections for the underlying concerns being voiced. • Listen for rumors and suppositions, then replace them with facts. • Recognize that leaving something old sometimes requires a period of "mourning" before the new future can be faced.

accomplishment of the change plans. The resources include funds, people, and time. A change can require that money be applied to new physical space, new equipment and supplies, training, consultation, and a host of other items and activities. People must be made available, and production and other work schedules must be adjusted to permit the planning and implementation activities necessary to conduct the transition. The lack of any of these resources can mean insurmountable barriers to change.

An organization may also have existing arrangements or contractual obligations that act as barriers to desired changes. Union agreements specifying numbers and types of workers, job descriptions, and working conditions that are incompatible with a desired change may effectively stop the change from occurring. Similarly, contracts that require specific methods or other production details may be impossible to alter sufficiently to allow changes that appear necessary for the company's well-being.

Organizations can also create barriers to acting upon change simply through their own inertia. The need to change may be well understood, and the plans for change may be well accepted. The change may still not happen because the company as a whole is so accustomed to acting in certain ways. These are not formal contractual requirements as just described, but merely habit and convention. Ironically, inertia can be the result of successful performance.[22] Existing managerial procedures, job descriptions, schedules, and cultures have firmly supported the success associated with the status quo. Consequently, carrying out changes that affect those areas requires someone finally acknowledging what is already known: that the organization must change, and is willing and ready to change. An example is provided in "Focus On: Barriers to Acting."

Focus On: Barriers to Acting

A relatively small development and construction company operated for many years with few employees and a simple organizational structure. During the early years, all involved worked hard, made adequate salaries, and were quite comfortable with their organization. Because they were skillful in the work they did, the two owners eventually had a very successful corporation. It grew steadily and gained a regional reputation for sound operation and good products.

The owners got to a point where they saw that work planned for the near future would be more than their simple organization could effectively manage. In collaboration with a new senior-level member of their management team, they debated and discussed their requirements and alternatives. They agreed upon the reasons that change was necessary. They agreed upon the timing of the needed changes. They spent numerous hours discussing the various possible forms the changes could take. A new reporting structure was devised and responsibilities were rearranged among the owners, the senior manager, and field superintendents.

The initial change steps attempted were not successful because the superintendents in the field did not have the skills to manage the increasingly larger projects the company was undertaking. They could not make the transition from relatively small residential projects to more complex industrial and commercial jobs. For a while this restrained the company's progress, slowing the startup of two key projects.

At the same time, the owners continued to conduct their activities in much the same way that they always had. They were involved in virtually every decision about every aspect of every project in progress. No decisions were considered routine or subject to set rules or procedures: all were viewed as fresh, new, and requiring infinite examination and attention. Activities on projects were soon suspended as crucial details awaited the owners' action. All the old procedures were still in effect, despite plans made to the contrary. Even when it was realized that this was happening, no one had time to stop and work on it. They were all too busy trying to get their jobs done.

The company looked again at its change plans. They were understood and accepted but could not be acted upon. The owners realized that the commercial projects could not be completed with their current field-management staff, and added qualified people. The owners examined once again the need to change their own managerial activities, decentralizing the decision making to others in the company to avoid the bottlenecks. The company sits at this point even now: knowing what it must do to change, accepting that it must change, but unable to overcome the inertia of the past.

Activities for reducing barriers to acting.

What activities can be used in anticipation of these generalized barriers to acting? Barriers to acting are some of both the easiest to recognize and the most difficult to deal with of all the barriers. Reducing them can be accomplished in some cases by a particularly long-range view of the future. Having employees without proper qualifications can often be anticipated and altered before it becomes a significant problem. Internal training and new employee-selection programs can create the necessary human resources in advance of the need for them. This solution can work only with long enough planning horizons.

When other resources such as time and money are unavailable, the solutions become more situation specific. If there is no money for external consultants, internal resources must be more completely investigated. Perhaps a team of internal employees, each with his or her own skills, can work together to produce what a single outside consultant might have been hired for. When money or time is the perceived issue, cost-benefit studies assessing all costs and benefits to the organization and its members often reveal that the revenues lost to change activities are more than recouped within a short time of the changes being implemented.

Barriers caused by contracts with suppliers, unions, and customers can often be better understood through cost-benefit studies of buying out the contracts. As with barriers involving employee skills, longer planning horizons can help avoid some problems.

When organizations undertake a major, systemwide organizational change, they typically face many barriers to acting; successful implementation demands that they deal with these barriers. If employees haven't the skills to do all of the tasks asked of them, they should be provided in-depth training in group processes and facilitation, data gathering, analysis, and presentation skills. Where union agreements and other contracts restrict change, those management and unionized groups are given roles to improve relations; foster better and more cooperative working agreements; and improve the organization's products, services, and delivery modes. Methods for reducing barriers to acting are summarized in table 7.5.

People have many roles to play in organizational change. Someone who serves as a catalyst change agent in one change may simply be a recipient of change in the next. Change managers in one event will find themselves in a

Table 7.5
Reducing Barriers to Acting

1. Ensure that employees have the necessary training, skills, and personal characteristics to meet new requirements.	• Keep human planning horizons sufficiently long to anticipate probable future personal needs. • Use ongoing training to keep existing employees current in skills needed for changed or changing conditions.
2. When lack of resources appears to stop change effort, reassess.	• Assess truthfully the costs and benefits of not implementing needed changes. • Compare them to a true assessment of the costs and benefits of implementing the change. • Seek alternative means of gaining the needed resources for change.
3. If inertia is preventing change, go back to the beginning and refocus on the needs for change.	• Be certain that everyone understands the short-term and long-term needs for change. • Create a scenario of the future based on not making the needed changes and compare that to what the future will look like with the changes.

totally different role in the next one. And recipients of today's change may be the leaders of tomorrow's change efforts.

Emotional Appeals and Change

Much of our discussion on change and dealing with change recipients' resistance to change has focused on the cognitions associated with change. In other words, we have outlined how change-recipient resistance can best be overcome by providing information to change recipients so that they can better understand the logic behind the need for change. We have to note, however, that communication is composed of both cognitive and emotional components. Therefore, although rational arguments are useful, emotional appeals are also necessary.

In particular, emotional appeals can first help to establish a sense of urgency for the change before change managers and change agents outline the vision to accomplish the desired objectives and form coalitions of employees who embrace the change plan. Important elements with respect to emotions and change include (1) the creation of a core message that includes emotional arguments and vivid metaphors, (2) the packaging of the message through emotional communications and the displaying of emotions—including humor—by change managers and agents; (3) the characteristics of the change leaders and the importance of credibility, competence, and openness; (4) the behavior of change managers and agents and how they treat change recipients in fair and honest ways while allowing the recipients to raise objections; and (5) the setting, the use of ceremonies, and the existence of powerful groups who believe change is necessary.[23]

CHANGE ALLIES

A companion concept to emotional intelligence is that known as emotional capacity. Emotional capacity refers to an organization's collective ability to acknowledge, recognize, monitor, discriminate, and attend to members' emotions.[24] An emotionally capable enterprise understands the relationship between emotion and change.[25] Furthermore, emotionally capable organizations institutionalize routines that attend to emotions and devote resources to achieving relevant objectives.

Change arouses both positive and negative emotions. Specifically, change can create uncertainty and even toxicity[26]—two of the more obvious and relevant negative reactions in organizations. Consider the effect of mergers or downsizing on emotions as individuals grapple with such questions as (1) Why is change happening now? (2) What will change mean to me? and (3) What are the costs (or benefits) associated with supporting the change?

We propose that change agents are not the only individuals who must confront and deal with the negative emotions experienced by change recipients.

Change allies are also key individuals during the change process. Change allies are not necessarily change agents or recipients, though they could be. Instead, a change ally is simply an individual who plays a critical, yet *informal* role in alleviating negative emotions during the change process and consequently helps to sustain change initiatives.

There are two change allies—the "toxic handler" and the "organizational sage"—that best exemplify what we mean by change ally. Both, through the informal roles played, help to create and sustain emotionally capable organizations. Like that of the change agent, the role of change ally is taken on by an individual in addition to his or her assigned organizational roles. Because of the trust they engender, change allies are sought out by the very individuals experiencing negative emotions. Change managers or agents invariably have little say in who plays these roles, though they have a vested interest in creating an environment that gives rise to their very existence.

A toxic handler is one who "voluntarily shoulders the sadness, frustration, bitterness, and anger that are endemic to organizational life."[27] How do toxic handlers do this? They listen emphatically, in nonjudgmental and compassionate ways, so that workers walk away less troubled. They suggest solutions and solve problems. They work behind the scenes to prevent pain, sometimes buffering coworkers from difficult decisions or reframing difficult messages.

The organizational sage is similar in many ways to the toxic handler. Both rely on their relational skills and abilities to process information. Sages, however, are focused on reducing uncertainty, not toxicity. They enhance and transmit knowledge in organizations—by encouraging change by speaking up, creating understanding through sense making, and communicating meaning.[28]

Sages are experienced individuals whose broad vision, expert knowledge, cognitive and emotional maturity, and process and relational skills allows them to create, extend, retain, and transfer knowledge and understanding throughout the organization. In effect, these individuals play an important role in helping others understand the organizational system while fostering individual and group-level dynamics that reinforce shared values and support of the discussion of subjects—even those that are taboo—important to change initiatives. They process complex data, transform it into meaningful information for organizational members (i.e., change recipients, change agents, and change managers and leaders), and create organizational meanings that develop over time.

CONCLUSION

Effective organizational change depends on a number of people, playing a number of roles. As a general proposition we suggest that the wider the involvement on the part of change managers, agents, and recipients, the greater the chance for success. That said, the question then becomes this: Who needs to be involved; whose voice needs to be heard?[29] In discussing the importance of "widening the circle of involvement," Richard Axelrod suggests the following criteria for answering this question:

- *Information:* Invite and involve people who have information, knowledge, or expertise to contribute to the particular issue being worked on.
- *Impact:* Invite and involve people who will be affected by the changes in question.
- *Authority:* Invite and involve people who have authority to make the changes happen.
- *Responsibility:* Invite and involve people who will have to live with the results of the changes, who will have responsibility for making the changes work.
- *Opposition:* Invite and involve people who don't think the proposed changes are a good idea, don't think they'll work—in other words, who are opposed to the changes under consideration.

The purpose of all this is to truly *engage* organizational members—not merely include them—in a change effort. When they are engaged, people do a number of good things: They understand and relate to the issues, they expend energy in creative ways, they collaborate across organizational boundaries, they share information (rather than hoard it), and they increase their appetite and capacity for change.[30] In short, by making sure that those who can affect either the design or the implementation of a change process are invited and involved, by making sure that their members are truly engaged, organizations increase the chances for success of planned changes.

NOTES

1. R. M. Kanter, B. A. Stein, & T. D. Jick (1999), The challenges of execution: Roles and tasks in the change process, in D. Ancona, T. Kochan, M. Scully, J. Van Maanen, & D. E. Westney (Eds.), *Managing for the future: Organizational behavior and processes,* Cincinnati, OH: South-Western.

2. Ibid.

3. G. Zaltman & R. Duncan (1977), *Strategies for planned change,* New York: John Wiley, p. 187.

4. Q. N. Huy (2001), Time, temporal capability, and planned change, *Academy of Management Review,* 26, pp. 601–623.

5. Discussion based on previous treatment by R. Havelock found in P. L. Hunsaker (1982), Strategies for organizational change: The role of the inside change agent, *Personnel,* September–October, pp. 18–28.

6. W. W. Burke & A. H. Church (1992), Managing change, leadership style, and intolerance to ambiguity: A survey of organization development practitioners, *Human Resources Management,* 31 (4), pp. 301–318.

7. D. Buchanan, T. Claydon, & M. Doyle (1999), Organisation development and change, *Human Resource Journal,* 9, pp. 20–37.

8. I. G. Mauksch & M. H. Miller (1981), *Implementing change in nursing,* St. Louis, MO: C.V. Mosby.

9. Strictly speaking, the librarian has changed policy through a structural method (introducing a rule), using a political (coercive) strategy.

10. Hunsaker, Strategies for organizational change.

11. H. M. Trice & J. M. Beyer (1993), *The cultures of work organizations,* Englewood Cliffs, NJ: Prentice-Hall, p. 39.

12. Discussions of characteristics of change agents can be found in Hunsaker, Strategies for organizational change; N. M. Tichy (1974), Agents of planned social change: Congruence of values, cognitions, and actions, *Administrative Science Quarterly,* 19, pp. 164–182; M. London (1988), *Change agents: New roles and innovation strategies for human resource professionals,* San Francisco: Jossey-Bass.

13. P. Salovey & J. D. Mayer (1990), Emotional intelligence, *Imagination, Cognition, and Personality,* 9, pp. 185–211.

14. A. D. Brown & K. Starkey (2000), Organizational identity and learning: A psychodynamic perspective, *Academy of Management Review,* 25, pp. 102–120.

15. L. C. Harris & E. Ogbonna (1998), Employee responses to culture change efforts, *Human Resource Management Journal,* 2, pp. 78–92.

16. R. Gilbreath (1990), The myths about winning over resisters to change, *Supervisory Management,* January, pp. 1–2.

17. Resistance to change is included in virtually all discussions of organizational change. The treatment of it here borrows from A. G. Bedian (1984), *Organizations: Theory and analysis* (2d ed.), Chicago: Dryden Press; D. R. Hampton, C. E. Summer, & R. Webber (1987), *Organizational behavior and the practice of management* (5th ed.), Glenview, IL: Scott, Foresman; J. Pfeffer & G. Salancik (1978), *The external control of organizations—a resource dependence perspective,* New York: Harper and Row; J. Stanislao & B. C. Stanislao (1983), Dealing with resistance to change, *Business Horizons,* July–August, pp. 74–78; B. M. Staw (1982), Counterforces to change, in P. S. Goodman et al. (Eds.), *Change in organizations,* San Francisco: Jossey-Bass; and Zaltman & Duncan, *Strategies for planned change.*

18. Zaltman & Duncan, *Strategies for planned change.*

19. J. Goldstein (1988), A far-from-equilibrium systems approach to resistance to change, *Organizational Dynamics,* 17 (Autumn), pp. 16–26.

20. D. A. Nadler (1982), Implementing organizational changes, in D. A. Nadler, M. L. Tushman, & N.G. Hatvany (Eds.), *Managing organizations: Readings and cases,* Boston: Little, Brown, p. 444.

21. L. A. Isabella (1990), Evolving interpretations as a change unfolds: How managers construe key organizational events, *Academy of Management Journal,* 33, pp. 16–17.

22. K. E. Weick & R. E. Quinn (1999), Organizational change and development, *Annual Review of Psychology,* 50, pp. 361–386.

23. S. Fox & Y. Amichai-Hamburger (2001), The power of emotional appeals in promoting organizational change programs, *Academy of Management Executive,* 15, pp. 84–95.

24. E. H. Schein (1992), *Organizational culture and leadership* (2d ed.), San Francisco: Jossey-Bass.

25. Q. N. Huy (1999), Emotional capability, emotional intelligence, and radical change, *Academy of Management Review,* 24, pp. 325–345.

26. P. Frost & S. Robinson (1999), The toxic handler: Organizational hero and casualty, *Harvard Business Review,* 77, pp. 96–106.

27. Ibid., p. 98.

28. R. W. Stackman & J. M. Purdy (2001), *Sagacity, sages and organizational learning*, UW Tacoma Working Paper; R. W. Stackman & J. M. Purdy (1999), *Reflections on experience: Discovering organizational sages*, presented at the Western Academy of Management Meetings, Redondo Beach, CA.

29. The following is based on R. Axelrod (2000), *Terms of engagement*, San Francisco: Berrett-Koehler, pp. 52–55.

30. Ibid., pp. 35, 107–108.

8
Change Policy

Change is a paradoxical process, given the fact that one invites an energizing, disparate, invigorating, and unpredictable force into the organization.[1] In upsetting the status quo, the organization is attempting to use the chaotic energy that results and direct it toward ongoing organizational renewal.

The topics we have covered to this point have dealt with these questions:

- Why must the organization change?
- What is being changed?
- How will the change be accomplished?
- Who is involved in the change?

These are basic considerations, but they do not in themselves detail the full extent of the issues involved in managing change. Rather, they are concerned with how change would be pursued given ideal conditions. Because ideal conditions seldom exist, additional questions must be asked and additional issues must be considered.

These additional issues result from asking *these* questions:

- What blend of change and stability is desirable?
- What change resources are available, and how will they be allocated?
- How will the transition from the current state to the new state be staged?

These questions focus attention on some very practical elements of the change. Given the ideal course, what is actually practical or realistic?

Considering all of these questions—concerning what is ideal and what is practical—leads to the development of a change policy. *Change policy is the set of assumptions, diagnostic conclusions, and guidelines that serve as the basis for managing specific changes.* It combines the topics we've already covered—models of organizations and change, the objects and methods of change, the people involved, and the use of change strategies—with the practical topics of change versus stability, resource availability, and transition management.

CHANGE POLICY AND CHANGE MANAGEMENT

To discuss change policy fully, we must return to the idea of diagnosis. During diagnosis the organization's current state is first examined, then compared to some idealized or desired state. The comparison produces these conclusions: what is wrong or what must be changed (the objects), how it must be changed (the methods), who will direct the change (the change agents), and who must change (the change recipients). Actions are then suggested to transform the organization from the current state into one that is more like the idealized state.

The ideal state, of course, relates back to another of our previously discussed ideas—organizational models. A change manager's first attempt to visualize the new state depends on his or her conception of the ideal organization. All of the preliminary decisions about what, how, and whom to change are made in light of this conception.

For example, the current organization may use reporting relationships and decision processes that result in sluggish responses to new opportunities, whereas the change manager's ideal organization is streamlined and reacts quickly to the same opportunities. If so, the change manager's vision of the organization's new state will look much like her model of the ideal organization. The questions already presented will then result in answers that are compatible with the ideal organization.

Table 8.1 contains two sets of questions: those associated with change management, and those dealing with change policy. The aspects of change policy that we have yet to discuss are those that temper the answers to the change-management questions. Factoring these change-policy questions into the vision of an idealized future state results in a refined, more rational, more realistic vision of the organization's future state.

Considering what, how, and whom to change in light of the practical issues of the blend of change and stability, resource availability and allocation, and

Table 8.1
Questions Governing Change

Change-Management Questions	Change-Policy Questions
Why must the organization change?	What blend of change and stability is desirable?
What is being changed?	What change resources are available?
How will the change be accomplished?	How will resources be allocated?
Who is involved in the change?	How will the transition from the current state to the new state be staged?

transition management describes the full scope of change policy. In fact, the term change policy means that the answers to these many questions are to be arrived at not separately or independently, but as a whole and in relation to one another. In this way, the value of each individual decision is enhanced, and a coherent plan for managing the change is derived so that the momentum of the effort is sustained.

In this chapter we cover the second half of the decisions involved in change policy. We discuss the issues of change versus stability, resource availability and allocation, and transition management.

CHANGE VERSUS STABILITY

The degree of change—the number of organizational elements and the number of people involved—falls along a continuum. At one end is incremental or adaptive change that fine-tunes limited numbers of elements or levels of the organization over time. At the other end is large-scale, quantum, or transformational change, which causes numerous, significant alterations of nearly all aspects of the organization, sometimes in a fairly short time.[2] A discussion of time and intervention types with respect to large-scale change is provided in "Focus On: Time, Interventions. and Large-Scale Change."

Focus On: Time, Interventions, and Large-Scale Change

Two general theories of change—theory E and theory O—have been defined by Beer and Nohria. Theory E favors altering tangible structures and work processes (i.e., the "hardware" of the organization). Theory O seeks to revitalize culture, including the beliefs and social relationships within the organization (i.e., the "software"). In considering theory E and theory O, it is important to recall three critical dimensions of change: what is to be changed (content), where the change will occur (context), and how the change is to happen (process). Another important consideration is that the timing and pace of change is tied directly to what is to be changed. Organizational elements differ in how fast they can be changed; invariably, changing the organization's hardware can be accomplished more quickly than changing the software.

Huy offers four intervention approaches (outlined here) in a discussion on large-scale change. Large-scale change involves the alteration of multiple organizational elements, and it requires that the change agent effectively sequence and combine the intervention approaches. For example, a change agent could pursue a pure sequencing approach (enacting one of the four intervention types at a time) or a pure combining approach (where all four types are enacted simultaneously).

Following are the four intervention approaches:

Commanding—changing formal structures. Here change agents apply directive and coercive actions to the change recipients, thus exacting compliance with proposed change goals. Such an intervention favors a near-term time perspective in that changes should produce fast improvement in the firm's economic performance; however, such an approach is unlikely to lead to lasting qualitative change in beliefs and values.

Engineering—changing work processes. The focus for change agents is on analyzing, understanding, and then redesigning work processes to improve the speed or quality of production, or both. By favoring a medium-term time perspective, engineering serves to produce moderately fast improvement in the organization's economic performance.

Teaching—changing beliefs. Change recipients are the focal point of the teaching approach. Through collaboration, recipients are actively involved in their own personal change as evidenced through changes in fundamental beliefs. Teaching favors a moderately long-term approach as change agents seek to develop the firm's organizational capabilities, both cognitive and emotional.

Socializing—changing social relationships. The socializing approach assumes that changes in behavioral interactions among individuals will lead to changes in organizational tasks, beliefs, and culture. In comparison to the commanding approach, socializing does not require change managers to have extraordinary strategic foresight. Instead, change managers and agents nurture an internal context where variation, divergences, and open debate about competing options are tolerated. Socializing is a long-term approach.

Huy goes on to discuss Jack Welch's legacy at General Electric, arguing that the same performance results at GE might have been achieved in less time and with less human and financial cost had the various intervention types been applied differently through better sequencing and by combining Welch's commanding approach with that of teaching and socializing. Only after Welch had earned the nickname "Neutron Jack" did he seek ways to rebuild employees' emotional commitment and GE's culture.

Sources: M. Beer & N. Nohria (2000), Cracking the code of change, *Harvard Business Review,* 78, 133–145; Q. N. Huy (2001), Time, temporal capability, and planned change, *Academy of Management Review,* 26, 601–623.

Most of us have experience with changes that do not involve altering all elements of the organization. New technologies are introduced, though many of the old managerial policies remain in effect. While new reporting relationships are established, accounting practices can stay the same. New physical locations coexist with old values and norms. These evolutionary changes are more common than larger, or revolutionary, changes. Not only is it unlikely that everything will require change at once, but it is also unlikely that such extreme degrees of change will be desirable. More likely, the new state will require some blend of change and stability.[3]

Suppose that a diagnosis leads change managers to conclude that there are several objects of change, a variety of recipients, and even several methods required to transform the current organization into the desired state. Change managers might have one of two responses at this point.

One response is to move swiftly into the change, proceeding directly from diagnosis to the implementation of all the changes indicated by that diagnosis. The other approach is to first determine what blend of change and stability is important for the organization. This determination can be made independently of the diagnosis. It is simply a statement of what is reasonable for this organization with respect to the tempo[4] of the change (i.e., rate, rhythm, and pattern of the change efforts).[5] It is the answer to a question that might be phrased, "Just how much change can this place take at once?"

Under consideration here is not whether there is sufficient cause to change, or even which things need changing. The answers to those questions have been arrived at through diagnostic efforts. If those efforts indicate numerous changes, each change suggested may be quite correct individually but absolutely wrong in the aggregate.

The goal is to choose to make only the number of changes that is suitable in each particular case. The following is not a prescription of how much to change and what to leave the same, but a framework for change managers to use in deciding whether to carry out all or only some of the indicated changes. That decision is aided by examination of the organization's culture, its people, the details of the proposed change, and the interaction among the proposed changes.

Organizational Culture

As we discussed in chapter 2, certain organizational cultures favor change. Does the culture include norms encouraging innovation and change (e.g., General Electric as discussed in chapter 4)? Is there a positive or negative history of change? Does the company experiment readily or reluctantly? Given past change initiatives, were there unexpected *positive* outcomes that remain memorable to employees? A company whose stories are about the time all the employees came in for a marathon weekend of retooling and rearranging machines and warehouse space so that the product line could be completely changed is a good candidate for successful implementation of many changes at once.

Representing the opposite view is a company whose beliefs about change are illustrated by another story. The subject of that story is the new director of human resources who was given full rein to make sweeping changes. Her new benefits, work schedules, and employee-recruitment and training programs upset the employees so much that a union organized—and won—an election within the first two months. This incident was so painful that it influenced the culture's view of change. This company would now be a poor place to propose to implement many changes at once.

Some organizations have no particularly positive or negative norms for innovation and change or have little experience with them. However, other cultural characteristics may indicate how likely the organization is to accept and implement many changes at once. When one Pacific Northwest manufacturer began planning to use robots to produce its advanced-technology product, the numerous changes were expected to cause few difficulties, largely because the suggestion came from the company's own engineering division. The norms for giving people a chance and for judging every idea on its own merits far outweighed the fact that there were no particular norms dealing directly with change. Rather, the norms that did exist created an environment that could accept even multipart changes.

People

Change managers further develop their change policies by assessing the general nature or characteristics of the people associated with the organization, as employees and as customers. Such assessments about receptivity are made to indicate the number of changes the people are likely to accept without additional accommodation. If the number of acceptable changes is fewer than the number desired, that indication becomes the basis for determining which augmentative strategies and tactics should be applied to make greater changes than would be acceptable naturally.

To assess the people involved, a change manager asks these questions:

- On the whole, do the people have the characteristics often seen in those who resist change?
- If some people have characteristics generally accepting or favoring change, are there many of those people, and are they influential?
- If people are expected to resist large-scale change, can the form of that resistance be anticipated?

Not only employees, but also customers and other stakeholders must be considered. Are customer characteristics well enough known and understood that their responses to extensive changes can be predicted? What is known about stakeholders' assumptions about the organization and their expectations of how they can get their needs satisfied there? Customers—whether internal or external—may be overwhelmed if they expect to place orders in an accustomed manner but suddenly confront new procedures and new payment requirements, as well as new faces with new attitudes at the order desk. They may then seek a different source for the necessary goods, one that does business in a more familiar way.

Are customers a captive audience—such as food-stamp recipients who depend on particular state welfare offices—or are they like automobile purchasers who can change dealers or brands? If captive, they will have to remain customers even if many changes are made. If not, will too many changes cause them to go elsewhere?

Several years ago two of the authors lived in the same small town, where they witnessed the installation of the area's first automated grocery checkout system. The changes resulting from this system were that customers had to unload their own grocery baskets since this was no longer part of the checkers' duties; prices were marked only on the shelves and not on the items themselves; prices were recorded by a scanner and not called out as the items were rung up.

Weeks before the actual changeover, explanatory materials were posted at the store and dispensed in handouts to customers. During the remodeling of the checkout stands, checkers repeatedly talked about how excited they were to be getting the new system (sometimes to convince themselves, we suspected). When the new machines were installed, extra checkers were stationed to assist people in placing their groceries on the conveyor belt and to explain just what would be happening next. They presented the merits of the system and boldly predicted that all stores would one day have automated checkout machines.

By now all of us are accustomed to such machines (not to mention the do-it-all-yourself checkout stands), but it was interesting to see that this store's management anticipated a particular response from its customers and developed strategies—educative and facilitative—and tactics—posters, handouts, helpers—to help them deal with the many changes they were being asked to accommodate.

In this town, customers could have chosen to shop elsewhere for groceries, so it was necessary to consider them. However, if the company had had a captive audience—as would have the only store in an isolated, even smaller town—such knowledge may well have led management to provide little or even no assistance. The point is, of course, that considering the customers caused the change managers to implement their change strategies in a particular way. If those people had different characteristics, the change strategies and tactics would have been different.

Details of the Proposed Change

A third place to look when trying to determine how many changes can reasonably be made at one time is at the details of the proposed changes. The strength and seriousness of the forces necessitating change—expressed both cognitively and emotionally—are important factors. If the company's entire future financial existence depends on it quickly doing many things very differently, then there is little point in debating over the number of changes. If the reasons for change are not so compelling but people are asked to make big changes anyway, those changes are less likely to meet with success.

The degree to which the changes can be modularized or bundled, and the effect of instituting only some of the modules, should also be considered. Can the changes be broken into parts? Does it make sense to do so? Does accomplishing one or more modules of the changes result in anything worthwhile? If only some of the proposed changes can be made, will they make enough of a difference that some of the other changes could be made at a later time? If so, which changes must be made now and which can wait? If the set of changes must be implemented all at once to have the desired effects, then there is no point in considering whether to do part or all of the change.

Another issue relates to the likely outcomes of the changes. What if the changes are implemented and they do not adequately fix the problems? Where do those changes leave the organization? Would it be in a position to proceed with additional changes? Would it be possible to retreat to the starting point—its position before the changes were implemented—to regain equilibrium or try another group of changes? Critical to any change effort is the linking of the change process to the measurement of organizational performance outcomes.[6] Ultimately, the change managers should be able to demonstrate the extent of success for the change effort. Such a demonstration of success should prove useful in instigating future change efforts.

After considering these details of a proposed change, a change manager may be quite sure that a particular course of change is good but may consider it unwise to make all of the changes at once. To test the waters, the change manager implements the change in a limited area of the organization or with a small number of people. These pilot studies or experiments allow change managers and recipients to "practice" with limited resources, fine-tune the implementation, then decide whether to go forward with a complete change program. A limited approach also allows for change agents to discover previously unexpected consequences.

The pilot or experiment can take place in a department or division within a company or a completely new business within a conglomerate. A hospital might institute a new automated patient-charting procedure on just one ward; a manufacturing company may choose to replace just one production line; a police department might issue new equipment to a single squad. There, the degree of change and stability can be tested to help answer some of the questions. The choice of a pilot site in itself bows more to stability than to change for an initial step.

Interactions among Changes

A final aspect to consider when determining the appropriate blend of change and stability is what interactions among the various changes can be anticipated, and whether those interactions are desirable. For example, a midsize company faced impending needs for changes on several fronts: it had outgrown its office space, the need to improve performance in the marketplace suggested a changed organizational structure, and it recognized a need to change to more professional management.

Each of these perceived needs necessitated significant changes. The changes could have been staged over time, with each being implemented only after the previous one was institutionalized. However, the change managers believed the organization would benefit from interactions among the changes. The move to the new location was seen as aiding the change in structure because people could be physically rearranged at the time of the move. Also, the professional management could be more easily insinuated into the changed structure. The company chose to move rapidly forward on all fronts.

Organizational change efforts result in a blend of change and stability. Although some things are changed, others are deliberately left the same. Studying the organization's culture and its employees and customers helps change managers determine just what degree of change will be accepted. If more change is required than is likely to be acceptable, strategies and tactics are applied not simply because of the nature of the changes, but also because of their numbers. Careful accounting of the numbers of changes and planning for the appropriate blend of change and stability is one more way a change manager can ensure the success of a particular change effort.

RESOURCE AVAILABILITY AND ALLOCATION

Conducting an organizational change requires the expenditure of people, time, and monetary resources. Changes can fail if change managers do not consider what resources are required, where they will come from, and how and when they will be applied. A major part of organizational change is left unmanaged when these questions are ignored.

To study resource requirements, the activities involved in managing a change can be loosely divided into three major phases, each with its own resource-allocation problems. All aspects of diagnosis—defining the problem, gathering and analyzing information, and suggesting future actions—require a variety of people and usually a great deal of time. Implementing a change—putting new operations in place, making adjustments and alterations in work activities—takes even more people, time, and money. Finally, institutionalizing the change—making certain that changes remain in place—is accomplished only through additional resource expenditures. Organizations don't want to run out of resources before institutionalizing the change.

Diagnostic Resource Requirements

In the early stages of a change, organization members and customers begin sensing problems without being directed to do so. They gather data in the ordinary course of their business activities. The problems are more formally investigated only when enough people have registered complaints and questions. The first committee formed, the first task force commissioned, or the first staff person assigned to study the problem is the beginning of many resource-allocation decisions.

The choice of who is to conduct the diagnosis may be determined more by resource availability than by people's suitability to the task. Each of the alternatives carries associated costs. If current employees are chosen, either their existing tasks suffer or additional resources must be assigned to carry out those tasks. If outside consultants are brought in or new people are hired, the search and initial orientation require time and money. Combined with fees and salaries, these are all additional costs tied specifically to the potential change.

The relative costs of the options may be the determining factor in, for example, the choice of a task force chairman. In fact, issues such as those discussed in chapter 7, however important, may no longer be the primary bases for deciding who should conduct diagnostic activities.

Where diagnosis involves people who have never participated in survey preparation, small-group brainstorming, data analysis, or cooperative investigation, such people must be trained even before the diagnostic process is undertaken. The quality of the diagnostic results cannot be as detailed, accurate, or reliable from untrained people, no matter how dedicated they are or how much time they apply to producing them.

Pursuing diagnosis beyond the initial investigation requires additional organizational resources. The people conducting the diagnosis must take others' time to gain the information they need, must often use secretarial or clerical support, or may require information that has to be purchased. Costs are increased if consultants are required for certain aspects of the diagnosis.

In addition, a diagnosis may go on for quite some time, with a great deal of effort at some times and relatively little at others. There are often unproductive but costly phases as committees or individuals devise what turn out to be only temporary solutions. Sometimes the people involved are not sufficiently impressed by the severity of the problems and choose not to pursue them, only to be forced again to attend to the problems at a future time. The costs of these anticipated inefficiencies (or delays) are factors in resource decisions.

Eventually, the change is moved through diagnosis, but only as rapidly as can be accomplished with the resources assigned. Indeed, the thoroughness or correctness of the diagnostic findings may be more a reflection of the amount and quality of resources applied than of the existing facts and logical conclusions.

Implementation Resource Requirements

Once the diagnosis is complete and a vision of the ideal state is drawn, the changes that are actually implemented are determined in great part by the resources that can be applied. After the diagnosis points to the objects and methods to be used, change managers must ask how much they can afford to accomplish those changes: What funds are available? Who can be spared from other tasks? How much time is there?

Gathering the resources together is not simply a series of financial decisions or locating activities. It is more than determining how much of which resources is needed and where these resources are located. Change managers must go beyond that to actually secure the identified resources.

All of the required resources are rarely under the control of a single person or group. Individuals or organizational units opposing the proposed change can refuse to allocate resources of information, time, people, or money to any part of its implementation.

Political strategies may be required to secure necessary cooperation. Without their own managers' cooperation, even employees who are eager for the change may not be available for the necessary training and orientation accompanying the change. A change manager may secure the overt cooperation of line managers who then make available only the poorest employees or the least effective hours of the day for work on implementing the changes. Under such conditions even the most creative and appropriate change plans are not transformed into the visualized new state.

Even managers and others who are neutral or in favor of the change may be unable to contribute resources for its implementation. Their resources may be too meager, or may be required elsewhere to accomplish tasks aimed at meeting other organizational goals.

Authority to require new actions from others is also required,[7] and a change manager without this authority can be stopped at implementation time. The costs of obtaining these resources must be considered in figuring allocation problems.

Even when implementation resources are freely given, if they are of poor quality or not the right kind, the change may still be imperiled. Change agents may be chosen who have personal or organizational characteristics that are inappropriate to fill the roles in a particular change. Money may be plentiful, but without proper plans or good change agents, its expenditure can be virtually useless in achieving the desired state.

Institutionalization Resource Requirements

After the changes have been introduced to the organization, additional resources must be applied to institutionalize those changes. Institutionalized changes are those that, once introduced and fine-tuned, persist in the organization.[8] Institutionalized changes succeed in solving the original problems or destabilizing forces that caused the organization to embark on the change. They make it possible for the company to meet its goals. Those changes are accepted as the ways the company now does its business.

There are two sources of institutionalization costs. The first involves discarding the old and replacing it with the new. The second source involves the costs of activities required to prevent the organization from reverting to its old ways.

The costs of substituting new for old may be readily identifiable, such as those involved in abandoning old forms and creating new ones, or purchasing new computers or other machinery. Visible costs also include moving to larger quarters, hiring additional employees or those who are more highly qualified, and the severance costs of laying off or firing employees.

There are also costs of institutionalization that are more difficult to account for. Employees may become less efficient while worrying and speculating about the effects of new methods, procedures, or structures. Increased absenteeism may result from a poor understanding of just what is expected in the new version of the organization. Settling in to new methods, organizational arrangements, reward systems, or offices takes time and sometimes temporarily diminishes productivity, even in people who are enthusiastic about the new organization.

Once the old has been replaced with the new, additional resources are required to prevent the organization from reverting to the old ways. For individuals, this may involve further training to advance in the careers made possible by the new state. Individuals may also be rewarded specifically for those behaviors the new organization requires. Such training and rewards may not be strictly required for the change to be introduced but are essential to its maintenance and therefore its success. The tabulation of all the required change resources is not complete until these costs are included. Ford's experience in the early 1980s provides such a tabulation example (see "Focus On: Ford in the Early 1980s").

Focus On: Ford in the Early 1980s

In the early 1980s, Ford Motor Company embarked upon a large-scale, organization-wide change from its traditional authoritarian management culture to a more participative and employee-centered culture. Nearly 400,000 employees, locations throughout the world, and product lines that varied from automobiles to satellites and microprocessors demanded that huge resources be devoted to accomplishing such an all-encompassing and fundamental change.

In a presentation to an Academy of Management symposium in 1984, company spokespersons spoke to the enormity of the task, and one specifically addressed the heavy commitment of resources throughout the project. Resources of all types were applied at every stage and substage of this project.

Even though many outsiders recognized that all American car manufacturers were in deep financial trouble, for some time internal forces at

Ford resisted investigating the changes necessary for the company to succeed, or even to stay in operation. Because both the forces compelling change and the inertia and resistance to change were so great, Ford had to apply enormous resources to first determine what the goals of the changes were, then to detail what was required to accomplish the goals, and finally to actually accomplish them.

At various points in the process, entire work teams were sequestered in brainstorming and planning meetings, taking them away from their regular work. Initially reluctant, then with greater enthusiasm, management committed these resources in the belief that such large-scale changes could never be accomplished without them.

What was originally a small staff of internal consultants grew throughout the change so that resource needs in training, facilitation, and coordinating could be met. Technical expertise was gathered from within and hired from outside to ensure that all phases would be successful. Change targets had to commit both organizational and personal resources—practicing new ways of interacting, even when they were uncomfortable or felt foolish—until they fully internalized and successfully implemented the changes that fundamentally altered how they conducted their work lives.

Looking at Ford's experience might lead one to marvel at the richness of resources that the company applied to a major change, then to dismiss its example as irrelevant to most ordinary changes solely because Ford had such a bounty of resources to apply. However, it is more to the point to examine the relative proportions of the change resources to the task being undertaken. When the numbers of employees, work sites, and product lines are considered, then the resources applied are seen as appropriate in scope to the undertaking. What made Ford's change program work was not simply that it was able to throw many resources at it, but that it threw enough resources, compared to what had to be accomplished.

Sources: N. L. Badore et al. (1984), "Cultural change within a large system," Ford Motor Company presentation to the annual meeting of the Academy of Management, Boston, August 12–15, 1984; J. T. Walsh (1984), "Creating the conditions for large-scale systems change," presentation at the annual meeting of the Academy of Management, Boston, August 12–15, 1984.

Resource Allocation Decisions

Each of the major phases of organizational change has demonstrated resource requirements. In no organizations are resources unlimited. Almost always, a decision to apply resources in one area means they cannot be applied elsewhere. Change managers must look realistically at how many resources are required and whether they are able to obtain them. Further, if the only resources obtainable are too few or of poor quality, change managers must determine whether it is possible to attain the desired new state. In this way, resource availability and allocation becomes a practical consideration tempering the pursuit of the ideal new state.

TRANSITION MANAGEMENT

Blends of change and stability and resource allocation are two of the three practical issues involved in managing organizational change. The third is the impact of transition management on the actual process of change. The transition referred to is the movement of the organization from the current, troubled state to the new state. Transition management is managing not just the current organization, but also the transitional organization and the new organization.[9] It focuses on the acts—and the sequencing of the acts—necessary to propel the organization forward along the path of change while still conducting the organization's business.

A discussion of transition management depends heavily on change and stability and resource-allocation issues. It also involves three timing questions: where should the first intervention occur, when must the change be essentially complete, and what are the optimal sequence and timing for strategy application? Managing the transition is the final step in developing a change policy. The transition profile is a useful tool for understanding and managing that transition.

Transition Profile

The management of a manufacturing company decided to change from a functional organization to one organized around product lines. The executive managing the change spent a great deal of time planning the transition from the original state to the new organization. The change manager wanted to coordinate the change implementation schedule with the company's seasonal production variations.

She determined that from January to May the employees' primary concern had to be meeting the company's heavy production requirements, so company routines and procedures had to be held relatively stable during that time. Also, the entire plant was closed for routine maintenance during two weeks over Labor Day, so no changes could be introduced then. During the rest of the year, the slightly lighter production schedules would free employees to spend more time implementing additional elements of the change. Her transition-management plan was based on differing requirements for change and stability and the availability of resources.

The change manager designed a profile of the change before it was implemented. She first determined a goal date for the full implementation of all changes. Then she looked at the availability of various employees and funds.

Finally, she developed a schedule for applying tactics to accomplish the change by her goal date.

In this example, considering the blend of change and stability is useful in two ways. First, it is a conscious choice made as a result of considering the culture, the people involved, the details of the change itself, and the availability of resources to implement the designed changes and bring them into the organizational routines. Second, the exact composition of the blend of change and stability is a measure of how much of the change has been accomplished at any point in time.

Figure 8.1 depicts the progression of this manufacturing company's organizational change. The graph divides time into the three major change stages: diagnosis, implementation, and institutionalization. The measure of progress of this change is the upward movement of the line. Points along that line represent the new or changed activities as a percentage of all the activities carried out in the company.

From January through mid-May, the change was in the diagnostic stage, as a small committee began investigating some reported problems. As a result of the investigation, methods and objects of change were decided upon. Although no explicit changes were officially implemented during diagnosis, some employees slightly altered their actions merely as a result of discussing existing problems.

The new organizational structure was announced on June 1. The new structure required immediate changes in several employees' jobs. In figure 8.1, those changes are represented by the sharp increase in the percentage of new activities at the beginning of June. Additional new procedures and policies were introduced every few weeks until August 1. The percentage of new or changed activities to the whole group of activities remained stable through the shutdown and did not increase again until late September.

When second-quarter earnings figures came in, the change manager was allowed to hire a team-building consultant, increasing the number of changes beginning October 1. There followed a two-and-a-half-month period of stability designed as a time to fine-tune the incorporation of the early portion of the changes.

In late December, a final effort implemented the last of the elements of this planned change. This was just before the heavier production season arrived.

What lesson can we learn from the transition profile in figure 8.1? This change manager carefully staged the application of strategies and tactics to take full advantage of resource availability. She accounted for time and her ultimate goal for the number of individual change elements that had to be implemented to fully achieve this major structural change. By plotting a profile of the change in advance, she increased her chances of managing the events of the change.

Table 8.2 contains some observations about the transition profile of figure 8.1. The one most important to the people managing the change is noting that

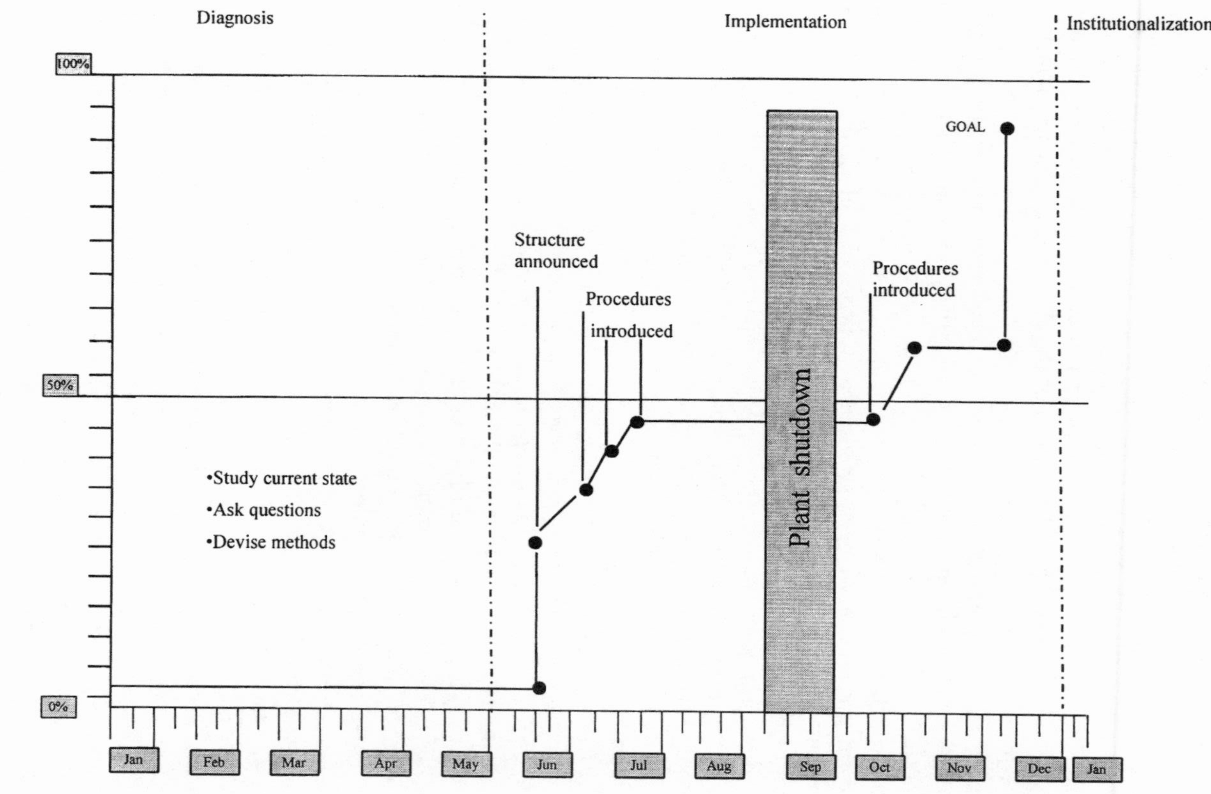

Figure 8.1 Transition Profile

Table 8.2
Transition Profile Observations

Change Stage	Profile Condition	Possible Causes
Diagnosis	Slight increase in percentage of new activities	Just talking about what is wrong with current state encouraged some change
Implementation/ Institutionalization	No negative slope	Employees are rewarded for engaging in new activities Only people who participate are retained Means for doing past activities are removed when new ones are introduced

the line never has a negative slope: at each point, there are as many new activities as there were at any prior points, or there were more.

There are several reasons for this to occur. First, the means for accomplishing any task in the old way may have been removed or made difficult. If so, it would not be possible to revert to the old ways, causing the percentage figure to stay up. Second, rewards for using the new ways may have operated. Intrinsic rewards operate when the changed activities are obviously and inherently rewarding to employees, allowing them to do their jobs better, or faster, or more easily. Extrinsic rewards such as praise and formal performance review restructuring can also be used to maintain the changed behaviors. Finally, only those employees who completely favor and follow the new ways may be retained. In that way, the percentage of new activities can also be expected to stay level or increase over time.

The transition profile in figure 8.1 is useful to a change manager in two different ways. It might be used as a planning device and become part of the package that constitutes change policy. Indicating both the time when all the new activities must be in place and the level (given in percentages) of changed activities establishes the goal of the change effort. Adding known resource constraints on the availability of time, money, and people assists in scheduling activities.

The transition profile can also be used in a second manner. Once the change has been effected, it becomes a device to assess the success of that change.

Transition management is the final element of change policy. When combined with thorough diagnosis and consideration of the desired blend of change and stability and resource availability and allocation, it offers change managers a powerful means of managing large and small organizational changes as well as the opportunity to assess the success of the change with respect to organizational performance outcomes.

NOTES

1. S. G. Gryskiewicz (2000), Positive turbulence, *Executive Excellence*, 17, p. 18.

2. Discussions of the contrasting degrees of change can be found in T. G. Cummings & C. G. Worley (2001), *Organizational development and change* (7th ed.), Cincinnati: South-Western; G. Barczak, S. Smith, & D. Wilemon (1987), Managing large scale organizational change, *Organizational Dynamics*, 16 (Autumn), pp. 22–35; R. H. Kilman, T. J. Covin, et al. (Eds.) (1988), *Corporate transformation: Revitalizing organizations for a competitive world*, San Francisco: Jossey-Bass; J. R. Gordon (2001), *A diagnostic approach to organizational behavior* (7th ed.), Upper Saddle River, NJ: Prentice-Hall, pp. 665–667; D. Miller (1982), Evolution and revolution: A quantum view of structural change in organizations, *Journal of Management Science*, 19, pp. 131–151; and G. J. Skibbins (1974), *Organizational evolution*, New York: Amacom.

3. L. S. Ackerman (1982), Transition management: An in-depth look at managing complex change, *Organizational Dynamics*, 11 (Summer), pp. 46–66; D. Nadler (1982), Implementing organizational change, in *Managing Organizations: Readings and cases*, D. A. Nadler, M. L. Tushman, & W. P. Anthony (Eds.), Boston: Little, Brown, p. 448; W. Bridges (1991), *Managing transitions*, Reading, MA: Addison-Wesley.

4. K. E. Weick & R. E. Quinn (1999), Organizational change and development, *Annual Review of Psychology*, 50, pp. 361–386.

5. A. M. Pettigrew, R. W. Woodman, & K. S. Cameron (2001), Studying organizational change and development: Challenges for future research, *Academy of Management Journal*, 44, pp. 697–713.

6. L. G. Hrebiniak (1978), *Complex organizations*, St. Paul, MN: West, p. 281.

7. P. Goodman et al. (1982), *Change in organizations*, San Francisco: Jossey-Bass, p. 229.

8. Ackerman, Transition management, p. 49; Nadler, Implementing organizational changes, pp. 447–448; R. Beckhard & R. T. Harris (1987), *Organizational transitions*, Reading, MA: Addison-Wesley; Bridges, *Managing transitions*.

9

Conducting the Change

Following its publication in late 1998, *Who Moved My Cheese?* became the top-selling business book for three years running—1999, 2000, and 2001.[1] The book contains a pithy story about four mice and how one pair embraces change while the other pair does not. The lessons of the book are simple:[2]

- Change happens.
- Anticipate change.
- Monitor change.
- Adapt to change quickly.
- Change.
- Enjoy change.
- Be ready to change quickly again and again.

Given the book's popularity, these lessons must resonate with readers. We all face change, and we all want to know how best to cope with and manage change. Other authors (see "Focus On: Summary of Key Elements for Successful Organizational Change") have also outlined their own lessons for managing change. However, when we take a closer look at these lists and the information conveyed, one important conclusion is clearly evident. The lists tell us only *what* should be done when managing change. They fail to tell us *how* to manage change.

In the first eight chapters we examined important elements of organizational change. We discussed the origins of change and the use of a diagnostic approach in managing change. We then discussed various objects, methods, recipients, and change agents, defining and describing them. Underlying that discussion was an implicit model of change relating the elements and processes to one another.

In this chapter, we make that implicit change model—the how—explicit and provide sample diagnostics that either exist or can be fashioned to assist in managing a change. These activities, which will incorporate the key elements

Focus On: Key Elements for Successful Organizational Change

Four Key Principles [Axelrod, pp. 33-35] Widen the circle of involvement. Connect people to each other. Create communities for action. Embrace democracy.	The Ten Commandments for Executing Change [Kanter, Stein, & Jick, p. 383] Analyze the organization and its need for change. Create a shared vision and common direction. Separate from the past. Create a sense of urgency. Support a strong leader role. Line up political sponsorship. Craft an implementation plan. Develop enabling structures. Communicate, involve people and be honest. Reinforce and institutionalize change.
Key Factors in Vision-Driven Change [Beckhard & Pritchard, p. 25] Create and set the vision. Communicate the vision. Build commitment to the vision. Organize people and what they do so that they are aligned with the vision.	Three Keys in Vision-Driven Change [Kirkpatrick, pp. 112-150] Empathy (with employees). Communication. Participation.
Principles of Strategy for Effecting Institutional Change [Benne & Birnbaum, pp. 330-334] To change a subsystem or any part of a subsystem, relevant aspects of the environment must also be changed. To change behavior on any one level of a hierarchical organization, it is necessary to achieve complementary and reinforcing changes in organization levels above and below that. The place to begin change is at those points in the system where some stress or strain exists. In diagnosing the possibility of change in a given institution, it is always necessary to assess the degree of stress and strain at the points where change is sought. Both the formal and informal organization of an institution must be considered in planning any process of change. The effectiveness of planned change is often directly related to the degree to which members of all levels of an institutional hierarchy take part in the fact-finding and in the diagnosing of needed changes and in the formulating and reality testing of goals and programs of change.	Eight Steps of Successful Large-Scale Change [Kotter & Cohen, p. 3-7] Increase urgency. Build the guiding team. Get the vision right. Communicate for buy-in. Empower action. Create short-term wins. Don't let up. Make change stick.

Eight Responsibilities of Transition Management [Duck, p. 109-118]	Prescriptions for Organizations in Transition [Lippett, Langseth, & Mossop, pp. 99-101]
Establish a context for change and provide guidance. Stimulate conversation. Provide appropriate resources. Coordinate and align projects. Ensure congruence of messages, activities, policies and behaviors. Provide opportunities for joint creation. Anticipate, identify and address people problems. Prepare the critical mass.	Involve all employees in planning for change. Communicate and use feedback. Consider effects on working environment and group habits. Inform employees about the change effort before it commences. Build a trusting work climate. Use problem-solving techniques. Involve people in the implementation of change. Ensure an early experience of successful change. Quickly stabilize and spread successful change.
Activities to Reinvent an Organization [Goss, Pascale, & Athos, pp. 97-108]	Ten Steps for Shifting an Organization [Mariotti, pp. 52-54]
Assemble a critical mass of key stakeholders (employee involvement described). Do an organizational audit. Create urgency; discuss the un-discussable. Harness contention. Engineer organizational breakdowns.	Develop a vision, mission, strategy and operating plan as a guide for the organization. Set high expectations with specific goals and objectives, but do not be unrealistic. Build trust. Define each person's and group's roles, responsibilities and job content. Agree on measures that the people can use to track how they are doing. Give frequent, balanced feedback about "how things are going." Continuously update the people on external situation – customers, market status, competition and other factors such as legislation and regulation. Recognize and praise success and progress. Reward success and the desired behavior, both psychologically and financially in multiple ways. Celebrate successes together, and share/grieve over setbacks together.
The Lessons [Johnson, p. 74]	Guiding Propositions [Margulies & Wallace, p. 157]
Change happens. Anticipate change. Monitor change. Adapt to change quickly. Change. Enjoy change. Be ready to quickly change again and again.	Any change effort in which changes in individual behavior are required, regardless of initial focus, must include means for ensuring that such changes will in fact occur. Organizational change is more likely to be met with success when key management people initiate and support the change process. Organizational change is best accomplished when persons likely to be affected by the change are brought into the process as soon as possible. Successful change is not likely to occur following the simple application of any technique. Successful change programs rely upon informed and motivated persons within the organization if the results are to be maintained. No single technique or approach is optimal for all organizational programs, contexts and objectives; diagnosis is essential.

Sources: R. H. Axelrod (2000), *Terms of engagement,* San Francisco: Berrett-Koehler; K. Bechhard & W. Pritchard (1992), *Changing the essence,* San Francisco: Jossey-Bass; K. Benne & M. Birnbaum (1969), *The planning of change: Principles of changing,* New York: Holt, Rinehart and Winston; J. Duck (1993), *Managing change—the art of balancing,* Harvard Business Review, 71, November–December, 109–118; T. Goss, R. Pascale, & A. Athos (1993), *The reinvention roller-coaster—risking the present for a powerful future,* Harvard Business Review, November–December, 97–108; S. Johnson (1998), *Who moved my cheese?,* New York: G. P. Putnam's Sons; R. M. Kanter, B. A. Stein, & T. D. Jick (1992),

The challenge of organizational change, New York: Free Press; D. L. Kirkpatrick (1985), *How to manage change effectively,* San Francisco: Jossey-Bass; J. P. Kotter & D. S. Cohen (2002), *The heart of change: Real-life stories of how people change their organizations,* Boston: Harvard Business School Press; G. L. Lippett, P. Langseth, & J. Mossop (1985), *Implementing organizational change,* San Francisco: Jossey-Bass; J. L. Mariotti (1998), Ten steps for shifting an organization, *Management Review* 87(1), pp. 52–54; N. Margulies & J. Wallace (1973), *Organization change: Techniques and application,* Glenview, IL: Scott, Foresman.

documented in the "Focus On," can be conducted by a person serving as an ongoing change manager or by any number of people filling particular change-agent roles.

EXPANDED CHANGE MODEL

Figure 9.1 is the expanded change model that has been the basis for all previous discussions on managing change. It represents topics we've previously presented and shows relationships among the various processes we prescribe as the means of properly planning and conducting a complex organizational change.

Although we've made the point before, we now repeat it: Models form a useful basis for dealing with complex processes and complex organizations. When managers see the need for large-scale change, they may fear that chaos will result. That fear can cause them to not go forward or to do it timidly.[3] A model of change can help hold that fear at bay. It brings order and understanding to what otherwise seems chaotic and incomprehensible. With a map, a leader knows where to lead her troops. With a model, a change manager sees his course; he can use it to explain that course to change agents and change recipients.

The processes in the model in figure 9.1 have been broken into four phases: initiating, envisioning, crafting, and conducting. Each process in the figure is numbered to correspond to the numbers in the section of text describing that process.

First Major Phase: Initiating

In the first phase are the initiating processes. In this phase, we describe the change from the acknowledgment of the problems affecting the organization to the formulation of an ideal solution.

(1) Acknowledge the Destabilizing Forces

An organizational change begins with the recognition that a change is required. Someone must acknowledge that the organization is no longer stable, that forces are operating to destabilize it. If those forces are strong enough, the

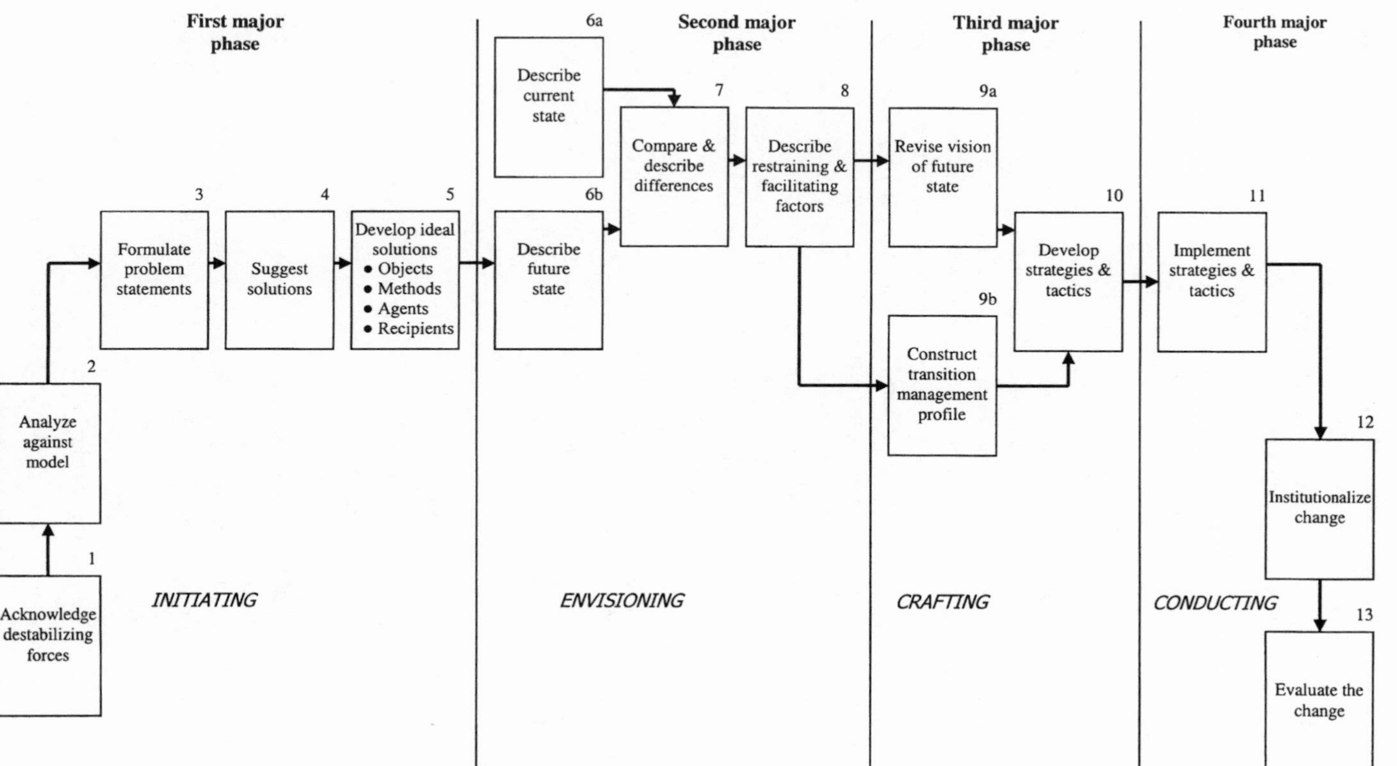

Figure 9.1 Expanded Change Model

organization must change various elements of its operation until stability is achieved[4] or the movement to the next change is under way.[5]

Before destabilizing forces can be acknowledged, they must be recognized. Doing this presents at least three significant problems. First, problems may be noted but their significance remains unclear. During their initial occurrence, for example, it may be difficult to distinguish short-term deviations from desired outcomes and results that are indicative of a system's poor performance. Having insufficient inventory to fill a routine order, unexpectedly having to call in an extra shift, or failing to land a new account can be minor, temporary aberrations, or they can be significant indicators of even more serious and continuing problems. Recognizing their seriousness and the need to do something about them is acknowledging that destabilizing forces are at work.

A second factor—organizational systems—may make it difficult to recognize that destabilizing forces are at work. An organization's communication and decision-making systems may route small, isolated pieces of information to so many different people that no one person can clearly see the big picture and recognize the pattern of deteriorating performance.

Third, an organization's culture may contain norms that make it difficult for problems to be recognized and acknowledged. A norm admonishing employees not to take bad news to their bosses shields the truth from those people who could do something about it. An acknowledged problem may be considered an unfavorable reflection on a manager's ability to do the job in some companies. The logic may read: Good managers never have problems; only poor ones do. So, those who wish to be viewed as "good" managers never appear to note or respond to problems.

What signs might indicate that destabilizing forces exist and a change is needed? Warner W. Burke offers three ways of knowing that "fundamental change" is needed:[6]

1. The same kinds of problems keep occurring.
2. A variety of techniques are used to fix the problem, but none of them really work.
3. Morale is low, with no single causal factor.

Of course, any one or all three may exist for a single work group, a department, or an entire enterprise.

Larry E. Greiner has his version of the three signs that stagnation and complacency have crept into an organization.[7] He sees it in managerial behavior that

1. is oriented more to the past than to the future;
2. recognizes obligations of ritual more than challenges of current problems, and
3. owes allegiance more to departmental goals than to overall company objectives.

This stagnation can settle in on companies whose cultures do not factor into daily operations changing environmental conditions, new technologies, or a changing workforce.

Gerald Skibbins offers a simple checklist for signaling the need for what he calls radical change—a large, systemwide change.[8] It is presented as questionnaire 9.1. A change manager or change agent noting a significant number of yes answers should investigate further, possibly concluding that change is required.

A final list is offered here, one that enumerates a different classification of danger signs, that of unethical behavior within the organization. If the behaviors in table 9.1 are found in organizations, they could spell serious trouble, not simply on a moral plane but on a legal or financial one as well.

(2) Analyze against Standards/Model

Once people acknowledge destabilizing forces, they soon compare the organization's current conditions to their personal standards for organizations. These standards or models are what they use to judge the adequacy of the organization around them. People's general models of organizations and how they should run are the bases for their beliefs about how their particular organization should operate and are important in the development of problem statements and proposed solutions.

What affects these standards and models? Personal experience and values, and personal and professional characteristics are all central. However, organi-

Questionnaire 9.1
Checklist of Organizational Behavior That Signals Need for Radical Change

Check your answers in the appropriate column.

Yes	No	In your organization:
( )	( )	Is there a constant need to manipulate employees?
( )	( )	Does downward communication contain a great deal of exhortation, of attempts to develop "positive" attitudes of cooperation?
( )	( )	Do you have substantial numbers of employees and managers who could be described as disaffected, alienated, unsympathetic, resentful?
( )	( )	Have the last three top management changes of personnel proved to have little effect on solving basic issues?
( )	( )	Has the system been increasing its pressure on individuals to conform?
( )	( )	Does your recruiting produce fewer good employees compared to five years ago?
( )	( )	Is the organization's future honestly confusing?
( )	( )	Are you locked into outmoded technology?
( )	( )	Are charlatans beginning to win promotions?
( )	( )	Are competent managers selecting early retirement more frequently?
( )	( )	Is the long-term trend on real profits downward?

Source: G. J. Skibbins (1974), *Organizational evolution*, New York: Amacom, p. 47.

Table 9.1
Danger Signs of Unethical Behavior

- Emphasizing short-term revenues over long-term considerations
- Routinely ignoring or violating internal or professional codes of ethics
- Looking for simple and quick solutions to ethical problems
- Being unwilling to take an ethical stand if there is a financial cost to doing so
- Maintaining an internal environment that discourages ethical behavior or even encourages unethical behavior
- Handing ethical problems off to the legal department
- Viewing ethics solely as a public relations tool
- Treating employees differently from the way customers are treated
- Employing unfair or arbitrary performance-appraisal standards
- Having no procedures or policies for handling ethical problems
- Having no mechanisms for internal whistle-blowing
- Lacking clear lines of communication
- Being sensitive only to shareholder needs and demands
- Encouraging employees to ignore their personal ethical values

Source: Based on R. A. Cooke. "Danger signs of unethical behavior: How to determine if your firm is at ethical risk," *Journal of Business Ethics* 10, 1991, pp. 249–53.

zational values and norms also play their parts. In many nonprofit organizations, problem and solution statements tend to focus on activities rather than expenditures for equipment, additional personnel, or more facilities because those resources are especially scarce. Other organizations may operate with the norm that only the newest, most modern technologies are used, creating a perpetual need for change because the current situation always is lacking when compared to those standards.

Making explicit the models or standards people hold helps articulate problem statements. People indicate that their model includes a standard for time when they say a certain organizational process takes too long. Or, people reveal standards of the quantity and quality of communication that should exist when they say that communication is poor in the organization.

As destabilizing factors begin affecting an organization, a change agent in the catalyst role may appear. That person will demonstrate to others the existing forces calling for change.

Catalyst change agents, having noted destabilizing forces, compare the organization to their own organizational models and declare that there is a problem. The models they hold play an integral part in the construction of both problem statements and the suggested solutions. The change agents then produce plans to study the situation further, conduct surveys, or administer formal or informal questionnaires. There must be someone who is appointed or who spontaneously takes on this catalyst role to move the change forward.

(3) Formulate Problem Statements

Once it is recognized that forces are acting to destabilize the organization's operations, the exact nature of the forces can be explored. The question is, now that the consequences of the problems are known, what are the exact problems at work?

Here it is essential to explore the important distinction between problems and symptoms.[9] In medical terms, fever is only the outward sign—the symptom—of the problem of infection. A headache is not the problem, but a symptom of muscle tension, vascular problems, or an allergy. It is essential to work beyond the list of symptoms to discover the true underlying problems.

Sorting symptoms from problems is tricky, and it requires diligent questioning and tracking. A useful question is "Why?"

"Our sales are off for the sixth straight week."

Why? Because our market share is down.

Why? Because the Robson Company is getting more and more of our old customers.

Why? Because they give good service and make calls when customers want them, and we don't.

Why? Because we never have. We have a weekly schedule, and that's it.

Why? Because we think our product is good enough that customers will flock to it without our doing much.

Why? Because when it came out it was the first, and for a long time it was the best, but now maybe it isn't.

Why? Because we've done nothing to improve it, and we haven't tried to find out what our customers would like to have changed about it.

Ferreting out the real problem underlying the more obvious symptoms is not as easy as the preceding dialogue indicates. Somewhere along this line of questioning people are likely to become defensive about divulging the truth or may choose not to acknowledge it—even to themselves. However, the dialogue illustrates the general path that must be taken until the symptoms are set aside and the true problems discovered.

Finding problems may involve examining every aspect of the company. It means finding symptoms, then digging for true problems. When questioning fails to disclose the essential problems, specific aspects of the organization may be studied using other investigative techniques.

Individual task behaviors.

A number of instruments are available for examining existing jobs for those characteristics that result in improved employee performance and satisfaction. One such diagnostic tool is the job diagnostic survey discussed in chapter 4.[10]

Organizational processes.

Control, information transmittal, and decision making—among other organizational processes—may need revision as a result of new economic, technological, or social circumstances. Is the company being beaten to the marketplace by the competition too often? Is this a symptom of decision making that is so centralized and formalized that nothing can be done quickly? Do good projects get stuck in R&D while legions of managers and their staffs review, inspect, analyze, and criticize requests to initiate their manufacture? (The reader is reminded of the "Focus On: Xerox" example in chapter 5.) Do good decisions get made and assignments handed out, only to be lost because there are no clearly drawn lines of responsibility or accountability for carrying them out? Does it frequently occur that ideas are good, and something would definitely be done, if only the right people got the right information at the right time? These are clear indications of problems in organizational processes.

One way to assess organizational processes is to conduct a postmortem when failure occurs. The objective is to determine whether organizational processes—as they are designed and as they actually operate—are at fault, or whether some other factor was the main contributor to the failure. Questionnaire 9.2 is an example of how a postmortem might be conducted.

A more generalized approach is illustrated in questionnaire 9.3 The intent of this questionnaire is to uncover stumbling blocks to efficient and effective operations that have been created by existing organizational processes.

Strategic direction.

An organization's self-identity is central to its functioning. When an enterprise's strategic direction changes, the consequences are felt throughout the organization. (The reader is reminded of the "Focus On: Microsoft" example in chapter 3.) These changes require careful diagnostics to determine not only when they are needed, but also how employees' actions to maintain the identity will be overcome as well as how the planned changes will affect other parts of the organization.[11] Organizations must have regularly scheduled procedures for reassessing overall strategy and supporting managerial objectives. When strategic direction is altered, organizational resources are allocated. Organizational elements are evaluated to see which aid in the accomplishment of new managerial objectives, and which do not. Change is required to maximize the efforts in supporting the new strategic direction.

Questionnaire 9.2
Assessing Failed Projects

Think of the last time a project you favored was not put into action.

Briefly describe the project:

How far did the project go before it was shelved?

__ talking stage
__ minor resources informally applied to check into it
__ official investigation, with resources assigned
__ formal presentation of idea to decision maker
__ short trial application (process) or model (product)
__ lengthier application or prototype
__ full adoption okayed, then denied
__ full adoption denied

What person or group stopped the project?

__ peers said it wouldn't work
__ actual potential users said it wouldn't work
__ my boss
__ my boss's boss
__ a committee designed to review such projects
__ I don't know
__ people just stopped talking about it; now no one is working on it.

Organizational culture.

Finally, efforts may also be spent on attempts to modify an organization's culture. Terence E. Deal and Allan A. Kennedy offer these symptoms of "cultural malaise":[12]

- Inward focus—overemphasis on internal budget, financial analysis or sales quotas; no talk about customers, competitors
- Short-term focus
- Morale problems—accompanied by high turnover
- Fragmentation/inconsistency
- Emotional outbursts—"rampant emotionalism" to a degree outside the norms for the company
- Subculture values that preempt shared company values

An organization's problems often have a cultural dimension to them when:[13]

- Internal people are aware of problems and talk about them.
- Problems are not new, but chronic.
- Problems resist efforts to change over a significant time.
- Problems are widespread within the organization.

Questionnaire 9.3
Decision, Control, and Information Outcomes

	Always	Sometimes	Never
1. How often do these *decision* outcomes occur?			
Decisions aren't made in any formal manner.	___	___	___
Decisions are made by those without authority to make them.	___	___	___
The first person asked for a decision doesn't make it. It is referred elsewhere.	___	___	___
2. How often do these *control* outcomes occur?			
Control procedures are directed at financial matters.	___	___	___
Control is scattered among so many people or departments that no one person really knows what is going on.	___	___	___
3. How often do these *information* outcomes occur?			
Information arrives too late to assist in daily decisions.	___	___	___
Information is sent to those who don't need it.	___	___	___
Information does not arrive in the form required for action to be taken.	___	___	___
Information is used as barter.	___	___	___

- People in the organization express a sense of fatalism about the problems.

The sense of fatalism is particularly telling because it speaks of the degree to which a problem is simply part of life, and the prevalent expectation that it is unchangeable.

Determining whether culture is the part of the organization that needs changing requires first determining what the culture is. It means explicating all of the elements discussed earlier: values and beliefs, stories, rituals, language, symbols, norms, and attitudes.

Diagnosing a culture can be difficult for someone who is part of it, however. Because a culture so shapes perceptions and understandings, it sometimes cannot be seen by those who have internalized it. Cultural outsiders, too, have difficulty. They are forced to translate the culture they study through a medium of their own culture—language. Outsiders can recognize that another culture is different, but cannot readily describe it in anything but terms from their own culture, thereby distorting it.[14] Essentially, someone with one worldview—a culture—cannot fully understand someone from another worldview—another culture.

Those diagnosing a culture should be aware of these issues and account for them in their procedures. Knowing the type of bias that is introduced, depending on whether the diagnostician is an insider or an outsider, will also help interpretation of the investigation's results.

Despite the difficulties posed, culture can be made explicit enough so that it can be determined whether it poses a problem to the organization's operation. For diagnostic purposes, cultural elements can be divided into three parts, based on how readily observable they are (see figure 9.2).

Organizational stories, rituals, language, and symbols are the most observable. They are public representatives of the deeper-level values. Because they are so publicly displayed, simply careful observation and close listening will disclose many of them.

At the next level lie norms. These too represent values but are closer to the organizational surface. Observation discloses behaviors from which norms might be inferred, but questioning reveals far more. Through questioning, norms can be made explicit and their relative strengths and importance made known.

Questioning people about the norms under which they operate can be slow and tedious. At first, people often cannot think of any because they take them so much for granted. Sometimes the questioner must offer illustrations to get people started.[15] Listing norms in a group setting can be helpful because one person's offering triggers others to contribute. In short, "a good way to find the central faith of a tribe is to get its members to see who can formulate the biggest blasphemy."[16]

The third and final level is the deepest, and it contains values and assumptions. Organizational values and assumptions are sometimes stated explicitly by organization members or in advertising and other literature. The true values of an organization can be inferred from the information gathered at the other two levels. Interestingly, discrepancies may exist between what the organization says it values and the values expressed in the organization's action. For example, an organization may publicly proclaim that it values individuality and freedom. However, if its norms operate to squelch individual initiative and encourage only conformity, then we may logically conclude that the stated value is false. Likewise, a company that says it values equality obviously does not if top executives occupy spacious, private, well-appointed offices while the rest are thrown together in large areas with their small spaces barely partitioned.

Observability	Cultural Element	Technique Used
Directly Observable	Stories, rituals, language, symbols	Observation • Look at symbols of power relationships between people and functions. • Listen for jargon or characteristic language structures. • Listen to stories and identify heroes. • Observe rituals.
	Norms	Questioning • What are the unwritten rules of behavior? • What are the meanings of the stories and symbols? • What happens to those who violate the norms?
Difficult to observe directly	Values and assumptions	Inference • What values and assumptions are inferred by the stories, rituals, language, symbols, and norms?

Figure 9.2 Relation of Observability and Diagnostic Techniques Used on Cultural Elements

Diagnosis.

Methods for gathering information about cultural elements are portrayed in questionnaire 9.4, which also contains suggestions for the information-gathering phase of diagnosing an organization's culture.

W. Jack Duncan has detailed the application of a multiple-method technique called "triangulation" to study organizational culture.[17] Duncan's use of obtrusive observation, self-administered questionnaires, and personal interviews recognizes that the clearest view of a culture requires interpretation from within and outside of that culture and the people who operate in it.[18] Like the other methods suggested here, triangulation recognizes the complexity and multidimensionality of culture; the result of using these multiple methods is a holistic view of the organization's culture.

To determine whether the culture is a problem and needs changing, the information must be gathered and analyzed. The analysis is to determine whether the culture is congruent with other structural, strategic, and managerial aspects of the organization. If there is no congruence, changes must be made, and culture may become an object of change.

(4) Suggest Solutions

Once problems are clearly identified and defined, solutions can be generated. They may appear spontaneously or be derived only after considerable study. Organizations often have normative as well as more explicit rules governing who is eligible to propose suggestions. For instance, in some institutions, committees or task forces are made up only of managers. Line workers or supervisors are excluded; only those who are managers, directors, or vice presidents are officially included as acceptable sources for solutions. In other enterprises, quality circles may be established, enabling all workers to play a part in defining problems and developing solutions.

Change agents play some of their various roles at this stage. Sometimes the solution-giver change-agent role is filled indirectly by those people or groups sanctified as solution developers. This can be seen in organizations where everyone knows that ideas must appear to come from the president.

Process-helper change agents may be very active at this stage of change. They may actually create or facilitate the forums for generating solutions, if the change manager wishes to solicit solutions from a broad group of people. Of course, numerous solutions may be suggested for fixing the identified problem. Proposed solutions may be directed to only a portion of the problem or to all of it. The change that is actually undertaken may incorporate implementation of several proposed solutions.

(5) Develop Ideal Solutions

After considering the variety of solutions that could be implemented, the change managers choose certain ones, and a complete picture of the ideal or-

Questionnaire 9.4
Questionnaire on Cultural Elements

FIRST LEVEL CULTURAL ELEMENTS

1. Study the *physical setting.* Is apparent attention given to creating messages through the use of physical space? Does it display pride? attention to detail? consistency or differences among sites, department, or areas housing different classes of people? Is it over crowded, grand, tacky, ostentatious?

2. Observe the *rituals.* Do the rituals serve to smooth out uncertainty in daily working life, or do they exist to convey messages about what is important in organizational life? What events are ritualized? What important ceremonies exist to highlight accomplishment? How does the company greet strangers – formal or informal, relaxed or busy, and what is the entrance ritual?

3. Listen to the *language.* Is the language unique for the words it uses or the meanings it gives them? Is any particular technical discipline featured in the language used?

4. Listen to the *stories.* Are stories an important part of passing on the culture of this organization? Who are the heroes and what makes them heroes? Are today's stories – heroes, plots, and outcomes – like yesterday's stories?

SECOND LEVEL OF CULTURAL ELEMENTS

5. What are the unwritten rules of behavior?

   a. How much effort should be expended?
   b. Where should effort be directed – maintaining status quo or innovation?
   c. What image is important – hard worker, creative thinker, hard taskmaster, helpful coworker?
   d. How are other members to be dealt with – derisively, cautiously, openly, with decorum, casually?

6. What norms are conveyed by the stories, rituals, language, and symbols?

   a. What are the "rules" illustrated by the stories?
      Follow the leader.
      Don't rock the boat.
      Close the sale at any cost.
      Work is more important than family
      People are to be respected and dealt with fairly.
      The customer is always right.
      Everyone is out to get you.
      Be careful.
   b. Does the language serve to exclude or include groups?

THIRD LEVEL OF CULTURAL ELEMENTS

7. What values do stories' heroes, fools, and villains represent?

8. From whose point of view are stories told?

9. Which cultural view is most often represented in stories and language?

10. Are the cultural messages imparted by stories, rituals, language, symbols, and norms consistent?

11. Do organizational values match cultural values, or are they in conflict?

Source: Compiled by authors, except for items 1, 2, and 5d, which are from *Corporate Cultures* by Terrence E. Deal and Allen A. Kennedy. Copyright © 1982 by Addison-Wesley Publishing Company, Inc. Reprinted by permission of Perseus Books Publishers, a member of Perseus Books, L.L.C.

ganizational change is drawn. The change objects, methods, agents, and recipients are named.

As the ideal solution is being developed, its architects may need to return to previous steps. They may redefine or more completely define the problems, or may question the organizational models or standards that shaped the problem statements. They may require additional diagnostics before they can clearly identify the objects and recipients, choose the methods, or select change agents. Ultimately, the architects must assess the organizational members' motivation to change, opportunity to change, and ability to change with respect to the ideal solution.[19]

Along with objects, methods, agents, and recipients, the ideal solution includes the goal of this change. Naturally, it is linked to the problem statement. Returning to the company whose sales were depressed, the goal for the change would be to increase sales. The objects might be organizational processes and culture; the methods, managerial and people. The recipients would be the sales force and their supporting departments; the change agent, the sales manager.

Second Major Phase: Envisioning

In the second major phase, change managers and their agents determine whether the ideal solution can be implemented. If necessary, they prepare a revised set of solutions, envisioning the changes required to lead to the new state.

(6a) Describe the Current Organizational State

Describing the current organizational state can occur at the same time as describing the future state. It also is preliminary to two other steps. It first serves as the control state against which the future state is viewed and evaluated. Comparing the current and future states produces a list of differences between the two. Describing the current state is also necessary to discover which of its elements will facilitate, and which will restrain, the transition from the current to the desired future state.

(6b) Describe the Future Organizational State

After identifying the ideal solution and detailing the objects, methods, agents, recipients, and goal, the change managers can draw a vivid picture of the organizational elements, with the changes in place.[20] Individual jobs and routines can be described, procedures can be outlined; even norms, rituals, and symbols can be envisioned.

The answers to these questions can produce a picture of the future state of the organization.

- If this element is the object of change, then how will it operate once it is changed?

- If this element is changed and these methods are used, what other things will also change?
- What additional changes must be made to allow or encourage the primary changes?

To be able to draw the details of the future state, one must imagine the effects of the intended change on the everyday life of the organization. In this future state, how will the building, offices, and common areas look? Who will do what, at what time? What relationships will exist between particular individuals and groups? Will some individuals or groups be unnecessary? Will new people or groups be required? What procedures will be easier or more difficult? How will schedules and routines change? Will some people exercise more or less authority, have broader or narrower jobs, and/or be more or less isolated or integrated?

The future state must be viewed not just from the top of the organization, and not even just from the perspective of the employees who must change the most. It must also be seen from the eyes of other stakeholders, including customers, suppliers, and sometimes the general public. How will customers and clients approach the enterprise in this future state? How will they be reached? Who will interact with them and how will they do it? Will suppliers have to develop new delivery schedules, credit terms, or quality standards? Will the public view the organization as a more-responsible or less-responsible institutional citizen?

Trying to imagine life after the ideal change, in the future state, is not particularly easy. Not everyone has the imagination or vision to picture the myriad results of seemingly simple changes. Going through this process can save change agents and change managers many future headaches. It serves as a basis for determining how extensively the change will affect the organization and people's lives. It also is the primary piece of information used in developing strategies to ensure that the change can be successfully implemented and communicated (both cognitively and emotionally).

(7) Describe the Differences between Current and Future States

Discovering the real differences between how things are now and how they will be tells a change manager where she must provide strategies and tactics to be certain the changes are accomplished. The itemized differences help the change manager see the true scope of the change. For example, to say that we are installing new machines to cut and stitch seat covers sounds simple. Imagining what other operations and arrangements it will affect helps the change manager see all the differences between the organization with the old machines and the organization with the new machines. Work schedules will be rearranged to add a third shift to make the machine's purchase financially practical. Inspectors' and supervisors' offices will be moved off the shop floor into a second tier to make room for the larger equipment. The scope of nearly all cutters' and sewers' jobs will be narrowed. And finally, most employees will be required to have computer keyboarding skills to change and monitor designs on the new machines. The actual set of differences may be even longer. It is worth the time to discover the differences in detail, both to recognize where resources will have to be applied and to determine where problems may arise.

(8) Describe Restraining and Facilitating Factors

In chapter 6 we noted that in any organizational change there are some factors that restrain the organization from changing and others that facilitate changing. The factors are influenced by an organization's culture, the characteristics of the people in it, the proposed change itself, the availability of resources, and the need for change versus stability. An organization with a culture that looks favorably on change (the reader is reminded of the "Focus On: General Electric" example in chapter 4), a workforce with previous experience in the introduced technology, an accomplished training department, and abundant monetary and personnel resources has many facilitating factors for change. On the other hand, an organization with a culture resistant to change, with more senior employees who have worked in no other industries or for no other employers, and that must make the change rapidly on a tight budget displays many factors that will restrain change.

Most change managers planning a change will discover both restraining and facilitating factors at work. Specifying those factors and assessing their importance requires asking more questions:

Q: What obstacles will I face in trying to move from one daily shift to two shifts?

A: People may say they won't work nights.

Q: Why would they say that?

A: For years they've had their off-work time arranged to accommodate family and personal activities—they have joined bowling leagues, card clubs, followed favorite TV programs.

This is clearly a restraining factor. Facilitating factors can also be found:

Q: What can I do to encourage people to make this change?

A: You can punish them for not doing it, or you can reward them for going along with it.

Q: Would something like that work here?

A: Punishment is not acceptable in our company's culture. But employees always react favorably to a reward of bonuses or company-sponsored activities.

Sometimes the greatest restraining or facilitating factors are related to people's previous experience with change. Questionnaire 9.5 is designed to survey employees' degree of acceptance of change.[21]

Questionnaire 9.5
Index of Acceptance of Job Changes

The following five questionnaire items are used to collect information about acceptance of job changes.

1. Sometimes changes in the way a job is done are more trouble than they are worth because they create a lot of problems and confusion. How often do you feel the changes which have affected you and your job at (name of organization) have been like this?

 (1) ____ 50% or more of the changes have been more trouble than they're worth
 (2) ____ About 40% of the changes
 (3) ____ About 25% of the changes
 (4) ____ About 15% of the changes
 (5) ____ Only 5% or fewer of the changes have been more trouble than they're worth

2. From time to time changes in policies, procedures, and equipment are introduced by management. How often do these changes lead to better ways of doing things?

 (1) ____ Changes of this kind never improve things
 (2) ____ They seldom do
 (3) ____ About half of the time they do
 (4) ____ Most of the time they do
 (5) ____ Changes of this kind are always an improvement

3. How well do the various people in the plant or offices who are affected by these changes accept them?

 (1) ____ Very few of the people involved accept the changes
 (2) ____ Less than half do
 (3) ____ About half of them do
 (4) ____ Most of them do
 (5) ____ Practically all of the people involved accept the changes

4. In general, how do you *now* feel about changes during the past year that affected the way your job is done?

 (1) ____ Made things somewhat worse
 (2) ____ Not improved things at all
 (3) ____ Not improved things very much
 (4) ____ Improved things somewhat
 (5) ____ Been a big improvement
 ____ There have been no changes in my job in the past year

5. During the past year, when changes were introduced that affected they way your job is done, how did you feel about them at *first*?

 At first I thought the changes would:
 (1) ____ Make things somewhat worse
 (2) ____ Not improve things at all
 (3) ____ Not improve things very much
 (4) ____ Improve things somewhat
 (5) ____ Be a big improvement
 ____ There have been no changes in my job in the past year

Source: M. Patchen (1965), *Some questionnaire measures of employee motivation and morale*, Ann Arbor, MI: Survey Research Center, University of Michigan.

Descriptions of restraining and facilitating factors unearthed by this process aid in deriving strategies and designing tactics. The change manager would work to remove or dampen as many restraining factors and create and augment as many facilitating factors as possible with her custom-designed package of change strategies and tactics.

Third Major Phase: Crafting

In the third major phase of the expanded change model, the actual plans for carrying out the change are crafted. Before continuing, however, it is important to consider three points. First, at any given time, other destabilizing forces may erupt. Second, and related to the first point, the entire change process is iterative, meaning that change managers and change agents do not conduct change in a predetermined, direct path. Sometimes—and maybe more often than they would like—change managers and change agents may need to loop back to earlier phases. Finally, the larger the organization, the greater the likelihood that it is combining a number of changes at the same time, and thus creating the need for coordination among leaders and agents.[22]

(9a) Revise Vision of Future State

Facilitating and restraining factors can change the picture of the ideal change. The revised vision of the future state is one that reflects the existing situation—the need for change, the elements of the organization, its resources, and so forth—and what is practical and possible. The revision takes into account restraining and facilitating factors in the current state and the comparison of current and future states.

If the ideal change results in so many differences that it cannot be accomplished, then a revised vision might entail less-aggressive goals and approaches. If the change is large but many facilitating factors are discovered, the revision may be grander than the original ideal changes. Activities at this point simply offer the opportunity to factor all that has been learned into the determination of what will be changed, the method for the change, who will be the recipients, and who will serve as change agents.

(9b) Construct the Transition-Management Profile

We introduced the transition-management profile in chapter 8. Transition is the movement of the organization from the current troubled state to the desired future state. The profile represents activities undertaken both to work toward the new state and to provide for the organization's management requirements during the transition.[23] Producing a profile takes into account the restraining and facilitating factors, including such givens as heavy production seasons, slack sales periods, when and to what extent resources will be available, and employees' characteristics. Ongoing business requirements accounted for might include such things as when shipments must go out, inspections by regulating agencies, and union agreements. Constructing the profile may uncover conflicts or may indicate the need for additional management action to ensure that both the company's business is accomplished and the change is managed and moved forward.

Making public the transition profile and appointing the transition-management team encourages positive expectations for the time of transition.[24] People are encouraged to prepare themselves and others for the change that is coming, because they know when and how it will unfold.

A process-helper change agent will be useful in pointing out where and when change activities should occur to ensure the desired outcome. A resource linker will help identify the necessary resources and where they can be found.

(10) Develop Strategies and Tactics for the Change

By the time a change manager arrives at this step, she will have gathered much information and made many decisions. She knows what and who will change, has chosen a method, and clearly understands that the organization will be different once the change is enacted. Because she knows where the organization is and where she wants it to be, it is now time to plan the details of getting there. Strategies and tactics must be developed to accomplish the primary change and all those changes that will or must occur as a result.

Strategies will be chosen to accomplish the change, to exploit facilitating factors at work in the current state, and to diminish the force of restraining factors now present. As we noted earlier, choosing strategies and designing strategy and tactic combinations are not easy tasks. In chapter 6, we offered four key aspects to consider when determining the most appropriate strategies.

1. Time—how much is available to implement the change?
2. Extent of the change—what are the scope and depth of the advocated change?
3. Favorableness of the change recipients—are recipients aware of the need to change, do they believe in it, and are they committed to it?
4. Favorableness of the change agent—how much authority, knowledge, and adeptness at cooperating does the change agent have, and to what degree is she able to conceptualize?

Questionnaire 9.6 is based on these guidelines for choosing a change strategy. A change agent could assess a given situation using this questionnaire.

Decision tree.

Figure 9.3 illustrates a process for choosing strategies. As the figure shows, the process is based on a consideration of key aspects of a change situation. The ordering of the aspects in this decision-tree format allows us to demonstrate how they affect the choice of strategies, and that the effects are cumulative. The particular ordering also indicates our beliefs as to the relative impact

Questionnaire 9.6
Examining the Change

I. TIME AVAILIABLE

1. How soon must this change be accomplished?

    ___ next week
    ___ 1 month
    ___ 2-3 months
    ___ 6 months
    ___ 1 year
    ___ 2 years
    ___ other (specify)

2. If partial changes can be implemented within a short period, and other changes follow, what are the time requirements?

    Within ________________ for partial; ________________ for others,
    Specify:

II. EXTENT

Scope	*Number*	*Depth*
1. How many individuals will have to change?	_____	Physical Space
	_____	Tasks
	_____	Reporting relationship
	_____	Supervision
	_____	Status relative to others
	_____	Career paths
2. How many units will have to change?	_____	Scope of responsibilities
	_____	Responsibility for task completion
	_____	Status relative to other units
	_____	Autonomy
	_____	Relationships to organizational environment

III. CHANGE RECIPIENTS

1. Few people perceive the need for change. They are

    ___ at upper levels of the organization
    ___ at lower levels of the organization
    ___ in technical areas
    ___ in nontechnical areas
    ___ scattered throughout

2. Many people perceive the need for change. They are

    ___ at upper levels of the organization
    ___ at lower levels of the organization
    ___ in technical areas
    ___ in nontechnical areas
    ___ scattered throughout

(continued)

Questionnaire 9.6 (Continued)

---

3. Those who perceive the need for change

___ have authority to initiate changes
___ haven't authority to initiate changes
___ have a high stake in maintaining the status quo
___ have a lot to gain by initiating changes

4. Cultural views of change in the organization

___ negative, suspicious, overtly resistant
___ cautious, covertly resistant
___ neutral; response is situation-specific
___ acceptance of change as a fact of organizational life
___ embraces and thrives on changes

5. Knowledge about changing in general and this change in particular

___ is dispersed throughout the organization
___ is held by only a few insiders
___ will have to come from outside consultants

---

of each on the choice of strategies—that is, of the first three, time is considered first because it is the most crucial factor. Moreover, the amount of time needed is generally dictated by the entire change situation rather than only by the change manager. It is accepted as a given and is considered first. The extent of the change is considered next, and the favorableness for change of the recipient is considered third. The fourth factor considered, that of the favorableness of the change agent, actually becomes the crux of the decision: Now that we know the strategies most appropriate for the change situation, do we have a change agent able to accomplish it?

Our discussion to this point has stressed that these aspects influence the choice of a strategy package. By working through the decision tree in figure 9.3, we can see how they work that influence. To use the tree for a particular situation, one asks the first question on the left and then follows the appropriate *yes* or *no* branches.

In the figure, letters representing the four strategies are written on the lines following the question boxes when they survive the question (see *key,* in the figure). In other words, whenever a particular strategy is not ruled out by the *yes* or *no* answer to the question, it is carried forward as a feasible candidate, to be treated by the next question. After the third question, the strategies remaining are those that, on the basis of these three considerations, are still feasible. For added clarity, column four of figure 9.3 describes the eight different change situations that are depicted by the combinations of answers to the three questions. The fifth column repeats the set of feasible strategies for each com-

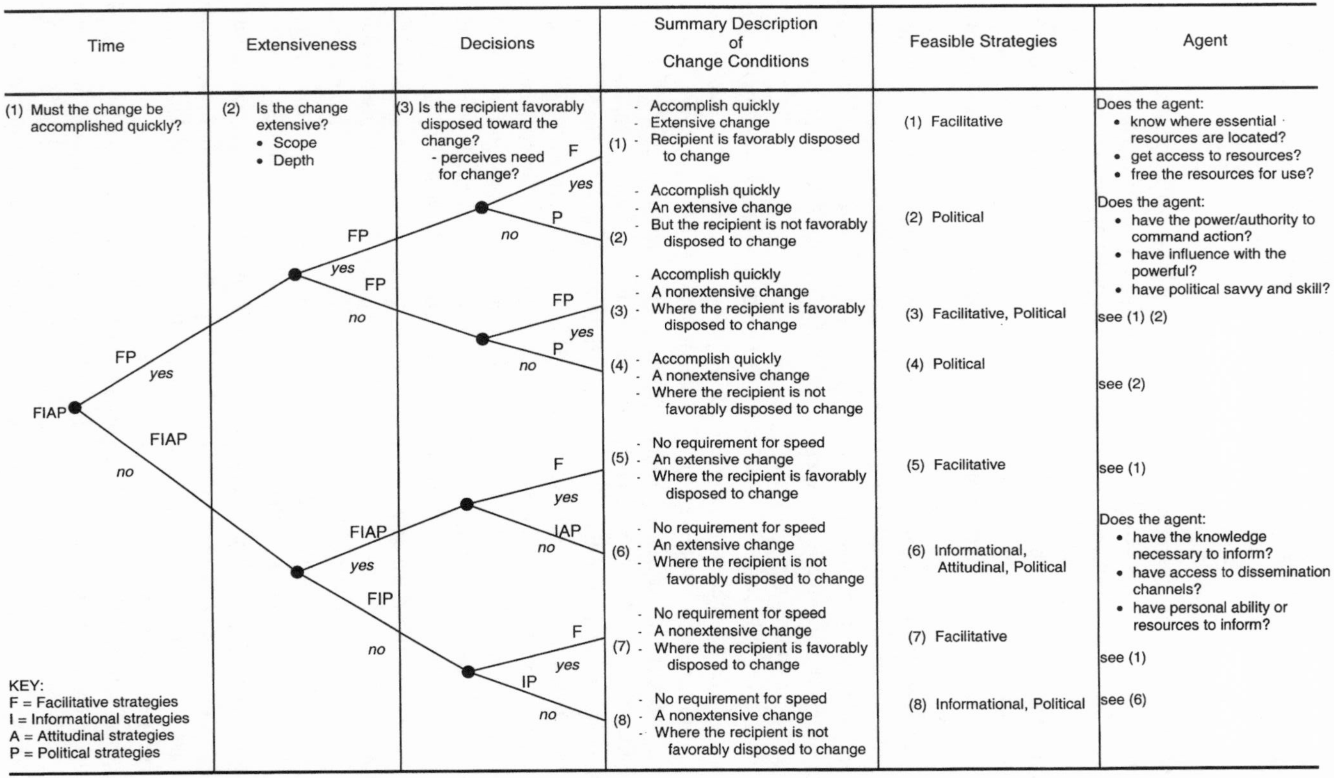

Time	Extensiveness	Decisions	Summary Description of Change Conditions	Feasible Strategies	Agent
(1) Must the change be accomplished quickly?	(2) Is the change extensive? • Scope • Depth	(3) Is the recipient favorably disposed toward the change? - perceives need for change?			
FIAP — yes — FP	yes — FP	yes — F	(1) - Accomplish quickly - Extensive change - Recipient is favorably disposed to change	(1) Facilitative	Does the agent: • know where essential resources are located? • get access to resources? • free the resources for use?
		no — P	(2) - Accomplish quickly - An extensive change - But the recipient is not favorably disposed to change	(2) Political	Does the agent: • have the power/authority to command action? • have influence with the powerful? • have political savvy and skill?
	no — FP	yes — FP	(3) - Accomplish quickly - A nonextensive change - Where the recipient is favorably disposed to change	(3) Facilitative, Political	see (1) (2)
		no — P	(4) - Accomplish quickly - A nonextensive change - Where the recipient is not favorably disposed to change	(4) Political	see (2)
no — FIAP	yes — FIAP	yes — F	(5) - No requirement for speed - An extensive change - Where the recipient is favorably disposed to change	(5) Facilitative	see (1)
		no — IAP	(6) - No requirement for speed - An extensive change - Where the recipient is not favorably disposed to change	(6) Informational, Attitudinal, Political	Does the agent: • have the knowledge necessary to inform? • have access to dissemination channels? • have personal ability or resources to inform?
	no — FIP	yes — F	(7) - No requirement for speed - A nonextensive change - Where the recipient is favorably disposed to change	(7) Facilitative	see (1)
		no — IP	(8) - No requirement for speed - A nonextensive change - Where the recipient is not favorably disposed to change	(8) Informational, Political	see (6)

KEY:
F = Facilitative strategies
I = Informational strategies
A = Attitudinal strategies
P = Political strategies

Figure 9.3 Conditional Model for Selecting Change Strategies

plete branch. The final column questions the favorableness of the change agent. If he or she is not favorable in the ways required by the feasible strategies, then thought must be given to either restructuring the change or choosing a new change agent.

Using the decision tree: Two examples.

Using the decision-tree model shown in figure 9.3, we will follow two separate branches to see how feasible change strategies can be selected. Beginning with the time dimension, we ask: Must the change be accomplished quickly? The *yes* answer eliminates the informational (I) and attitudinal (A) strategies as requiring too much time. Facilitation (F) and political (P) strategies are carried forward because they can be applied quickly. (Note that certain political strategies would not survive; only those that involve outright exercise of power would survive.)

A *yes* answer to the second question—Is the change extensive?—denotes a major change. Both facilitative and power/political strategies are useful in such extensive changes, but in somewhat different ways. Power/political strategies can be used for wide-scope changes, although facilitation strategies can effect either deep or wide-scope changes.

Regarding the third question—Is the recipient favorably disposed toward the change?—if the answer is *no,* and the recipients are not favorably disposed to change, only power strategies are left to accomplish an extensive change quickly. Through this series of ordered questions, we have arrived at a strategy that allows the appropriate management of a particular change situation.

In our second example, let us answer the time question—Must the change be accomplished quickly?—in the negative. This *no* answer means we have at least a reasonable amount of time to accomplish the change. Since speed is not necessary, none of the strategy types need to be eliminated, and all can be considered as candidates when the second question is asked. Second, if the change is extensive, then all of the strategies remain available for consideration. If the answer to the third question is *no,* the recipients are not favorably disposed to change. Facilitation strategies are therefore excluded. We are left with three feasible strategy types in this instance (no necessity for speed, an extensive change being required, and a recipient not favorably disposed to change). Under such conditions, the simultaneous or sequential use of two or three strategies is most probably indicated. Further delineation of the recipients' specific unfavorable characteristics and other facilitating and restraining factors would assist the change manager in making the final choice(s) and determining their order of presentation.

The final column of figure 9.3 contains the questions that must be asked of a change agent to determine whether she or he has the characteristics favorable to accomplishing this change with the chosen strategies. Unfavorable change agents—as in the case when a political/power strategy is indicated and the agent is a staff person with little or no positional authority—are either removed or supplemented. Several senior managers may be asked to endorse a particular strategic move to supplement what the change agent can cause to happen individually. Other skills favorable to effecting particular strategies can be similarly "hired out."

Fourth Major Phase: Conducting

Here, in phase four of the expanded change model, change managers and agents implement and then evaluate the changes. Conducting the change is rarely a quick process like throwing a light switch. Rather, it can take place over weeks, months, or, in the case of very large scale changes, years.

(11) Implement Strategies and Tactics

Once the initiating, envisioning, and crafting are accomplished, it is time to implement the strategies and tactics that have been designed. The characteristics of the change itself and the facilitating and restraining factors have led the change manager and agents to a particular course of implementation. Now it is time to advance on that course. Realistically, some activities have likely already been initiated. An informational or educational program may have been started early in the process, explaining that problems exist and a change is on its way. Persuasive talks, posters, and newsletter articles also may have been disseminated. Political activities may have begun in the cafeteria or at the watercooler. Communication throughout the change process is critical. Besides explaining the planned change process, change managers and agents should also communicate why the change is necessary and the impact of not changing, as well as identifying what is not changing and what the organization will be like after the change.[25] Thanks and acknowledgment should be expressed before, during, and after the change process.

The implementation of the strategies will follow the transition-management profile developed. If chosen, a transition manager and transition team will be in place.

Despite the extensive work done to this point, it is unlikely that all eventualities were anticipated, and contingency plans must be in place for unanticipated costs, consequences, or resistance.[26] During implementation, new facilitating and restraining factors may appear, necessitating additional activities. The business's environment may change, making more or fewer resources available. Indeed, the financial position of the company may deteriorate, forcing the change manager to push for the accomplishment of the needed changes more rapidly than planned or abandon the effort entirely. The previous careful planning provides greater safety and certainty that those ad hoc choices that must be made are congruent with those that enjoyed more thorough planning.

(12) Institutionalize Changes

Institutionalization of change "refers to the organization's continued reliance on the change and durability of its effects."[27] A change that persists over time is an institutionalized change.[28] Few activities are undertaken specifically to ensure that the change is institutionalized. Rather, if the destabilizing factors have been correctly diagnosed, the solution intelligently developed, the recipients and agents chosen wisely, and the facilitating and restraining factors noted and dealt with by well-designed strategies and tactics, then the change could be expected to persist. On the other hand, changes do not take hold, or persist, when they are ill-conceived solutions to poorly understood problems, delivered without adequately recognizing the cogent factors at work.

Strategies and tactics may have to be implemented to ensure that the change persists when some organizational conditions are expected to change. For instance, a change that is successfully implemented during a company's winter slack season may not be assured of continued success once summer's hectic activities begin. Specific new tactics may be required to deal with the changed conditions. Whereas the old methods may have allowed few people to accomplish the necessary jobs, the new methods may require that additional people be added during the summer to sustain the changes.

Other institutionalization activities might include discussions recalling the difficulties experienced in the original state, and the advantages to life in the new state. Such discussions, often conducted like college pep assemblies, serve to cement people's commitment to the changes that have taken place.

When culture is the object of change, creating new symbols and rituals that are in keeping with the change is essential. Keeping in place the symbols of the old culture while talking about a new one is too confusing and misleading and may result in backsliding, not institutionalization.

Two important institutionalization activities are essential. First, the reward system must reward the behaviors demanded by the new state of the organization. If raises, bonuses, and other perks reward behavior that is counter to the changes enacted, then the new state will never be institutionalized. Second, the people who are hired as the change is being conducted and after it is in place must be those who believe in and can support the changes. They must have the attitudes and behaviors to sustain the changes.

Sometimes institutionalization can be accomplished by removing the means required to perform in the old way and providing only the means to act in the new way. If all the paper forms are thrown out when a new computerized, online parts-ordering and inventory system is implemented, then those employees taking telephone orders will be forced to use the computer terminals provided them. No other course of action will be available.

(13) Evaluate the Change

As with any endeavor, the value in assessing the organizational change is to learn from mistakes and successes to apply the knowledge to future efforts. Although the people involved will evaluate a change individually and informally, there is great value in such an evaluation being a formal activity in a planned change process. Unless the change is evaluated in some manner, managers and others may not recognize which of their actions contributed positively or negatively to the outcome. Unfortunately, there is a real dearth of studies linking change capacity and action to ultimate organizational performance, thus limiting what can be learned from other organizations' attempts to change.[29]

Most discussions of evaluating a change effort include some mention of both the *results* of conducting the change and the *process* of conducting it. Included here are suggestions for both. The results can be evaluated from at least three perspectives: against the original change goals, against the described future state, and in terms of how well established, or institutionalized, the change becomes. The process can also be evaluated on three points: how rapidly the change was accomplished, the costs to individuals and the organization in conducting it, and the number of unanticipated actions and occurrences it generates. Finally, the process can also be compared to previous organizational change attempts, both successful and not-so-successful ones.

At an earlier point in our discussion of the expanded change model—(5), develop ideal solutions—we suggested making explicit the goal of the changes to be conducted. An obvious means of evaluating the change is to determine now whether that goal was met. The following are common change goals, easily evaluated for their success or failure:

- To halt the decline in number and profitability of sales
- To improve employee productivity
- To increase the response time to customer questions or complaints
- To decrease the marketing costs per each sale while keeping sales at their current level
- To reduce the amount of time between receiving a request and completing it

Clearly, the more precise and quantifiable the original goal, the easier it is now to assess whether the goal was met. In fact, the success of change goals aimed at altering attitudes or improving affective actions can be very difficult to evaluate. When the observable behavioral outcomes are stated, the underlying goals can be far more effective and considerably easier to evaluate. For example, the change goal "To improve employee morale" is made measurable when stated as "To improve employee morale, as evidenced by less time spent complaining about work within small groups, fewer union grievances, and a 1.5 percent average improvement in productivity." Similarly, "To improve employee service orientation" is more easily measured when stated "To improve employee service orientation, as evidenced by decreased mean response time to service requests, a 25 percent reduction in service complaint forms submitted, and a 35 percent improvement in the quarterly customer-satisfaction survey results."

Sometimes, change managers do not make explicit their goals for the change they undertake. If they have described the desired future state of the organization—as suggested in (6b), describe the future organizational state of the expanded change model—then it is that intended future state against which the changed organization is evaluated. If discrepancies are revealed, are there valid reasons for those discrepancies, and if so, should they stand? Or are they not valid, and therefore the change is incomplete and additional changes are necessary?

A change manager can prepare, based on the change's goal and the picture of the future state, a description of precisely what will constitute a successful change. That description—prepared in great detail, in advance, and revised as the view of the ideal state is altered—will provide the best and most accurate assessment of the success of a specific change effort.

A third measure for determining the successful outcome of a change effort is that the change "takes,"[30] or is institutionalized. It is successful if the implemented changes persist without additional or excessive controls to sustain the new behaviors, relationships, or activities.

An evaluation of the change must include not only the outcome, but the process of conducting it as well. First, was the change accomplished at the pace that was desired and planned? In some cases, the question is whether the change was conducted as rapidly as possible; in others, whether the pace was determined in advance and the change processes accomplished according to that timetable. Some outcomes simply cannot be met if the change does not take place in a timely manner. Therefore, the failure of a change may be not that the outcome wasn't correct, but that it didn't happen soon enough.

The process of change presents costs to organizations and the individuals in them. The costs for organizations are dollars, time, equipment, and other financially based costs, as discussed in chapter 8. The measure of a successful change in this regard is that these costs were adequately estimated and were controlled, keeping the change from going over budget in dollars, time, and so forth.

The costs of change for individuals are generally psychological or emotional—anxiety, reduced confidence, stress, disrupted friendships and relationships, uncertainty, and tension. A good change manager anticipates where costs may be too great for the people and works to avoid them. The successful change is then one where the costs to the organization and the individual are no greater than are essential, and that all costs that can be avoided indeed are avoided.

Finally, the process of change is successful when very few actions occur that were unanticipated.[31] The process, as described in the expanded change model, seeks to discover, in advance, what the change manager must know to plan and conduct strategies, tactics, and activities that will ensure the desired change results. The number of unanticipated or dysfunctional effects is a significant measure of how successfully the change manager managed the change.

Some organization-development theorists believe that the most successful organizational changes are those that help the organization in ways that are much broader than those we've discussed so far.[32] Those writers believe that a successful change

- produces positive changes in line and staff attitudes,
- prompts people to behave more effectively in solving problems and relating to others, and
- enhances the organization's potential for organizational renewal in the future.

Change managers evaluate the process of the change for the same reasons they evaluate the outcomes of change: to determine whether more work is required and to be better able to conduct the next change that comes along. For as we said in the beginning, change is a fact of organizational life. If this change was successful, there is a greater chance of the next one being successful, too. If the errors in this one go unnoted, the danger is that they will be repeated next time, and the time after that, and time and time again.

CONDUCTING AN ORGANIZATIONAL CHANGE

Managing organizational change is not a trivial undertaking. Because of this, our managed-change model is fairly complex. To be sure, many changes are so small and so well understood that it would be foolish to apply all of these steps. If the benefits gained from a change are not adequate to warrant the time and energy that this modeled process necessarily entails, then certainly the model should not be used. In those cases, a change manager often acts without conscious consideration of the elements we have deemed important.

However, when changes are complex or not well understood, then this change model is relevant. The warning to both seasoned and new change managers is that the complexities of a particular change are often not recognized unless such a complete and careful set of processes, as outlined here, is undertaken.

NOTES

1. *Business Week*, www.businessweek.com/bwplus/booksell.htm. As this book went to press, *Who Moved My Cheese?* had finally been supplanted atop the best-seller list.

2. S. Johnson (1998), *Who moved my cheese?*, New York: G. P. Putnam's Sons, p. 74.

3. A master class in radical change (1993), *Fortune*, December 13, p. 83.

4. D. A. Nadler & M. L. Tushman (1982), A model for diagnosing organizational behavior, in M. L. Tushman & W. L. Moore (Eds.), *Readings in the management of innovation*, Boston: Pitman, pp. 153–168. This article discusses congruence models for organizational elements, without specifying culture as one of those elements. T. G.

Cummings (1980), *Systems theory for organizational development,* New York: Wiley, p. 134, discusses organizational congruence, using culture as an organizational element.

5. Found in S. P. Robbins (2001), *Organizational behavior* (9th ed.), Englewood Cliffs, NJ: Prentice-Hall, and based on a perspective in P. B. Vaill (1989), *Managing as a performing art: New ideas for a world of chaotic change,* San Francisco: Jossey-Bass.
6. W. W. Burke (1982), *Organizational development,* Boston: Little, Brown.
7. L. E. Greiner (1970), Patterns of organization change, in G. W. Dalton P. R. Lawrence, & L E. Greiner (Eds.), *Organizational change and development,* Homewood, IL: Richard D. Irwin, pp. 213–219.
8. G. J. Skibbins (1974), *Organizational evolution,* New York: Amacon, p. 47.
9. Nadler & Tushman, A model for diagnosing organizational behavior, p. 245.
10. J. R. Hackman (1977), Work design, in J. R. Hackman & J. L. Suttle (Eds.), *Improving life at work: Behavioral science approaches to organizational change,* Santa Monica, CA: Goodyear.
11. A. D. Brown & K. Starkey (2000), Organizational identity and learning: A psychodynamic perspective, *Academy of Management Review,* 25, pp. 102–120, refer to these actions as ego defenses. Such ego defenses used to preserve identity include denial, rationalization, idealization, fantasy, and symbolization.
12. T. E. Deal & A. A. Kennedy (1982), *Corporate cultures,* Reading, MA: Addison-Wesley, p. 136.
13. G. Egan (1988), *Change agent skills b: Managing innovation and change,* San Diego: University Associates, p. 35.
14. K. Gregory (1983), Native view paradigms: Multiple cultures and culture conflicts in organizations, *Administrative Science Quarterly,* 28, pp. 359–376.
15. R. H. Kilmann (1982), Getting control of the corporate culture, *Managing,* 2, pp. 11–17.
16. N. M Tichy (1983), *Managing strategic change: Technical, practical political and cultural dynamics,* New York: Wiley-Interscience, p. 132.
17. W. J. Duncan (1989), Organizational culture: "Getting a fix" on an elusive concept, *Academy of Management Executive,* 3, pp. 229–236.
18. Ibid., pp. 229, 231.
19. H. R. Greve (1998), Performance, aspirations, and risky organizational change, *Administrative Science Quarterly,* 43, pp. 58–86.
20. L. S. Ackerman (1982), Transition management: An in-depth look at managing complex change, *Organizational Dynamics,* 11, p. 49.
21. M. Patchen (1965), *Some questionnaire measures of employee motivation and morale,* Ann Arbor, MI: Survey Research Center, University of Michigan, pp. 1–14.
22. A. M. Pettigrew, R. W. Woodman, & K. S. Cameron (2001), Studying organizational change and development: Challenges for future research, *Academy of Management Journal,* 44, pp. 697–713.
23. Ackerman, Transition management, p. 49; and R. Beckhard & R. Harris (1977), *Organizational transitions: Managing complex change,* Reading, MA: Addison-Wesley.
24. D. A. Nadler, M. L. Tushman, & N. G. Hatvany, *Managing organizations: Readings and cases,* Boston: Little, Brown, p. 448.
25. Prosci Benchmarking Report, Best practices in change management, www.prosci.com.

26. J. R. Gordon (2001), *A diagnostic approach to organizational behavior* (7th ed.), Upper Saddle River, NJ: Prentice-Hall, p. 689.

27. S. E. Seashore, E. E. Lawler III, P. H. Mirvis, & C. Cammann (Eds.) (1983), *Assessing organizational change,* New York: Wiley, p. 29.

28. P. S. Goodman et al. (1982), *Change in organizations,* San Francisco: Jossey-Bass.

29. A. M. Pettigrew et al., Studying organizational change and development.

30. M. Beer (1980), *Organization change and development,* Santa Monica, CA: Goodyear, p. 56.

31. Ibid.

32. See, for example, ibid., p. 100; and Greiner, Patterns of organization change.

10

Ethical Issues in Managing Change

> Unless and until otherwise advised by me in writing, you are each expected to report, instantaneously and directly to me, any legal violation or moral failure on behalf of any employee at Salomon Inc. or any subsidiary or controlled affiliate. You are to make reporting directly to me your first priority. You should, of course, report through normal chain of command when I am unavailable and, in other cases, immediately after reporting to me.
>
> Exempted from the above are only minor legal and moral failures (such as parking tickets or nonmaterial expense account abuses by low-level employees) not involving significant breach of law by our firms or harm to third parties.
>
> My private office telephone number in Omaha is . . . which reaches me both at the office and at home. My general office number in Omaha is . . . The Omaha office can almost always find me.
>
> When in doubt, call me.
>
> —Warren E. Buffett, Chairman and Chief Executive Officer[1]

In 1991 Salomon Brothers reported that its government desk had placed illegal bids in 20 of 230 auctions of government securities.[2] This admission from Wall Street's reputed "top-gun" trader of government securities led to the resignation of the company's chairman and CEO as well as its president. The memo is a testament to Warren Buffett's commitment to changing the organizational culture at Salomon Brothers after being named chairman and CEO. The culture under which employees had been working was no longer acceptable, and behaviors had to change. The company's survival depended on it.

Any time people try to affect someone else's behavior they run a risk. In fact, they run several risks—of being ineffective in that attempt, of outright failure, and of inciting the other party to rebellion.

The risk of which we speak, however, is not whether the attempt works, or how well; rather, it is whether the attempt is ethical. Is there misconduct on the part of the change manager or agent? Does the attempt lead to the abuse of members of the recipient group in some way? These sorts of questions concern the ethics of a change attempt.

Thomas H. Fitzgerald offers some cautions to those who would attempt to change organizations.[3] He reminds us that studies of other cultures are often influenced by the investigator's own cultural values and biases and suggests that change managers and change agents also may be guilty of arrogance:

> Perhaps workers have the right to be left alone, to do their jobs without M.S.W. counselors or other accredited professionals' training them in correct thinking and tinkering with local sentiments, notions, and prejudices. If I view as essentially insulting an uninvited attempt to make me over into someone else's vision of a better human being, should it be any less offensive to the hired hands?[4]

Fitzgerald also questions whether resistance to change should be viewed as the expression of a "frozen" attitude; doesn't that perspective portray the person holding that attitude as somehow wrong? Don't workers have the right to maintain their long-held values and purposes? Can't workers question any proposed changes that would fundamentally alter the organization's very identity? And at the practical level, perhaps resistance says something important about organizational realities. If so, shouldn't management examine them?[5]

The intent of the present chapter is to bring this book to a close by considering some ways in which ethical problems can arise for change managers and their agents. We begin by suggesting that one of the most important ways concerns the impact that change programs can have on three main aspects of justice.[6] Here's what we mean: Since organizational change usually involves redistribution of resources, issues of *distributive justice* can easily arise. Was the redistribution performed fairly—that is, equitably, equally, and in accordance with people's different needs?

Another issue in justice is whether the various parties to the change had sufficient "voice" in the matter—that is, did they have the opportunity to construct the policies and procedures that form the organization's new ground rules? And is a valid and working system of recourse available to those who challenge a change program's components or outcomes? These are questions of *procedural justice.*

Finally, did management deal with employees justly, by honestly giving explanations ("accounts") of why a change is needed, why a particular change is called for, why certain recipient groups and strategies were selected, and what outcomes were likely to occur? This is all a matter of *interactional justice.*

Failure to attend to matters of justice can get change managers and their agents into a great deal of ethical hot water. Louis P. White and Kevin C. Wooten have suggested that five major types of ethical difficulties are misrepresentation and collusion, misuse of data in change efforts, manipulation and coercion, value and goal conflict, and technical ineptness.[7] For our purposes, we have summarized the areas in which ethical problems can arise in four categories: strategy selection, recipient selection, managerial responsibilities, and manipulation.

Selection of a Change Strategy

As we have seen, a number of different strategies are available to a change manager: facilitative, informational, attitudinal, and political. We have also seen that different strategies are called for under different circumstances, depending on such things as the time available, how extensive the proposed change is to be, various characteristics of the recipient group, and the resources available to those wanting to implement the change.

These strategies and criteria were discussed in earlier chapters as constituting a fairly rational decision process for the change manager, a process by which the criteria were assessed and the corresponding strategies selected. Ethical problems come up when other criteria are introduced into the strategy-selection decision. For example, does the change agent have a vested interest in getting a pet educational program adopted, and so pushes for a strategy that will rely on that program? Does the change manager have a value bias toward a particular strategy—a bias that does not allow other strategies to be given a fair hearing?

On the latter point, Warren Bennis has reported a case called "the undercover change agent."[8] In this case an attempt was made to use a strategy that was contrary to the philosophy and desires of the firm's president. Upon discovering that his wishes had been contradicted, the CEO fired the change agent. The agent's general bias in favor of the strategy prevented him from perceiving the context of the change attempt clearly. It simply was not responsible in this case to go against the express desires of the company president. Management was poorly served, and so too were the recipients.

The other side of the coin is equally problematic. For example, it is possible that in another case an agent selects a strategy called for by his or her reading of the circumstances. However, the firm's president, having her own agenda, presses for a different strategy. Here, the agent may get fired just as abruptly as in the previous case. Bennis also provides an example of this situation.[9] It seems that a large Swiss company began a change effort that was rooted in the values of egalitarianism: full participation by all, equal treatment of employees regardless of seniority or organizational position, and so forth. These values clashed with those of the company president's Swiss army training—especially the idea that one's position in the organization hierarchy was all-important. As in the previous instance, this clash caused the program to be terminated. In both cases—although for opposite reasons—the aims of the change program were not met.

Selection of the Change Recipient

Managers are charged with investing, employing, and protecting the organization's resources. *Steward* is a classic term used to describe this basic responsibility. The obligations of stewardship often cause managers to design and implement changes. Unfortunately, this is often done with little attention paid to the wishes of those who will be affected directly by the changes. For example, it is generally contrary to most organizational philosophies to give employees a choice as to whether they wish to participate.

There is a potential ethical difficulty here. Should people be required or otherwise coerced into joining a team-building project, for example, when they do not wish to do so? Should employees, even at the managerial level, be required to participate in a change program that is contrary to some aspect of their personal philosophy? For example, the president of a small software-development firm had all of her managers attend a series of company-sponsored talks. These talks were given on the premises and on company time. They were offered by a well-known consultant and were peppered with his personal religious values. Because of this content, one manager declined to attend. As a result, he acquired a reputation for being uncooperative, of "not being a team player." Was this fair? More to our point here, was it right? What were his bosses' responsibilities and obligations in the face of his action? A companion ethical difficulty concerns not the right of employees to choose to participate, but their ability to do so. In this case, members of potential recipient groups can choose to participate *only if* they possess the requisite knowledge *beforehand.*

Information and access to information are central to change efforts' being seen as just and ethical. Consequently, consider these questions: How much information does ethical behavior require the change manager to impart? Is full and complete disclosure the only purely ethical action a manager can take? On the other hand, how well would anyone be served by full disclosure of management's concerns and intents, all at once, with no warning or preparation? What if there were a desire to proceed in some secrecy so as not to alert competitors? Would full and immediate disclosure still be indicated?

These questions indicate the essence of the ethical problem. On the one hand, a full and complete sharing of change-program information seems the honorable and right thing for management to do. On the other hand, such sharing is frequently dysfunctional, not only for management's objectives but for members of the recipient group as well.

Change Management's Responsibilities

The third major area of ethical difficulty concerns the responsibilities of change managers and their agents. These responsibilities involve three key issues: of goals, beliefs, and assumptions; of value systems; and of the nature of the manager-agent contract.

First, how compatible are the goals, beliefs, and assumptions of those designing and conducting the change with those of the recipients? Is it management's responsibility to disclose its goals, beliefs, and assumptions? Is it management's responsibility even to examine this issue? Or is it merely a technical matter, with the responsibility falling to the change agent to assess compatibility?

On the other side, what are the recipients' obligations in this regard? Are they responsible for fully disclosing their goals and beliefs about a proposed change? Or is it all a type of stud poker game, each side waiting to see what card the other puts down next?

The second responsibility issue is raised by the fact that managing change is not a value-neutral activity. In introducing this chapter we noted that change managers have value systems that almost certainly affect their management of a change program. Their agents do also, which affect their efforts to implement the program. And members of change-recipient groups have value systems that influence their response to a change attempt. The issue therefore is what values—or more practically, *whose* values—are to guide the change process.

The same questions posed a moment ago apply to this values issue: Should management make certain that the various value systems are placed on the table, that is, are acknowledged, articulated, and discussed so that everyone is aware of them? Or is this the agent's task? Or again, do the change recipients share in this responsibility?

A number of years ago David Hapgood and Meridan Bennett issued a scathing critique of the popular Peace Corps.[10] The critique rested on their indictment of idealistic and arrogant Americans striding into Third World countries determined to work changes in the image of American values and objectives. Would a similar indictment of many large-scale change programs in modern corporations and agencies ring equally true?

Finally, the third responsibility issue concerns the nature of the contract between change management and its agent(s). Contracts can be, of course, either formal or informal, explicit or implicit. Whatever form they take, contracts usually refer to such aspects of the change program as what is to be done, by whom, by when, and for how much.

Regardless of the exact wording of a contract, however, several unanswered questions usually remain. For example: Whom does the change agent serve? Is it the manager, or the organization as a whole? Certain key members of the organization? Or key members of the recipient group? How are conflicts in goals, beliefs, or values to be resolved? And finally, is the change agent free to opt out of the whole process if she or he believes that an unsolvable conflict exists?

In summary, then, it is clear that their responsibilities present those who would attempt to change organizations with a number of ethical difficulties. This is true all the way through a change effort, from beginning to end. Using a somewhat generic set of stages through which a change progresses, White and Wooten have identified several of these difficulties, shown in table 10.1.

Manipulation

The final area of ethical difficulty is the one that is probably the most common, the most discussed, and in fact the most important: manipulation. Manipulation is fundamentally an exercise of power. In particular, we can define it as an exercise in which power holders influence the behavior of others with-

Table 10.1
Possible Ethical Difficulties in Various Stages of Organizational Change

Stage	Purpose	Role of Change Agent	Role of Client System	Ethical Difficulty
Initiation	To share initial information	To provide information on background expertise and experience	To provide information on possible needs, relevant problems, interest of management, and representational politics	Misrepresentation of consultant's skill base and background; misrepresentation of organizational interest
Clarification	To elaborate on initiation stage	To provide details of education, licensure, operative values, and optimum working conditions	To provide a detailed history of special problems, personnel, marketplace, internal culture, and organizational politics	Inappropriate determination of who the client is; avoidance of reality testing; inappropriate determination of value orientation
Specification/ agreement	To specify needs, interest, fees, services, working conditions, and arrangements	To specify actual services, fees to be charged, time frame, and actual working conditions	To specify whose needs are to be addressed, goals, objectives, and possible evaluative criteria or end-state outcomes	Inappropriate structuring of the relationship; inappropriate definition of change problem; collusion to exclude outside parties
Diagnosis	To obtain an unfiltered and undistorted view of the organization's problems and processes, and to pinpoint change recipients and criteria	To collect data concerning organizational problems and processes, and to provide feedback	To assist change agent in data collection	Avoidance of problems; misuse of data; distortion and deletion of data; ownership of data; voluntary consent, confidentiality
Goal setting/ action planning	To establish the specific goals to be pursued and strategies to be used	To agree mutually with the client system on the goals and strategies to be used	To agree mutually with the change agent on goals and strategies to be used	Inappropriate choice of intervention goal and recipients; inappropriate choice of operative means; inappropriate scope of intervention
Intervention	To intervene into ongoing behaviors, structures, and processes	To intervene at specific targets, at a specific depth	To invest the energy and resources required by planned intervention	Assimilation into culture; inappropriate depth of intervention; coercion vs. choice, freedom, and consent to participate; environmental manipulation

Evaluation	To determine the effectiveness of the intervention strategies, energy, and resources used, as well as the agent-client system relationship	To gather data on specified recipients and report findings to the client system	To analyze the evaluation data and determine effectiveness of the intervention	Misuse of data; deletion and distortion of data
Alteration	To modify change strategies, depth, level, goals, recipient, or resources utilized, if necessary	To make alterations to meet original goals, or to develop new mutual goals and strategies with client system	To make known needs and expectations, and to provide the context for a modification of the original agreement, if necessary	Failure to change; lack of flexibility; adoption of inappropriate strategy
Continuation/ maintenance	To monitor and maintain ongoing strategies, provide periodic checks, and continue intervention based on original or altered plans and strategies	To specify the parameters of the continuation or maintenance of the intervention	To provide or allocate the resources required to maintain or continue the intervention	Inappropriate reduction of dependency; redundancy of effort; withholding of services
Termination	To have the change agent disengage from the client system and establish a long-term monitoring system	To fulfill the role agreed on in previous stages and evaluate overall effectiveness from feedback from the client system	To determine the organization's state of health and whether it has developed an adaptive change process	Inappropriate transition of change effort to internal sources; premature exit; failure to monitor change

Source: Adapted from L. P. White & K. C. Wooten (1983), Ethical dilemmas in various stages of organizational development, *Academy of Management Review*, 8, p. 695.

out making explicit the behavior that they want them to perform. This can happen either directly, through some sort of action, or indirectly, as through the use of symbols.[11]

By this definition, it is virtually impossible to design a change strategy that does not have some element of manipulation in it. For example, attempts to influence (or "manage," as some would have it) an organization's culture are doubtless fraught with the danger of such an ethical problem. Remembering that an organization's culture consists of its norms, beliefs, values, core assumptions, and so forth, attempts by management to change these would have to be amazingly explicit and public to avoid charges of manipulation.

In fact, even when merely selecting one strategy over another, a change manager is making trade-offs that will limit the options of the change recipients. Hence, some manipulation, albeit subtle, is taking place at the outset. Simply emphasizing the positive features of a proposed change and downplaying the negative aspects is a form of manipulation. Deciding which information will be transmitted to whom, on the premise noted earlier that it is impossible to provide full and complete disclosure and to transmit 100 percent of the available information to 100 percent of the potentially affected—this too is manipulation.

Is it possible to avoid *all* manipulative behavior? We've already said that the answer to this question is no. Thomas G. Cummings and Christopher G. Worley put the problem succinctly: The manager is placed "on two horns of a dilemma: (1) any attempt to change is in itself a change and thereby a manipulation, no matter how slight, and (2) there exists no formula or method to structure a change situation so that such manipulation can be totally absent."[12]

SOME ETHICAL GUIDELINES

So what is a manager to do? We believe there are in fact some things that can be done to reduce the unethical aspects of change management. For one thing, an organization may decide to develop formal standards for ensuring and guiding ethical behavior. Such standards apply not only to the management of change, but to all actions taken in the name of the organization. Allied Chemical, Boeing, Champion International, General Dynamics, General Electric, General Mills, GTE, Hewlett-Packard, IBM, Johnson & Johnson, Raytheon, and Whirlpool have all developed programs that focus their people's attention on ethical behavior.[13] Some of these programs spell out all details as precisely as possible; others are more informal, providing general statements that outline appropriate conduct in different circumstances. An example of the latter is the U.S. federal government's code of ethics, portrayed in table 10.2.

Regardless of how specific or vague their organization's code of ethics, or even if one doesn't exist, change managers and their agents can increase the likelihood of designing and carrying out a change program ethically if they *regularly* and *consistently* follow a few simple guidelines:[14]

Table 10.2
Code of Ethics for Government Service

Any person in federal government service should:

I.	Put loyalty to the highest moral principles and to country above loyalty to persons, party, or government department
II.	Uphold the Constitution, laws, and regulations of the United States and of all governments therein and never be a party to their evasion
III.	Give a full day's labor for a full day's pay, giving earnest effort and best thought to the performance of duties
IV.	Seek to find and employ more efficient and economical ways of getting tasks accomplished
V.	Never discriminate unfairly by the dispensing of special favors or privileges to anyone, whether for remuneration or not; and never accept, for himself or herself or for family members. Favors or benefits under circumstances which might be construed by reasonable persons as influencing the performance of governmental duties
VI.	Make no private promises of any kind binding upon the duties of office, since a government employee has no private word which can be binding on public duty
VII.	Engage in no business with the government, either directly or indirectly, which is inconsistent with the conscientious performance of governmental duties
VIII.	Never use any information gained confidentially in the performance of governmental duties as a means of making private profit
IX.	Expose corruption wherever discovered
X.	Uphold these principles, ever conscious that public office is a public trust.

Source: O.C.G.A. 45-10-2 12/3/01

- Identify the people who will be affected by any change.
- Identify the costs and benefits of various alternative change decisions to those people.
- Consider the relevant moral *expectations* that surround a particular change decision, such as identifying one or more objects of change, selecting recipient groups, selecting strategies, and so forth. These expectations might stem from professional norms, laws, organizational ethics codes, and principles such as honest communication and fair treatment.
- Be familiar with the common ethical dilemmas that are faced by change managers or change agents in your organization, industry, or profession.
- Discuss ethical matters, both with those who might be affected and with others. Don't think ethics without talking about ethics.

Of course, change managers should not depend solely on their organization's code of ethics. As the preceding guidelines suggest, they should be committed to acting ethically in any case. Following extensive study and discussion, the Human Systems Development Consortium has developed a set of ethical guidelines that anyone responsible for designing and implementing change could fruitfully follow.[15] The guidelines concern conduct relative to one's responsibility for professional development and competence, responsibility to clients and significant others, responsibility to the profession, and social responsibility. The complete statement is reproduced in this chapter's appendix.

Beyond the general guidelines shown in the guidelines here and in the appendix, Herbert C. Kelman has argued that the way to avoid unethical behavior, especially manipulation, is to maximize the freedom of choice for members of the recipient group.[16] We don't mean that in the reality of day-to-day organizational life every change recipient can (or even should) be given complete freedom of choice to participate or not in a change program. We do mean, however, that management should make sure that if anything, it errs on the side of giving members of change-recipient groups too much information, too much knowledge about options, rather than too little. (The same also applies to a group member's ability to voice concerns or to raise questions.)

In addition, Kelman argues, the problem of inherent manipulation can be confronted effectively by means of three steps. The three steps, and the corresponding conduct of change managers, are outlined in table 10.3.

First, the change manager and change agent need to be clearly aware of their own value systems, their biases, and the ways in which those values and biases intrude into the change-management process. This intrusion can take place when they initially identify a problem or select a change strategy, or when the change's consequences are felt by the recipients.

Table 10.3
Steps to Reduce the Manipulative Aspect of Change Management

Desirable Step	Change-Management Conduct
1. Increase awareness in manipulation	• Identify own values to self and to others • Evaluate the organization or unit that will be affected; consider how, by whom, and in what context the change will be felt
2. Build protection against manipulation	• Minimize management's values and recognize recipients' values as critical to the change process • Help recipient members protect their interests
3. Enhance recipient's freedom of choice	• Help and encourage recipients to increase their range of choices and their abilities to choose

Source: Adapted from H. C. Kelman (1965), Manipulation of human behavior: An ethical dilemma for the social scientist, *Journal of Social Issues*, 21 (April), pp. 31–46.

Too often, employees' values are confronted and evaluated only as they relate to organizational goals rather than for their inherent worth. Management thus finds itself in the position of attempting to shape the values of the so-called human resources to conform to organizational values (as perceived by management, of course).[17] Kelman's second step, therefore, calls for procedures to be built into the change process that will provide a measure of protection against manipulation. One way to do so is for management to recognize and consider change recipients' values and desires, while at the same time explicitly reducing the impact of their own.

The third step is an enrichment of step two. As Kelman puts it, "It is important to go beyond providing protection and resistance against manipulation that would encroach on the [recipients'] freedom of choice. The actual *enhancement* of freedom of choice should, ideally, be one of the positive goals of any influence attempt."[18]

There's no doubt: These steps are heavy-duty for the average manager trying to supervise the rapid implementation of a planned change, while at the same time trying to keep production at a competitive level. Still, Kelman is right: The ideal way to avoid the kind of ethical dilemma posed here is to bring those affected into the change process as completely as possible. In short, "An effective way to resolve [ethical difficulties] is to make the change effort as open as possible, with the *free consent and knowledge of the individuals involved.*"[19]

CONCLUSION: A NORMATIVE COMMENT

A reading of most current textbooks in management, organizational behavior, human-resource management, organization theory, or organization design will confirm the idea that traditionally, organizations serve three core values: rationality, technology, and efficiency.[20] Managers of change probably have served these values as well as any. We conclude this book by suggesting five alternative values to guide the management of change.

Before proceeding, however, we note that the core values identified by the Population Task Force of the Institute of Society, Ethics and the Life Sciences should be preserved and promoted:[21] freedom, or the capacity and opportunity to make choices and act on them; justice, or the equitable distribution of positive and negative rewards; and welfare, or the promotion of the vital interests of the larger society.

Such values make a great deal of sense as they relate to the external societal context in which organizations operate. At the managerial level, however, more pertinent values need to be identified. The first value we recommend is that of *integrity*. By this we mean that the change manager and agent should always remember what their responsibilities are, to whom, and why. In the early 1970s, when the war in Vietnam was still raging, a friend of one of the authors was attempting to obtain a research grant. This scientist was doing biochemical research on the viruses of cherries, an issue of some importance to his region of the country. His grant proposal was turned down by several national foundations. Finally, a military branch of the federal government offered to fund his research—providing that he changed his research program from cherries to *viruses of rice.* Although he was not a geopolitical genius, this biochemist knew that he did not want to participate in such a change in his program.

The second value we call *pathfinding.* By this we mean the need for change managers to do more than merely go down customary and well-worn paths. They need to do more than simply solve problems; they also need to find them. A colleague of ours has been a professor of engineering for several years. He recently said to us, "In engineering, we do a great job of teaching our students to solve problems *that other people pose,* but we do a lousy job of teaching them to find their own problems." Could the same be said of management education? In any event, the point is that it is not enough for managers to design and implement a change in response to a problem that suddenly confronts them. Effective change management also means finding—or even creating—those paths that will enable the organization and its people to develop and prosper.

Third on our list of recommended values is *learning.* In a rapidly changing world, both managers and nonmanagers need to be continually growing, developing, and improving. This can happen only through an enduring commitment to learning, and the commitment needs to be both personal and organizational. Individuals should devote a substantial part of their energies to learning, and organizations need to be major sponsors of all sorts of education and training. After all, when students graduate from school it's called "commencement," not "termination." Without a commitment to learning, there is no effective way to anticipate and respond to change.

The fourth value is that of *commitment.* Change managers and their agents need continually to ask themselves: What's important? What do I really want to accomplish? What values and goals do I really want to further?

Managing is a stressful business. Most managers are caught in a web of conflicting pressures: to be a successful employee, to be a loving spouse, to be an effective boss, to be a caring and nurturing parent—the list of roles is virtually endless. Several years ago a young supervisor acquaintance of ours was given a dramatic promotion to middle management. He found himself involved in a great deal of travel and extra effort as he worked himself into his new position. One night he came home late after a particularly long week to find that his three-year-old had been extremely upset and crying all evening. He told us that after being calmed down, the youngster finally sobbed, "I don't want you to be a 'boss'; I want you to be a daddy."

The point of this anecdote is this: One cannot hope to confront such a plea successfully without a clear idea of what one is committed to, and why. Managing change often (perhaps always) involves conflicting demands and responsibilities, usually between improving some aspect of the organization and maintaining the comfort of the status quo. Overcoming the stress of such conflicting responsibilities requires a clear understanding of their relative importance.

Finally, we suggest the value of *stewardship,* which in this context means maintaining, promoting, and improving the vital interests of the larger society. We used this term earlier in describing the manager as steward. But managers are stewards not only of their organization's resources. Owing to the incredible presence, power, even dominance of organizations in modern society, they are stewards of nothing less than the planet's resources. A corresponding responsibility accompanies this role. In other words, it is not enough to make decisions that effectively utilize the capital and labor that belong directly to the organization. Managers must also recognize that their decisions can profoundly affect resources that inhere to the larger community. Those, too, must be part of the decision calculus. There may be no better example of stewardship and the other four values than the late Katharine Graham of the Washington Post Company (see "Focus On: Katharine Graham and *The Washington Post*").

Focus On: Katharine Graham and *The Washington Post*

In 1963 Katharine Graham was a forty-six-year-old mother of four when she assumed control of *The Washington Post* following her husband's suicide. By her own admission, she possessed very modest journalism experience and little business knowledge; however, in her thirty years as chair of the board she turned a mediocre paper into an American institution while transforming the landscape of American journalism. During her tenure, the company went public and saw a twentyfold increase in revenues.

She did not seize this unexpected role with the intention of systematically building the Post Company's bottom line and the paper's stature to rival that of *The New York Times.* Her metamorphosis into savvy businesswoman—the first woman to lead a Fortune 500 company—mirrored the transformation of the paper. The two histories cannot be separated.

Two momentous decisions—steeped in values and ethics—made by her in the early 1970s could have brought financial ruin to the company as the *Post* withstood threats of criminal prosecution and enormous pressure from the White House.

First, the government attempted to block the publication of the Pentagon Papers, a secret report on the United States's involvement in the Vietnam War. With *The New York Times* already barred by court order from publishing excerpts from the report, Graham gave the final go-ahead, against the advice of lawyers and senior managers, to publish the *Post*'s own excerpted version. What followed was a landmark freedom-of-the-press win in the Supreme Court for the *Post* and the *Times.*

Second, she did not intervene as *Post* reporters—notably Carl Bernstein and Bob Woodward—followed the Watergate scandal that led to the resignation of then-president Richard Nixon. As the story unfolded, the White House threatened to not renew several licenses for TV stations owned by the Post Company. In a telling example of character, though she could have demanded the information, Graham died never knowing the identity of Deep Throat.

Though considered one of the most powerful women in the world, she also became a good study in leadership—applying intelligence, toughness, a willingness to listen and learn (Warren Buffett was a mentor), and an ability to judge character. It was her belief that journalistic excellence *and* profitability went hand-in-hand. She hired good people and gave reporters the independence necessary to cover the story. The *Post* (and *Newsweek)* reporters had her unconditional support. As Ben Bradlee, the famed executive editor hired by Graham, once said, "Katharine had the guts of a burglar" (Quinn, 2001).

Sources: M. Berger (2001), Katharine Graham, Washington Post executive, dies at 84, *New York Times,* July 17, on-line edition at www.nytimes.com; R. G. Kaiser (2001), The storied Mrs. Graham, *The Washington Post,* July 18, p. C1; Katharine Graham [editorial] (2001), *Washington Post,* July 18, p. A3; S. Quinn, What a spectacular dame (2001), *The Washington Post,* July 17, on-line edition at www.washingtonpost.com; J. Y. Smith & N. Epstein (2001), Katharine Graham dies at 84; led Post Company, *The Washington Post,* July 17, on-line edition at www.washingtonpost.com.

Books and movies also provide myriad examples of change, in general, and what we mean by stewardship, specifically. Two films, *Pleasantville* and *Chocolat,* are particularly noteworthy.

In both movies, individuals—by their very introduction into a community—are catalysts for societal change. The changes introduced are vivid and liberating. These communities spring to life in new and unexpected ways, much in the same way organizations should become more motivating and productive following planned change efforts. Though one can quibble with Hollywood's penchant for good-overcoming-evil plots and happy endings, what is correctly portrayed in these movies is that the change process is not always positive. There is mess. There are missteps. There is even discomfort and pain. And, of course, there is resistance.

The subplots of resistance are strong in both films. Powerful forces—most notably the mayors of both towns—are at the forefront of all-out efforts to stop the change, sometimes at great personal cost. What distinguishes the "resistors" from the "change agents," we would argue, is the existence of a reflective nature or conscience. While exhibiting integrity and being proactive, the change agents do question their roles in the change process. They are aware of how they themselves are changing. They are at times conflicted by their strong belief in the inherent goodness or correctness of the changes, and thus, they question the very means used to bring about change. What is important? What is proper? What is right?

Managers, including managers of change, need to take into account the fact that they are changing, manipulating, and rearranging a variety of elements—human and nonhuman alike. They need to do so thoughtfully, carefully, and with respect.

NOTES

1. This memo, issued to all Salomon senior executives, was reported in an SEC filing in 1991. It was reproduced in R. R. Sims (2000), Changing an organization's culture under new leadership, *Journal of Business Ethics,* 17 (May), pp. 65–78.
2. Ibid.
3. T. H. Fitzgerald (1988), Can change in organizational culture really be managed? *Organizational Dynamics,* 17 (Autumn), pp. 4–15.
4. Ibid., p. 13.
5. J. Goldstein (1988), A far-from-equilibrium systems approach to resistance to change, *Organizational Dynamics,* 17 (Autumn), pp. 16–26.
6. This discussion is based on A. T. Cobb, R. Folger, & K. Wooten (1993), Establishing justice in times of organizational change, *Academy of Management Proceedings,* pp. 191–195.
7. L. P. White & K. C. Wooten (1983), Ethical dilemmas in various stages of organizational development, *Academy of Management Review,* 8 (4), pp. 690–697.
8. W. Bennis (1969), *Organization development: Its nature, origins, and prospects.* Reading, MA: Addison–Wesley, pp. 67–70.
9. W. Bennis (1977), Bureaucracy and social change: An anatomy of a training failure. In P. H. Mirvis & D. N. Berg (Eds.), *Failures in organizational development and change: Cases and essays for learning,* New York: Wiley, pp. 191–215.
10. D. Hapgood & M. Bennett (1968), *Agents of change,* Boston: Little, Brown, pp. 23–42.
11. G. A. Theodorson & A. G. Theodorson (1960), *A modern dictionary of sociology,* New York: Thomas Y. Crowell, p. 241.
12. T. G. Cummings & C. G. Worley (2001), *Organization development and change* (7th ed.), Cincinnati: South-Western, p. 60.
13. J. B. Barney & R. W. Griffin (1992), *The management of organizations,* Boston: Houghton Mifflin, p. 724; R. B. Dunham & J. L. Pierce (1989), *Management,* Glenview, IL: Scott, Foresman, p. 125; H. Weihrich & H. Koontz (1993), *Management* (10th ed.), New York: McGraw-Hill, p. 73.
14. Based on J. A. Waters & F. Bird (1992), "A note on what a well-educated manager should be able to do with respect to moral issues in management," unpublished manuscript, cited in G. Johns (1992), *Organizational behavior,* New York: HarperCollins, pp. 440–441.
15. W. Gellermann, M. S. Frankel, & R. I. Ladenson (1990), *Values and ethics in organization and human systems development: Responding to ethical dilemmas in professional life,* San Francisco: Jossey-Bass, pp. 378–388.

16. H. C. Kelman (1965), Manipulation of human behavior: An ethical dilemma for the social scientist, *Journal of Social Issues,* 21 (April), pp. 31–46.

17. W. G. Scott & T. R. Mitchell (1985), The moral failure of management education, *Chronicle of Higher Education,* December 11, p. 35.

18. Kelman, Manipulation of human behavior, p. 41.

19. Cummings & Worley, *Organization development and change,* p. 60 (emphasis in the original).

20. With respect to the core value of rationality, see M. Weber (1946), *From Max Weber: Essays in sociology,* trans. H. H. Gerth & C. Wright Mills, New York: Oxford University Press, pp. 196–244; to that of technology, see J. Ellul (1964), *The technological society,* New York: Alfred A. Knopf; and to that of efficiency, see H. Fayol (1949), *General and industrial management,* trans. Constance Storrs, London: Pitman.

21. Population Task Force of the Institute of Society, Ethics and the Life Sciences (1970), *Ethics, population and the American tradition,* a study prepared for the Commission on Population Growth and the American Future by the Institute of Society, Ethics and the Life Sciences, Hastings-on-Hudson, NY. Cited in G. Zaltman & R. Duncan (1977), *Strategies for planned change,* New York: John Wiley, p. 332.

Appendix: Ethical Guidelines for Change Managers and Their Agents

I. Responsibility to Myself

A. Act with integrity; be authentic and true to myself.

B. Strive continually for self-knowledge and personal growth.

C. Recognize my personal needs and desires, and when they conflict with other responsibilities, seek whole-win resolutions.

D. Assert my own interests in ways that are fair and equitable to me as well as to my clients and their stakeholders.

II. Responsibility for Professional Development and Competence

A. Accept responsibility for the consequences of my actions and make reasonable efforts to ensure that my services are properly used; terminate my services if they are not properly used, and do what I can to see that any abuses are corrected.

B. Develop and maintain my individual competence and establish cooperative relations with other professionals.

1. Develop the broad range of my own competencies. These include:

a. Knowledge of theory and practice in

1. Applied behavioral science generally.

2. Leadership, management, administration, organizational behavior, system behavior, and organization/system development specifically.

3. Labor union issues, such as collective bargaining, contracting, and quality of working life (QWL).

4. Multicultural issues, including issues of color and gender.

5. Cross-cultural issues, including issues related to my own ethnocentric tendencies and to differences and diversity within and between countries.

6. Values and ethics in general and how they apply to both the behavior of my client system and my own practice.

7. Other fields of knowledge and practice relevant to the area(s) on which I concentrate.

b. Ability to

1. Act effectively with individuals; groups; and large, complex systems.

2. Provide consultation using theory and methods of the applied behavioral sciences.

3. Cope with the apparent contradiction in applying behavioral science that arises when my "science" is too particular or too theoretical to be applicable or when my real approach is intuitive and not clearly grounded in science.

4. Articulate theory and direct its application, including creation of learning experiences for individuals; small and large groups; and large, complex systems.

2. Establish collegial and cooperative relations with other professionals. These include:
   a. Using colleagues and consultants to provide me with feedback or suggestions about my own development and to minimize the effects of my blind spots.
   b. Creating partnerships with colleagues to enhance my effectiveness in serving clients whose needs are greater than I can serve alone.

C. Recognize my personal needs and desires and deal with them responsibly in the performance of my professional roles and duties.

D. Practice within the limits of my competence, culture, and experience in providing services and using techniques.

1. Neither seek nor accept assignments outside my limits without clear understanding by clients when exploration at the edge of my competence is reasonable.
2. Refer clients to other professionals when appropriate.
3. Consult with people who are knowledgeable about the unique conditions of clients whose activities involve specific areas in which I am inexperienced or not knowledgeable:
   a. In special functional areas (such as marketing, engineering, or R&D)
   b. In certain industries or institutions (such as mining, aerospace, health care, education, or government)
   c. In multicultural settings (such as when I practice in settings in which there is significant diversity in the race, ethnicity, or gender of the people involved)

E. Practice in cultures different from my own only with consultation from people native to or knowledgeable about those specific cultures.

III. Responsibility to Clients and Significant Others

A. Serve the long-term well-being of my client systems and their stakeholders.

1. Be aware of the beliefs and values relevant to serving my clients, including my own, my profession's, my culture's, and those of the people with whom I work (personal, organizational, and cultural).
2. Be prepared to make explicit my beliefs, values, and ethics as a professional.
3. Avoid automatic confirmation of predetermined conclusions about the client's situation or what needs to be done by either the client or myself.
4. Explore the possible implications of any intervention for all stakeholders likely to be significantly affected; help all stakeholders while developing and implementing approaches, programs, and the like, if they wish help and I am able to give it.
5. Maintain balance in the timing, pace, and magnitude of planned change so as to support a mutually beneficial relationship between the system and its environment.

B. Conduct any professional activity, program, or relationship in ways that are honest, responsible, and appropriately open.

1. Inform people with whom I work about any activity or procedure in which I ask their participation.
   a. Inform them about sponsorship, purpose and goals, my role and strategy, costs, anticipated outcomes, limitations, and risks.

b. Inform them in a way that supports their freedom of choice about their participation in activities initiated by me; also acknowledge that it may be appropriate for me to undertake activities initiated by recognized authorities in which participants do not have full freedom of choice.

c. Alert them to implications and risks when they are from cultures other than my own or when I am at the edge of my competence.

d. Ask help of the client system in making relevant cultural differences explicit.

2. Seek optimum participation by people with whom I work at every step of the process, including managers, labor unions, and workers' representatives.

3. Encourage and enable people to provide for themselves the services I provide rather than foster continued reliance on me; encourage, foster, and support self-education and self-development by individuals, groups, and all other human systems.

4. Develop, publish, and use assessment techniques that promote the welfare and best interests of clients and participants; guard against the misuse of assessment techniques and results.

5. Provide for my own accountability by evaluating and assessing the effects of my work.

a. Make all reasonable efforts to determine if my activities have accomplished the agreed-upon goals and have not had other undesirable consequences; seek to undo any undesirable consequences, and do not attempt to cover them up; use such experiences as learning opportunities.

b. Actively solicit and respond with an open mind to feedback regarding my work and seek to improve my work accordingly.

6. Cease work with a client when it becomes clear that the client is not benefiting or the contract has been completed; do not accept or continue work under a contract if I cannot do so in ways consistent with the values and ethics outlined in these guidelines.

C. Establish mutual agreement on a fair contract covering services and remuneration.

1. Ensure mutual understanding and agreement about the services to be performed; do not shift from that agreement without both a clearly defined professional rationale for making the shift and the informed consent of the clients and participants; withdraw from the agreement if circumstances beyond my control prevent proper fulfillment.

2. Ensure mutual understanding and agreement by putting the contract in writing to the extent feasible, yet recognize that:

a. The spirit of professional responsibility encompasses more than the letter of the contract.

b. Some contracts are necessarily incomplete because complete information is not available at the outset.

c. Putting the contract in writing may be neither necessary nor desirable.

3. Safeguard the best interests of the client, the profession, and the public by making sure that financial arrangements are fair and in keeping with appropriate statutes, regulations, and professional standards.

D. Deal with conflicts constructively and minimize conflicts of interest.

1. Fully inform the client of my opinions about serving similar or competing organizations; be clear with myself, my clients, and other concerned stakeholders about my loyalties

and responsibilities when conflicts of interest arise; keep parties informed of these conflicts; cease work with the client if the conflicts cannot be adequately resolved.

2. Seek to act impartially when involved in conflicts among parties in the client system; help them resolve their conflicts themselves, without taking sides; if it becomes necessary to change my role from that of impartial consultant, do so explicitly; cease work with the client if necessary.
3. Identify and respond to any major differences in professionally relevant values or ethics between my clients and myself; be prepared to cease work, with explanation of my reasons, if necessary.
4. Accept differences in the expectations and interests of different stakeholders and realize that those differences cannot always be reconciled; take a whole-win approach to the resolution of differences whenever possible so that the greatest good of the whole is served, but allow for exceptions based on more fundamental principles.
5. Work cooperatively with other internal and external consultants serving the same client systems and resolve conflicts in terms of the balanced best interests of the client system and all its stakeholders; make appropriate arrangements with other internal and external consultants about how to share responsibilities.
6. Seek consultation and feedback from neutral third parties in cases of conflict involving my clients, other consultants, or any of the systems' various stakeholders and myself.

E. Define and protect confidentiality in my client relationships.

1. Make limits of confidentiality clear to clients and participants.
2. Reveal information accepted in confidence only to appropriate or agreed-upon recipients or authorities.
3. Use information obtained during professional work in writings, lectures, or other public forums only with prior consent or when disguised so that it is impossible from my presentations alone to identify the individuals or systems with whom I have worked.
4. Make adequate provisions for maintaining confidentiality in the storage and disposal of records; make provisions for responsibly preserving records in the event of my retirement or disability.

F. Make public statements of all kinds accurately, including promotion and advertising, and give service as advertised.

1. Base public statements providing professional opinions or information on scientifically acceptable findings and techniques as much as possible, with full recognition of the limits and uncertainties of such evidence.
2. Seek to help people make informed choices when they refer to statements I make as part of promotion or advertising.
3. Deliver services as advertised and do not shift without a clear professional rationale and the informed consent of the participants or clients.

IV. Responsibility to the Profession

A. Contribute to the continuing professional development of other practitioners and of the profession as a whole.

1. Support the development of other professionals by various means, including:
   a. Mentoring with less experienced professionals.

b. Consulting with other colleagues.

c. Participating in reviews of others' practices.

2. Contribute to the body of professional knowledge and skill, including:

a. Sharing ideas, methods, and findings about the effects of my work.

b. Keeping my use of copyright and trade secrets to an appropriate minimum.

B. Promote the sharing of professional knowledge and skill.

1. Grant use of my copyrighted material as freely as possible, subject to a minimum of conditions, including a reasonable price based on professional as well as commercial values.

2. Give credit for the ideas and products of others.

3. Respect the rights of others in the materials they have created.

C. Work with other professionals in ways that exemplify what the profession stands for.

1. Establish mutual understanding and agreement about my relationships, including purposes and goals, roles and responsibilities, fees, and income distribution.

2. Avoid conflicts of interest when possible and resolve conflicts that do arise constructively (following guidelines similar to guideline III-D).

D. Work actively for ethical practice by individuals and organizations engaged in similar activities and, in case of questionable practice, use appropriate channels for dealing with it.

1. Discuss directly and constructively when feasible.

2. Use other means when necessary, including:

a. Joint consultation and feedback (with another professional as a third party).

b. Enforcement procedures of existing professional organizations.

c. Public confrontation.

E. Act in ways that bring credit to the profession and with due regard for colleagues in other professions.

1. Act with sensitivity to the effects my behavior may have on the ability of colleagues to perform as professionals, individually and collectively.

2. Act with due regard for the needs, special competencies, and obligations of colleagues in other professions.

3. Respect the prerogatives and obligations of the institutions or organizations with which these colleagues are associated.

V. Social Responsibility

A. Accept responsibility for and act with sensitivity to the fact that my recommendations and actions may alter the lives and well-being of people within my client systems and within the larger systems of which they are subsystems.

B. Act with awareness of my own cultural filters and with sensitivity to multinational and multicultural differences and their implications.

1. Respect the cultural orientations of the individuals, organizations, communities, countries, and other human systems within which I work, including their customs, beliefs, values, morals, and ethics.

2. Recognize and constructively confront the counterproductive aspects of those cultures whenever feasible, but with alertness to the effects my own cultural orientation may have on my judgments.

C. Promote justice and serve the well-being of all life on earth.

1. Act assertively with my clients to promote justice and well-being including:

a. Constructively confronting discrimination whenever possible.

b. Promoting affirmative action in dealing with the effects of past discrimination.

c. Encouraging fairness in the distribution of the fruits of the system's productivity.

2. Contribute knowledge, skill, and other resources in support of organizations, programs, and activities that seek to improve human welfare.

3. Accept some clients who do not have sufficient resources to pay my full fees and allow them to pay reduced fees or nothing when possible.

4. Engage in self-generated or cooperative endeavors to develop means for helping across cultures.

5. Support the creation and maintenance of cultures that value freedom, responsibility, integrity, self-control, mutual respect, love, trust, openness, authenticity in relationships, participation, and respect for fundamental human rights.

D. Withhold service from clients whose purpose(s) I consider immoral, yet recognize that such service may serve a greater good in the longer run and therefore be acceptable.

E. Act consistently with the ethics of the global scientific community of which my professional community is a part.

Finally, I recognize that accepting these guidelines as a guide for my behavior involves holding myself to standards that may be more exacting than the laws of any countries in which I practice, the ethics of any professional associations to which I belong, or the expectations of any of my clients.

Source: Adapted from W. Gellermann, M. S. Frankel, & R. I. Ladenson (1990), *Values and ethics in organization and human systems development: Responding to ethical dilemmas in professional life,* San Francisco: Jossey-Bass, pp. 378–388.

Selected Bibliography

Axelrod, R. (2001). *Terms of engagement.* San Francisco: Berrett-Koehler.

Beer, M., Eisenstat, R. A., & Spector, B. (1990). Why change programs don't produce change. *Harvard Business Review,* 68, 158–166.

Bennis, W. G., Benne, K. D., & Chin, R. (Eds.). (1961). *The planning of change.* New York: Holt, Rinehart and Winston.

Bolman, L. G., & Deal, T. E. (1997). *Reframing organizations: Artistry, choice, and leadership* (2d ed.). San Francisco: Jossey-Bass, 1997.

Bridges, W. (1991). *Managing transitions.* Reading MA: Addison-Wesley.

Buono, A. F., & Nurick, A. J. (1993). Intervening in the middle: Coping strategies in mergers and acquisitions. *Human Resource Planning,* 15, 19–33.

Burke, W. W., & Church, A. H. (1992). Managing change, leadership style, and intolerance to ambiguity: A survey of organization development practitioners. *Human Resource Management,* 31 (Winter), 301–318.

Church, A. H., & Burke, W. (1993). What are the basic values of OD? *Academy of Management ODC Newsletter* (Winter) 1, 7–12.

Cobb, A. T., Folger, R., & Wooten, K. (1993). Establishing justice in times of organizational change. *Academy of Management Proceedings,* 191–195.

Connor, P. E. (1991). Developing managers: A case study in laying the groundwork. *Journal of Management Development,* 10, 64–76.

Crosby, P. B. *Completeness: Quality for the 21st century.* New York: Penguin.

Cummings, T. G., & Worley, C. G. (2001). *Organizational development and change* (7th ed.). Cincinnati: South-Western.

Deming, W. E. (1982). *Quality, productivity, and competitive position.* Cambridge, MA: MIT Center for Advanced Engineering Study.

Duncan, W. J. (1989). Organizational culture: "Getting a fix" on an elusive concept. *Academy of Management Executive,* 3, 229–236.

Egan, G. (1988). *Change-agent skills b: Managing innovation and change.* San Diego: University Associates.

Federman, I. (1992). Can turnaround be this simple? *Journal of Management Inquiry,* 1, 57–60.

Fitzgerald, T. H. (1988). Can change in organizational culture really be managed? *Organizational Dynamics,* 17 (Autumn), 4–15.

Fox, S., & Amichai-Hamburger, Y. (2001). The power of emotional appeals in promoting organizational change programs. *Academy of Management Review,* 15, 84–95.

Frost, P. J., Moore, L. F., Louis, M. R., Lundberg, C. C., & Martin, J. (Eds.). (1991). *Reframing organizational culture.* Newbury Park, CA: Sage.

Gellermann, W., Frankel, M. S., & Ladenson, R. I. (1990). *Values and ethics in organization and human systems development: Responding to ethical dilemmas in professional life.* San Francisco: Jossey-Bass.

Gilbreath, R. (1990). The myths about winning over resisters to change. *Supervisory Management* (January), 1–2.

Goldstein, J. (1988). A far-from-equilibrium systems approach to resistance to change. *Organizational Dynamics* (Autumn), 16–26.

Goodstein, L. D., & Burke, W. W. (1991). Creating successful organization change. *Organizational Dynamics,* 19, 5–17.

Greiner, L. E. (1967). Patterns of organization change. *Harvard Business Review,* 45 (May-June), 119-130.

Hackman, J. R., & Oldham, G. R. (1980). *Work redesign.* Reading, MA: Addison-Wesley.

Huber, G. P., & Glick, W. H. (Eds.). (1993). *Organizational change and redesign.* New York: Oxford University Press.

Hunt, J. G. (1991). *Leadership: A new synthesis.* Newbury Park, CA: Sage.

Hurst, D. K. (1992). Cautionary tales from the Kalahari: How hunters become herders (and may have trouble changing back again). *Academy of Management Executive,* 5, 74–86.

Huy, Q. N. (1999). Emotional capability, emotional intelligence, and radical change. *Academy of Management Review,* 24, 325–354.

Huy, Q. N. (2001). Time, temporal capability, and planned change. *Academy of Management Review,* 26, 601–623.

Isabella, L. A. (1990). Evolving interpretations as a change unfolds: How managers construe key organizational events. *Academy of Management Journal,* 33, 7–41.

Juran, J. M., & Gryna, Jr., F. M. (1980). *Quality planning and analysis.* New York: McGraw-Hill.

Kanter, R. M. (1999). Change is everyone's job: Managing the extended enterprise in a globally connected world. *Organizational Dynamics,* 28, 7–23.

Kanter, R. M., Stein, B. A., & Jick, T. D. (1992). *The challenge of organizational change.* New York: Free Press.

Kotter, J. P. (1996). *Leading change.* Boston: Harvard Business School Press.

Kotter, J. P., & Schlesinger, L. A. (1979). Choosing strategies for change. *Harvard Business Review,* March-April, 106-114.

Lawler, E. E. (1981). *Pay and organization development.* Reading, MA: Addison-Wesley.

Lawler, E. E. (1988). Gainsharing theory and research: Findings and future directions. In W. A. Pasmore & R. Woodman (Eds.), *Research in organizational change and development* (Vol. 2). Greenwich, CT: JAI Press.

Lewin, K. (1951). *Field theory in social science.* New York: Harper & Row.

London, M. (1988). *Change agents: New roles and innovation strategies for human resource professionals.* San Francisco: Jossey-Bass.

Manzini, A. O. (1988). *Organization diagnosis: A practical approach to company problem-solving and growth.* AMACOM.

Marshak, R. J. (1993). Managing the metaphors of change. *Organizational Dynamics,* 11 (Summer), 44–56.

McCall, Jr., M. W., Lombardo, M. M., & Morrison, A. M. (1988). *The lessons of experience: How successful executives develop on the job.* Lexington, MA: D.C. Heath.

Miller, C. S., & Schuster, M. H. (1987). Gainsharing plans: A comparative analysis. *Organizational Dynamics,* 16 (Summer), 44–67.

Morison, E. (1966). Gunfire at sea: A case study of innovation. In E. Morison, *Men, machines and modern times.* Cambridge, MA: MIT Press.

Pettigrew, A. M., Woodman, R. W., & Cameron, K. S. (2001). Studying organizational change and development: Challenges for future research. *Academy of Management Journal,* 44, 697–713.

Posner, B. Z., & Schmidt, W. H. (1992). Values and the American manager: An update updated. *California Management Review,* 34, 80–94.

Seashore, S. E., Lawler III, E. E., Mirvis, P. H., & Cammann, C. (Eds). (1983). *Assessing organizational change.* New York: Wiley.

Stackman, R. W., Pinder, C. C., & Connor, P. E. (2000). Values lost: Redirecting research on values in the workplace. In N. Ashkanasy, C. P. M. Wilderom, & M. F. Peterson (Eds.), *Handbook of organizational culture & climate* (pp. 37–54). Thousand Oaks, CA: Sage.

Trice, H. M., & Beyer, J. M. (1993). *The cultures of work organizations.* Englewood Cliffs, NJ: Prentice-Hall.

Vaill, P. B. (1989). *Managing as a performing art: New ideas for a world of chaotic change.* San Francisco: Jossey-Bass.

Walton, R. E. (1972). How to counter alienation in the plant. *Harvard Business Review,* November-December, 70-81.

Warrick, D. D. (1984). Managing organization change and development. In J. E. Rosenzweig & F. E. Kast (Eds.), *Modules in management.* Chicago: Science Research Associates.

Weick, K. E. (1979). *The social psychology of organizing* (2d ed.). Reading, MA: Addison-Wesley.

Weick, K. E. (1995). *Sensemaking in organizations.* Thousand Oaks, CA: Sage.

Weick, K. E., & Quinn, R. E. (1999). Organizational change and development. *Annual Review of Psychology,* 50, 361–386.

Weisbord, M. R. (1982). Organizational diagnosis: Six places to look for trouble with or without a theory. In M. S. Plovnick, R. E. Fry, & W. W. Burke, (Eds.), *Organization development: Exercises, cases, and readings.* Boston: Little, Brown.

Wilhelm, W. (1992). Changing corporate culture—or corporate behavior? *Academy of Management Executive,* 6, 72–77.

Zaltman, G., & Duncan, R. (1977). *Strategies for planned change.* New York: Wiley.

Index

About the Authors

PATRICK E. CONNOR is Professor of Organizational Analysis, Atkinson Graduate School of Management, Willamette University in Salem, Oregon.

LINDA K. LAKE is a consultant in Kirkland, Washington, a suburb of Seattle, working with start-up and emerging firms in the health services industry. She also chairs the Washington State Board of Health.

RICHARD W. STACKMAN is Assistant Professor of Business Administration at the University of Washington, Tacoma.